Stage Fright

Kevin Killian

Stage Fright

Selected Plays from San Francisco Poets Theater

Kenning Editions

Stage Fright
by Kevin Killian

First Printing

Published by Kenning Editions,
3147 W Logan Blvd, Ste 7
Chicago, IL 60647
Kenningeditions.com

Distributed by Small Press Distribution,
1341 Seventh St,
Berkeley, CA 94710
Spdbooks.org

ISBN: 978-0-9997198-2-4

Library of Congress Control Number:
2018938746

Cover design and interior composition by
Brian Hochberger

Photograph by Ryan Thayer:Kota Ezawa
as Kevin Killian Senior in *THAT*

This book was made possible in part by
the supporters of Kenning Editions: Charles
Bernstein, Julietta Cheung, Carol Ciavonne,
Steve Dickison, Craig Dworkin, Kristin
Dykstra, Laura Elrick, Jais Gossman, Kaplan
Harris, Tom Healy, Lyn Hejinian, Edward
McAdams, Krishan Mistry, Dee Morris,
Chris Muravez, Sawako Nakayasu, Caroline
Picard, Janelle Rebel, Kit Robinson, Jesse
Seldess, Tyrone Williams, and Steven
Zultanski

Kenning Editions is a 501c3 non-
profit, independent literary publisher
investigating the relationships of aesthetic
quality to political commitment

Contents

dedicated to the poets and artists who have worked in my plays, and especially to those who have passed on:

Lawrence Braithwaite, Ethel Chase, kari edwards, Arturo Galster, Barbara Guest, Philip Horvitz, Rick Jacobsen, George Kuchar, Akilah Oliver, Rex Ray, Leslie Scalapino, and Nancy Shaw

Introduction

Interview with Heidi Bean

This interview was conducted in 2006 for a planned special
issue of Iowa Journal of Cultural Studies which never materialized

Heidi Bean: Tell me a little about this history of the poets theater in San Francisco. Is there a founder or a founding event? What's your personal involvement?

Kevin Killian: Thirty years ago there was quite a bit of activity with the poets theater in San Francisco. They were always putting on plays, not only their own work but "classic plays" too, like that canto of Zukofsky's "A" that calls for singers and actors. I came to SF too late for that, but little by little I got to meet most of the key players. As you know, many of the early scripts were published in Bob Perelman's magazine *Hills*. Consider me the second wave of poets theater.

At some slightly later stage I realized that there had been an original poets theater movement in the Bay Area in the 1940s, 1950s and 1960s led by the very poets whom I was researching and writing about for the biography I was writing about Jack Spicer (1925-65). One of the amazing things has been to usher into print and/or act on the stage in some of the vintage poets theater plays such as James Broughton's *Mission to Gomorrah* ("This play was especially written to amuse poet friends and was performed by them for the first time in April 1958"), Helen Adam's play *Initiation to the Magic Workshop* (1957), and several by Spicer himself—*Young Goodman Brown, Troilus, Nobody at the Bar* (1946-1957).

The first play I worked in was called *Fist of the Colossus* by Carla Harryman and Tom Mandel. Eileen Corder and I played the leads, a pair of archaeologists who were trying to raise the Colossus from the deep sea waters of Alexandria Harbor. (I believe the authors were inspired by a contemporary news story.) This was a one act play for six actors, I think, later published in the Language Poetry vehicle *Writing* magazine in Vancouver.

At the same time I could see the first wave of poets theater dissolving into something else. I think most of the poets stopped writing plays in the early 80s. Except for Carla of course, and Leslie Scalapino. whose interest in the theater paralleled my own. Some of the Language poets, like Lyn Hejinian or Ron Silliman, never really wrote for the stage, but many of the others jumped in wholeheartedly. But there was a vacuum into which, I thought, I could harness some New Narrative energy. And gay it up a bit—it was a terribly straight place. Maybe not earnest, but stra ght.

HB: How would you describe poets theater to someone who's never seen it?

KK: This is a good question but I hardly know how to answer it. Of course it's startlingly similar to conventional theater in look. Except that the actors are all holding scripts in their hands, ar d their movements are somewhat hampered by having only one hand to do all their "acting" with, as well as having to keep their eyes trained on the scr pt most of the time, which cuts down on their gazing, ordinarily half of actinc. Outside of that, the theater we work in is largely free of "acting" gestures, sjch as pretending to be someone whom you are not. You know the way Robert Bresson disdained using professional actors? Instead he preferred amateurs and others whom he called "models"? I like that too. They are often working artists of one kind or another. Do they bring authenticity to their parts? No, but the plays they appear in are haunted by the specter of lost authenticity.

HB: Who creates poets theater? In particular I'm wondering what are the goals of people involved in creating poets theater? Is it a political practice? A social one? An aesthetic challenge?

KK: Although I think of it as a political practice, I can hardly justify myself thinking so. The place of theater inside the "direct actions" of ACT UP and like minded groups was a good model for me, in the late 1980s, of a theater that might dare to address political topics. But soon I found myself embracing the social, rather than the political side of things. I wanted not one but a whole slew of results: I wanted, as did many of the "first wave" poets, a place from which to attack what we saw as the solipsism of the actual poem (and also of the poetry reading, despite what anyone might recognize as the sometimes immense theatricality of individual readers—Tina Darragh, Susan Howe, Robin Blaser, John Wieners, dozens of such cases). I wanted also to yoke the energies of the poetry world in San Francisco with the New Narrative crowd, and then on top of that to bring in the art world and give ourselves that ersatz glamor. It then became an aesthetic challenge, every time out, to be able to employ a very large cast, an ensemble that had grown quite sizeable, not to say top heavy, like having to write a symphony every time you wanted to hear a little tune in your head.

HB: What's the relation between written texts and live performances in poets theater (if it's possible to generalize)? Are the texts simply "scripts" for performance? Can a written text alone be a form of fully realized poets theater?

KK: I didn't understand this question at first, too impatient to follow its implications. Leslie Scalapino and I wrote a play, which was published, *Stone Marmalade*, and yet it has never seen a production, and anyone who reads it through might see why, because of the immense scenic demands it calls forth, you'd have to be Wolfgang Wagner with the stage resources of Beyreuth to put it on! Is it "fully realized" without a production? I don't know. I do know that many perfect productions of different plays exist only in my head. I have written some plays I haven't even written, for that matter. I don't think that a play has been fully realized, even if the production came off marvelously, if the performance was not videotaped for posterity. Thus some of our best shows, those that weren't taped, don't exist in the same way, and eventually, even though the scripts survive, the performances don't.

Yes, the performances consist of much more than is noted in the script. In Carla Harryman's piece, *Memory Play*, I was allowed to write my own dialogue, none of which shows up in the published script, but I suppose must still be on the video (though I don't know since I haven't seen it).

HB: What strategies do you employ as a poet-playwright and how are they different from the strategies that you employ as a poet?

KK: Writing for other bodies, not only voices, but other bodies than my own, is a practice in which I am forced to think about work and words in a different way than when I write my own poems. That said, my own poetry is enriched, I think, by being able to think of it as a score for one or more voices. Different people can come in and read it in different ways, thus more of what Blaser calls the "randonnee"! In my book *Argento Series* you can see a few poems that have stretched out the lyric in this way, one of them employing choruses, another a call and response pattern I use writing drama for the poets theater.

I guess I'm trying to say that eventually the two worlds meet on the other side—like the moon!

HB: Has poets theater changed since you first became involved in it in 1985? I'm wondering in particular if the conditions that initially gave rise to an interest in poets theater have changed and, if so, how poets theater has been affected.

KK: Today I think that poetry audiences are less isolated than before due to developments in contemporary art, and the involvement of their peers in art is welcomed more and more. That's the way I always wanted it to be, just didn't know how to make it happen. Except for what I did. Now you see poets at art openings and, wonder of wonders, you see some artists at poetry events.

I would also guess that today in San Francisco poetry there is more of an open interest in narrative, including plot and including comedy.

The technology has also changed and thus it is easier, more tempting to incorporate elements of what was once called video into our performances.

HB: In what way has the collaborative nature of the San Francisco poets theater community affected you personally and/or your work?

KK: Personally? For me, as I realize more and more, I have worked in the theater to counteract the terror of **AIDS**, with its Agatha Christie-like shrinking of one's social world. I need to gather around me an army of like minded cultural workers, their bodies interposed between me and the void. Working communally has comforted me in this time of psychic and physical strength, yes, and strengthened me too. I don't think my own work is important any more. It's what we do as a people that matters.

(That said of course I'm still morbidly vain about writing and stuck-up about it.)

HB: In your experience, who attends poets theater? Is it an "academic" art? A "popular" art?

KK: Oh dear, would anyone but an academic think of such a question or characterize art as "academic"? This one I can't figure out. I don't think of poets theater as an academic art, though it is an avant-garde one. It's time based, performance oriented, ephemeral, in the long run inconsequential. It's not only time based but fun based. I don't know if it's popular. If it was, you'd think there would be more of it, in New York, London, and other poetry capitals. It might be too lightweight for these lacustrine cities.

Who comes to the shows? Here, a cross section of just the same kinds of people who are working up on the stage—poets, film makers, curators, novelists, playwrights, painters, photographers and editors. And the boyfriends of the above.

HB: What has been the critical response, if any, to poets theater? I get the feeling very little has been said or written about it beyond its specific community. Any thoughts on why that is?

KK: Heidi, you are so right. We are doing this dramatic thing, and spending our whole lives doing so, and it is going undocumented. I think I know why, people don't like to say what they saw. And theater and dance critics, those used to notating on their feet as it were, shy away from on the one hand the bravura and on the other the non-theatrical elements of the performances. The best review I ever got was by Warren Sonbert, the late experimental filmmaker. He could get it.

We wanted a theater like Charles Ludlam's, in which the audience would, perhaps, recognize the same players over and over again in different roles. Or the Warhol films of the Silver Factory, in which superstars are born out of repetition alone. The other night Dodie and I watched Norman Foster's 1943 RKO film *Journey into Fear*, startled to see so many of Orson Welles' actors from *Citizen Kane* appear in it, all playing very unfamiliar roles (except Ruth Warrick, who plays almost the same part.) It was all perfectly unearthly, then I realized, that's what I wanted my audiences to feel, the comfort of the familiar, but always torqued a little bit to the left or right. The formula shifted each time the sugar bag is opened up.

We've done it so long that some of our stars have left us, and some have actually died, left this sorry planet. Of them I think continually, of, for example, Rick Jacobsen, Ethel Chase, Philip Horvitz, Barbara Guest. Often enough I forget that working communally involves working with the dead as well as the living. We reach out our hands and sometimes the living grab at them, hold us in life for a bit.

HB: What do you think one walks away with from a poets theater performance? An experience? An idea? A fresh perspective (on life, theater, writing, collaboration)? Something else?

KK: I think people might come away thinking, I could do that! Isn't that the best kind of work, something generative? Action painting was sort of like that, wasn't it, big messy canvases that left even Philistines thinking better of their own kindergarteners' finger paintings. When we have our poets theater marathon at Small Press Traffic every winter, I can feel the audience start to race, like finely tuned engines at the Indy 500, and I can see new plays being born at every curtain call.

In our case it seems as though audiences feel they can not only write as I do, they can act too, inhabit other realities than their own, or participate in direct political action. It's a blanket permission, as if the magical hills of San Francisco didn't already give us all the permission we needed, to be someone else, even just for one night.

> *If we shadows have offended,*
> *Think but this, and all is mended,*
> *That you have but slumber'd here*
> *While these visions did appear.*

THAT

characters

ALFRED CHESTER

BARBARA HUTTON,
world's richest woman

PAUL BOWLES

JANE BOWLES

SARA SEARS,
a girl from Kansas

HER CONSCIENCE

GLADYS SEARS,
her grandmother.

HAROLD SEARS,
owner of the Sears Building

KEVIN KILLIAN,
the missing boy

"CHERYL WILSON,"
the vagabond poet

LT. KEITEL

KEVIN KILLIAN, SR.

OFFICER WAYNE SMITH

[*ALFRED CHESTER and BARBARA HUTTON onstage, seated.*]

ALFRED CHESTER: By four a.m., the desert was already warm to the touch, though the dark was an absolute curtain of black. Tangier gleamed in the distance, a bowl of jewels, jewels without color.

BARBARA HUTTON: Oh, Alfred . . . that's a lot of jewels.

ALFRED CHESTER: I'd been living on the desert face a good six months, a pauper of flesh, thrown to the wolves. Cholera cut through my gut as native boys began to lay out barley and dates for the camel train that would take us there. I couldn't breathe. My face began to pulse and flush like the sun.

BARBARA HUTTON: You had a terrible time of it.

ALFRED CHESTER: And I thought I saw—Liza Minnelli . . .

[*Enter HAROLD SEARS.*]

HAROLD SEARS (*on the telephone*): Get me the police. This is Harold Sears—the Harold Sears, of the Sears Building! Chief, I want you to send over your best men. My lovely storefront here on Capp Street, has been overrun by—artists. Eliminate them all—cast them out like the Gadarene swine in the Bible. You say you'll send over your two best men? That's a relief, I can happily sleep in my Capp Street hideaway bed. Artists are sitting right inside my space and I can see them hatching artistic plots the way you or I can smell a daisy.

ALFRED CHESTER (*to HAROLD SEARS*): Mr. Mahmoudi, you have the best datoun in all Tangier. You one very sweet individual.

HAROLD SEARS: This is not Tangier, this is the Mission! And you two are spoiling my setup. I don't like artists, I never have, I want to attract—bowlers here to my tasteful space. Strikes and spares, splits, tenpins,—in short, suburban money. But you artists spoil it for everyone. Where are those cops?

[*Exit HAROLD SEARS.*]

BARBARA HUTTON: Oh, Alfred, I've never seen Mr. Landlord so incensed. I guess living in Tangier all these years makes some people wiggy.

[*Enter WAYNE SMITH.*]

WAYNE SMITH: San Francisco police. Pull over.

ALFRED CHESTER: You can pull me over till you're black and blue, but this is Barbara Hutton, elegant, feeble, many times married.

BARBARA HUTTON (*extending her hand to SMITH*): You may now kiss the bride.

ALFRED CHESTER: We're here in Tangier because this is a haven for artists.

LT. KEITEL [*offstage*]: Officer Wayne Smith! May I ask—what the fuck is going on?

WAYNE SMITH: Lt. Keitel!

[*Enter LT. KEITEL.*]

LT. KEITEL: I'm, like, what's the problem?

BARBARA HUTTON (*to ALFRED*): Give them some, I don't know, pieces of money, they'll go away.

LT. KEITEL: Why, you! Smitty, lodge that shotgun down her throat. Dislodge that silver spoon stuck there like two dogs rutting.

ALFRED CHESTER: Barbara, it's easy to say, "Give them money," but I'm not a Picasso, my pockets are bare. [*To LT. KEITEL.*] Did you say "San Francisco"?

LT. KEITEL: Yeah, the city of little gray sweaters. Show me, big boy, show me with your mouth. Smitty, what's the delay? Slap 'em in clappers, the squad car's purring at the curb.

ALFRED CHESTER: Nurse, we're two adorable library lions, don't take us away from Tangier, it would be cruel and airless. We're not packages, we're artists.

BARBARA HUTTON: Except for me. Jumping Jiminy, where's my purse? I have purses the size of trees but I can't find the forest at the moment—not with this pair of officials looking at my aura.

LT. KEITEL: Ain't that the cat's erection. Book 'em, Smit. No, don't book 'em, just give them a few shots of the Taser and we'll dump their bodies in the Yerba Berba Sewer Center or whatever.

WAYNE SMITH: What about their Miranda rights?

LT. KEITEL: What about them, Slim Jim? I fucked that Miranda, and she was lousy. She and two little pooch cocksuckers licked my stick till it cooed like a dove. [*To ALFRED CHESTER and BARBARA HUTTON.*] There's a tin shed, walls like sardine tins, where no one will hear your screams. Let's move it on out!

ALFRED CHESTER: He is a nurse?

BARBARA HUTTON: Oh, he's something, I forget, a blue thing.

WAYNE SMITH (*leading out ALFRED CHESTER AND BARBARA HUTTON*): You have the right to remain silent—

LT. KEITEL: —Not.

WAYNE SMITH: You have the right to an attorney—

[*Exit WAYNE SMITH, BARBARA HUTTON, ALFRED CHESTER.*]

LT. KEITEL: Yeah, let me get Johnnie Cochran on the walkie talkie. [*On walkie talkie phone.*] Hello, is this the Bar Association—of Hell? [*Satanic laugh. Disconnects, tries another number.*] Pauly? I know you covered me 15K on the Dodgers, how was I supposed to know Strawberry 3 to 2. Let it ride till tonight's game. Tomorrow I'll be taking candy from a baby! Thirty thousand dollars, spread on a heart-shaped bed of red crack, got any? You gotta do this for me, Marone. That's straight from my dick, Pauly. This isn't Michael Jackson asking for the latest child star, this is the SFPD and this is an order.

[*Enter KEVIN KILLIAN, SENIOR.*]

KEVIN SENIOR: Oh, there you are, Lieutenant. My son is missing—my only son, Kevin Killian, and he owes me money.

LT. KEITEL: How much?

KEVIN SENIOR: Thirty thousand dollars. Find him for me and I'll give you it all. I miss having him around.

LT. KEITEL: Good enough. How old is the boy?

KEVIN SENIOR: The perfect age.

LT. KEITEL: I see. What's your name?

KEVIN SENIOR: Kevin, Senior. Little Kevin was last seen on the corner of Haight and Presidio in the uniform of a Catholic schoolboy, rope burns round his neck and testicles. I keep him on a short string, lots of yanks like a flight of Blue Angels.

LT. KEITEL: You're a wise pop. So often thieves slip the cork on a man.

KEVIN SENIOR: He's here in the Sears Building—my intuition tells me so. Look, Lieutenant, I've got my end of the rope.

[*Enter PAUL BOWLES and ALFRED CHESTER, Alfred leaning on Paul's arm, wilted.*]

LT. KEITEL (*to KEVIN SENIOR*): We'll go into the dugout and talk turkey. You know why they call it the Sears Building, don'tcha? The Sears live here. I'm on their pad, like every other cop in the city.

KEVIN SENIOR: Find my boy, it's a must.

[*Exit LT. KEITEL and KEVIN SENIOR.*]

PAUL BOWLES (*to audience*): Hi, I'm playing the part of a happily married man with a real problem. [*To ALFRED.*] Alfred, what's up?

ALFRED CHESTER: I feel dazed. The sun's beating on my thick black hair like lashes of a jellyfish. But Paul, Paul Bowles, give me some wisdom, tell us about your long life as expatriate, addict, homo rictus.

PAUL BOWLES: As a kid I always wanted to be a policeman, or rather, a police boy, sleeping with the Dalmatians in some secret part of the station. My parents had this pet dog, Lester, kind of a mutt but with a real cute face and almost a human expression. I loved that pooch so much. Now I'm forty-five, living in San Francisco, has anything changed?

ALFRED CHESTER: You never used to bore me. Time was, whenever I felt the old ennui, I could trot over to Paul and Jane's and get some pep. No longer. Goodbye, or, as we say here in Morocco, Allah-ben-azzam.

[*Exit ALFRED CHESTER.*]

PAUL BOWLES (*to audience*): This is my apartment. My wife's a very talented writer, praised to the hilt by Truman Capote and Carson McCullers! So why am I hiding a runaway boy in the coal cellar? For purposes of exposition only . . . She, Jane Bowles, is such a natural and nonchalant person. But he, Kevin, is sleeping under a name that doesn't make it, correct?

[*Enter KEVIN KILLIAN, the runaway boy, walking in his sleep.*]

KEVIN KILLIAN (*in his sleep*): The powdered prisms of the past mix together like colored sand. You run from the arms of your dark intimate through thickets of converging paths into the dead-end of thought. Gloved fingers pry open your mouth.

PAUL BOWLES: He is sleeping under a name. That doesn't make it correct. And he drinks a lot, over and over the limit of the house.

JANE (*offstage*): Paul, don't just stand there in your own little world, help me get ready for the Sears Building party.

KEVIN KILLIAN (*in his sleep*): Guilt, hate, no-breath, death.

PAUL (*continues*): Under the glamorous coverlet of the baby hardly a hair moves on his long Hindu body.

[*Exit KEVIN KILLIAN, repeating speech about "Guilt, hate, no-breath, death."*]

One day Amnesty International will come to me hat in hand, to ask me everything I know about planet Earth, and why I am keeping a runaway boy in the cellar. It won't be pretty, my explanation.

[*Enter JANE BOWLES, with a wrapped present.*]

JANE: Paul, just think, you and I have been tenants for years, yet this is the first time Mrs. Sears and her husband have asked us to a party. They must be softening with age. Up to this point they've been hard as—volcanic glass.

PAUL (*continues*): Is he dead, do you think? This is some touch if so, for the wedding of the year, in which I will let him into the country, out of the country, and of which he is only one man, and now as it turns out, possibly a dead man.

JANE: This is some touch if so . . . When Mrs. Sears came to invite us to her party—I thought she wanted to evict us. You and I aren't her favorite tenants—

PAUL: We're a touch too artistic.

JANE: Now I feel like Cinderella in her new ball gown, sewn by rabbits and blue-birds out of pink silk. Still, the old lady wore an odd expression, almost triumphal, as though she had more than one ace up her sleeve, and wouldn't hesitate to play them if need be. She's hatching a plot and I don't need an egg timer to tell me so. She must be unveiling some secret weapon at this so-called reception, and I for one intend to be prepared.

PAUL: Jane, don't fuss so. She and Mr. Sears are introducing their granddaughter, Sara, to all their tenants. It's not a big deal—in fact, it'll be fun. How often do we get to meet an innocent corn-fed girl from Kansas, the corn state?

JANE (*wincing*): Don't remind me! Bumpkins aren't my type.

PAUL: They say she's five foot nine of—adorable!

JANE: Five foot nine—practically a silo. Paul, we've been married fifteen years— by the skin of our teeth—and give me enough credit to know the wheat from the chaff. Sara Sears and I will have nothing in common, and that's my dernier cri on the subject except—get dressed.

PAUL: If this was a soap, your defensiveness would signal the audience—that you and Sara will fall in love ASAP. It's always those with nothing in common who hit it off right at the start.

JANE: This is not a soap.

[*Enter BARBARA HUTTON—disheveled.*]

Why, Barbara, what happened?

BARBARA HUTTON: Don't ask me. I met this blue man with a silver shield, next thing I know the tortures of the damned were appealing next to what I felt in my tender thing.

JANE: Paul's been predicting I'll fall in love with Sara Sears. Did you ever hear of anything more ridiculous?

BARBARA HUTTON: I didn't even know she was in Tangier! But Jane, don't laugh about love. I've been in its mouth and been spewed right out. Married nine

times, always with dreams in my eyes. And look at me now! You know, Alfred was
with me when we had this strange, blue experience. I guess it took over, since he's
not here right now.

PAUL: Are you going to the party, Barbara?

BARBARA HUTTON: Have we met? Oh, are you Paul Bowles? Were we married
once—are you circumcised, were you the one?

PAUL: That's beside the point.

[*Enter WAYNE SMITH.*]

OFFICER SMITH: I'm the circumcised one! May I come in? It's a bridegroom's
right. Miss Hutton and I were married this morning down at the chop shop. I was
interrogating her, then the shoe was on the other foot.

PAUL: I'll look for Alfred. Think I saw him by the spice chest.

BARBARA HUTTON: Please do!

[*Exit PAUL BOWLES.*]

Because I never met this man in my life. Or your life, Jane, bizarre as it's been.
Alfred will back me up.

OFFICER SMITH: He was my best man, passed out huge cigars of some leafy
Moroccan tobacco. I asked my Chief, Lieutenant Keitel, but he just laughed, advis-
ing me of the wringer I'd caught my balls in. Yet who am I to care, when Barbara
Hutton is the new Mrs. Wayne Smith?

BARBARA HUTTON: Well, whatever you say, but I never thought I'd marry a
nurse. —At least I get to buy a trousseau. Those in my closet I share with the
moths, those pale, vacant insects, flying origami. —Is that Sara Sears with her
grandmother? She is tall—and thin, too: around the waist she's like Giacometti
with bows on. —Or she used to be.

JANE: She's a jerk.

[*Enter SARA and GLADYS SEARS, Sara nibbling on a corncrake; Mrs. Sears carries a tray
with four glasses—she dubiously offers one of them to Jane.*]

Whatever we expected, it was nothing like the real thing. Oh, we artists are blind sometimes! [*To MRS. SEARS:*] Love your party. And your outfit's a peach: Raisa Gorbachev prêt-à-porter?

MRS. SEARS: Hello, Mrs. Bowles. [*Sourly.*] It's party time. [*To WAYNE SMITH and BARBARA HUTTON:*] Never thought I'd see the day when a policeman would marry an artist. Did she entrap you, by any chance?

OFFICER SMITH: Barbara's good and true, at least half as true as the Steve Young rumors.

SARA (*to JANE*): The "real thing"?

JANE (*thrusts present at Sara*): You.

MRS. SEARS (*to WAYNE SMITH and BARBARA HUTTON*): Offstage, the pair of you. You should be locked up in a barrel pierced with nails. Then rolled down a hill.

WAYNE SMITH: Go ahead, pelt us with rice.

MRS. SEARS: Unholy duo, I'd pelt you with napalm.

[*Exit WAYNE SMITH and BARBARA HUTTON.*]

JANE (*to SARA*): Oh, gee, here's a tiny token of an undying passion. It's from Esprit, but it should have been—a rope of black pearls.

[*Pause while Sara appears to think about this.*]

SARA: Do you drink a lot, Mrs. Bowles?

JANE: Once or twice. —But let's get away from calling me "Mrs. Bowles" shall we? We're not after all at Church. Call me "Jane."

SARA: How country.

JANE (*taken aback*): Or maybe we are in Church—a kind of Church of romance. Oh, Mrs. Sears, I absolutely adore your granddaughter.

MRS. SEARS (*aside to audience*): I'm proud of my little kitten, yet wary of her.

[*Enter PAUL.*]

With the wisdom of the very provincial I know what's what, what's up, what's hot and what's not. [*To PAUL who's trying to take her picture.*] Would you stop fooling with that dark camera? [*To JANE.*] Sara's quite a ball of fire, isn't she?

PAUL (*to audience*): This monster of modesty sat for Mathew Brady's daguerreotype. She wiggled for Weegee and down through the ages for Robert Frank and Diane Arbus freak show. I know for a fact she's number one on Joel-Peter Witkin's wish list—why won't she pose for me, I feel—

JANE: A fireball? No! She's a uterine sphere—she's all fertility like a delta.

PAUL: —rejected.

JANE: She makes me wish I were a mother. No—a grandma like you.

MRS. SEARS: If that's the case, Mrs. Bowles, I advise application to your husband. I might remind you, however, your lease prohibits children of any sort. Even as visitors. Perhaps, while applying, you might remind your husband of that rule as well.

PAUL: Where's Kevin Killian? When I'm down, he makes me feel up. Like some elevator that brings grain to the moon.

MRS. SEARS:(*calling*): Janitor boy, artists have eaten here! Clean up after pigs!

SARA: That janitor boy has such wide brown eyes, almost like a fish.

MRS. SEARS: He's Swiss, not many fish in Switzerland . . .

SARA: Any more than in Kansas.

PAUL BOWLES: "Janitor boy," put me in your dustpan, wipe clean the smudged brightwork of my ego.

[*Enter KEVIN KILLIAN.*]

KEVIN KILLIAN: You come with me here now, I give you good Swiss chard, no say no. I give you big blow job, artist man. Guilt, hate, no-breath, death.

PAUL: Hmmm, whatever.

[Exit PAUL BOWLES and KEVIN KILLIAN.]

MRS. SEARS: The police were here today, Mrs. Bowles, asking questions about a young boy thief poet your husband has injected into the Sears Building. He's a bisexual, ain't he, like Daphne du Maurier.

SARA: Call her Jane: it's so much more neighborly. Treat her like just plain folks.

MRS. SEARS: May I speak to Sara alone for a moment, Mrs. Bowles?

JANE: I wish you wouldn't. Don't bogart this joint, this delicious, this Sapphic-flavored joint . . .

MRS. SEARS: If wishes were horses, Mrs. Bowles, than beggars would ride! I must insist. Goodbye. Enjoy the party.

[MRS. SEARS brings SARA downstage from JANE.]

Now, Sara. You must understand that Jane Bowles is not our neighbor. She is our tenant. We own the very bed she lies down on.

SARA *(slowly)*: If she's made her bed I suppose she must lie down on it.

MRS. SEARS: And when she lies down with dogs—

SARA: —She gets up with fleas. I see. Thank you, Granny.

JANE: I used to laugh and say I'd never fall in love.

MRS. SEARS *(drawing a relieved breath)*: I hope you do see, dear. This huge slate hovel has fallen on hard times. Though we haven't seen you since you were a tot, Harold and I perceive you nevertheless as our savior; you're the one who'll finally rid our building of artists. —At first a skeptic, something like a *coup de foudre* seemed to attack Jane Bowles as she watched you eat that corncrake.

SARA: This Mona Lisa smirk, Granny, isn't for you. I appreciate your feeling for me, all of it. You think me Messianic, and that's a compliment few teenage girls receive, in Kansas or anywhere else.

MRS. SEARS *(sharply)*: See that our faith is well deserved. Jimmy Swaggart and Chris Farley let Harold down badly—be sure you don't. Oh these artists! We've tried everything, from rent hikes to fluorocarbons, but still they cling like—barnacles, girl! Destroy the whole lot of 'em and you'll make an elderly couple very, very glad. Come now, enjoy your party.

[*Exit MRS. SEARS.*]

SARA: I could play her like bezique, I'm good at a con. What I need is a conscience but I don't want one.

[*Enter CONSCIENCE.*]

CONSCIENCE: Oh, you've got one, everyone has, we're the fingerprints of the unannounced.

SARA: You pesky shadow! Followed me from Kansas!

CONSCIENCE: You don't pick up and walk away, I'm not a movie set, or, in your case a pasture. I'm your conscience.

SARA: I'll do what I like.

CONSCIENCE: What about those teenagers you drowned in Spirit Lake?

SARA: They won the skating medal. They had it round their necks. It was mine, I had to eliminate them.

CONSCIENCE: They were just two ordinary kids.

SARA: Well, I forgot about them. Life goes on and I got away with it.

CONSCIENCE: How can you look at a lake again?

SARA: Luckily there are no lakes in the Mission. [*Pulls pendant from around neck, to the music of "My Heart Will Go On."*] Didn't you see "Titanic"? But I'm not throwing this skating medal away, I earned it, and I'll wear it, even though it's gaudy.

CONSCIENCE (*disgusted*): Go now, enjoy your party.

[*Exit CONSCIENCE. Enter party guests with champagne glasses: WAYNE SMITH, BARBARA HUTTON, ALFRED CHESTER, PAUL BOWLES, MRS. SEARS.*]

ALL: Welcome to the Sears Building, Sara Sears.

PAUL: And now, Barbara, sing. Sing, sing!

WAYNE SMITH: It isn't a party without a song from Barbara.

ALFRED CHESTER: Streisand? I didn't know she was in Tangier! Is Liza here too,—is that her name? The one with the spider haircut and the bright eyes, ringed with black oil?

WAYNE SMITH (*coldly*): Is she an auto mechanic? May I present the one and only Barbara Hutton?

[*Applause.*]

MRS. SEARS: Call her what you will, she's a blight to bourgeois eyes. Harold Sears, bring the Raid!

BARBARA HUTTON: Thank you, all.

[*Enter KEVIN SENIOR.*]

KEVIN SENIOR: I loved him the way you or I would love a pet, I brushed his fur with a number of awkward strokes. If it went against the grain, am I to blame?

JANE (*vaguely*): Sing, Barbara, sing . . . while my heart breaks in two like matzoh.

KEVIN SENIOR: With his little snub, he nosed open my combination, withdrew my deposit. I'm out only thirty grand, but he needs a human pal.

BARBARA HUTTON (*ignoring KEVIN SENIOR*): This is a little song Paul wrote as incidental music for Tennessee Williams or someone.

[*Sings, "Merry Widow Waltz," to these lyrics:*]

Night is falling,
Birds are calling
Sweet and low.

And what things
The future brings
We cannot know.

Not a word is spoken
Just that I love you.

Oh, my dear,
I long to hear
You love me, too.

[*All on stage join BARBARA HUTTON for second verse, as follows:*]

Music playing,
Dancers swaying,
To and fro.

And the night
Is filled with light
From long ago.

Silence is unbroken,
Just that I love you.

Oh, my dear,
I long to hear
You love me, too.

[*All on stage applaud BARBARA HUTTON and hopefully audience will too.*]

ALFRED CHESTER: Liza, you've never sung better.

SARA: Goodness, what a mess. I must find the janitor to clean up this—mess.

JANE: Don't leave me now!

SARA: Tell me, where does that janitor dwell, in what coal-smeared fiery dell? Give me corn or give me bread, I'll grind his light to make my bed.

[*Exit SARA, forgetting her present. Resentfully MRS. SEARS collects it for her.*]

JANE (*to PAUL*): I'll follow her, like a numbing drug, like clozapine. I can't let her go: not like this. Her dampness shall be my perception, my fog.

PAUL: Well, I'll help if I can—but it's a long shot. She strikes me as a tough, oh, what did they use to say, cookie.

[Exit JANE and PAUL.]

ALFRED CHESTER (*to BARBARA HUTTON*): Liza Minnelli, like jewels the lights of Tangier twinkled—in synesthesia each dot of light made its way through my cerebral cortex like a Fellahin fucking a snake.

WAYNE SMITH: That's all very well, but Barbara and I have a lifetime to share. "We've only just begun—"

BARBARA HUTTON (*to* WAYNE *SMITH*): Who was that singing, Nurse? That wonderful burst of fruit flavor?

WAYNE SMITH: "—to live . . . white lace and promises . . . A kiss for luck and we're on our way. . . ."

[Exit WAYNE SMITH and BARBARA HUTTON.]

ALFRED CHESTER: Life's no cabaret when you're Liza Minnelli. In each dot I read my history like bumps on a shaved black head. [*To MRS. SEARS:*] Liza, remember Ben Vereen in *All That Jazz*? The twinge I felt about leaving the States. The logorrhea—river of words!—ran lickety-split onto the page of desert I had scrawled farewell to.

MRS. SEARS: You're as bad as the rest, and that's the sum total of garbage.

ALFRED CHESTER: Are you Cherifa? Cherifa, mix me a brew of kef, mash in my usual dose of brown heroin. I have taught you enough English to be of use to all weary travellers.

MRS. SEARS: I am not Cherifa, I'm a landowning matron twice your age, and all-American, thank you. I'm from San Francisco.

ALFRED CHESTER: Don't thank me, Cherifa, I was proud to teach you A, B, and C, so you could order my boys from brothels all over Tangier, as in "one from Column A," and so forth. Is my hashish hot? Light a match, do, quick, dear, I'm getting cold chills—feeling straight when I should feel . . . askew.

MRS. SEARS: I hate tenants! They're creeps to a man. Harold Sears, fetch the butterfly net. Alfred's chestering worse than ever.

[Exit MRS. SEARS.]

KEVIN SENIOR: Have you seen my boy, Kevin Killian? He's tall, white, and precious.

ALFRED CHESTER: Like Lot's wife. I'm Alfred Chester, bon vivant, beggar, practically a priestess. My religion: poetry—and the stars. Do you have any strong narcotic juice or twig? You've a strong smell of hemp about you.

KEVIN SENIOR: You're smarter than you look. That's my rope you smell. This was the rope that used to bind my boy to my side, near to these hands, that caressed him without thinking.

ALFRED CHESTER: Liza, you're great at singing, but leave the brainwork to Martha Graham. You're expressive enough in your own right—Betty Ford?

KEVIN SENIOR: The nights are bitter—

ALFRED CHESTER (*excitedly*): I know, I know! "The stars have lost their glitter!" Come departez, me show you best boy house in all Tangier. And all because of the man who got away.

[*Exit ALFRED CHESTER and KEVIN SENIOR. Enter WAYNE SMITH and LT. KEITEL.*]

WAYNE SMITH: Chief, I've got a problem.

LT. KEITEL: What problem, Smitty? You're sitting in gravy, just let it enter your colon in one great spasm after another. I still have to find that missing boy, but you've landed an heiress.

WAYNE SMITH: But she doesn't know me as a person. She thinks I'm some kind of nurse.

LT. KEITEL: Here's my advice, for what it's worth. Just put a pillowcase over your head. Take her money, and I'll invest it. You think Strawberry's gonna live forever? By tonight we'll be rolling in it, if I find that missing boy, which I will, if I have to rip this building apart with my teeth and hair.

WAYNE SMITH: I've looked up to you since I was a lad in rompers. But now I'm a man and I have to find my own path.

LT. KEITEL: You! You couldn't find a slug in a carload.

[Enter SARA.]

SARA: Police presence, in the building that will soon be mine. Reassuring.

LT. KEITEL (*lecherously*): Got any crack in your awesome body parts?

SARA: No. Have either of you seen this lovely, Swiss, blue-eyed goatherd who works in the coal cellar? Tag him if so, property of Sara Sears? [*To WAYNE SMITH.*] Young one, take me to the coal cellar.

WAYNE SMITH: Yes, Miss Sears.

LT. KEITEL: Pelt 'im with rice, mice, or ice, every cop I know's got some hincky little thing he goes for. Say—is that the Kansas Skate Medal you've got round your neck?

SARA (*proudly*): Yes, in French we call it the Jewel of the Plains.

[Exit SARA and WAYNE SMITH.]

LT. KEITEL (*on walkie-talkie*): Pauly? Keitel here. Keep your dick on, I've got a lead. Tell those goombahs they'll have their money by midnight. I'm tearing down the Sears Building brick by brick till I find the kid. Already I've torched two flats and a dumbwaiter. How dumb was he? I'll tell you how dumb, he ast me did I eat with a knife and fork, I told him, I've eaten kids like you for breakfast and spat them out for lunch. So I'm bulimic, sue me.

[Enter PAUL and JANE.]

PAUL: Frankly, I don't see the attraction.

JANE (*tugs at PAUL's sleeve, indicating KEITEL*): Ask me later.

LT. KEITEL: I was just out the door. Wanted to ask Mrs. Bowles how she gets her hair so brown. Wouldn't that hair feel good in my mouth.

[Exit LT. KEITEL.]

PAUL: What do you see in Sara, Jane?

JANE: Oh, a box of tinder, that's all—a little less than TNT—but still—awfully combustible. At first—those pigtails—put me off I admit,—and all that gingham. Had I died, I wondered, and woken up in the arms of Mary Pickford? No—Belinda

Carlisle—no! Louise Lasser! But Paul, trying to explain women to you is like—like spitting in the wind. You'll never understand all that happens between two women.

PAUL: "All"? Far from it.

JANE: I think I'll invite her to—to Marin County.

PAUL: Invite Sara?

JANE: Yes—It's a much more vivid mise-en-scene than this, the Sears Building. Remember that time you and I, Paul, drove to Marin on that Folsom Mystery Tour? And all the hills were burnt black—

PAUL [*reminiscent*]: . . . Like after Bambi's mother died—

JANE: Yes. That is exactly the place where someone like Sara Sears might fall in love with—someone like me. You see, I think of Sara as a child of the—what did they call it—the Triangle Shirtwaist Factory Fire. I'm only a firehose . . . pelvically screwed into the hydrant of desire. A hose, fat with gushing pressure, she makes me feel fat. And it's all water weight.

PAUL: Fat? You? You're about as fat as a minute.

[*A knock at the door. JANE jumps up, startled, but PAUL is more casual.*]

JANE: If that's Mrs. Sears tell her—tell her we will pay the rent if she'd lend me her granddaughter. Even for twenty minutes, Paul . . . If she loves me I know I'll make good.

PAUL: Relax—it's Kevin Killian. Come in, Kevin.

[*Enter KEVIN KILLIAN.*]

KEVIN KILLIAN: I'm here with my trademark smirk.

PAUL: You know, Jane, who would have thought that when this young boy disappeared off the corner of Haight and Presidio in his Catholic school uniform that the next day he'd be hiding out in the Sears Building basement, disguised as a goatherd, playing the janitor?

JANE (*peevishly*): I don't like it. I don't like the idea of that boy in this building. It's like harboring a fugitive. Why, a few weeks ago he was on the cover of *People*, and this week he's on the cover of *Rope Digest*. They want him to star in *The Bettie Page Story*. It makes me nervous, Paul. This time you're playing with fire.

KEVIN KILLIAN (*pointing ominously at Jane, and at the various parts of her body he mentions; she recoils*): Your body jerks from sleep. Something throbs inside your stomach, rots inside your vagina, death crowding your hair like gray strands of parasite.

JANE: Is that your idea of polite conversation? What is so funny, Kevin Killian? There are one million and one pederasts in San Francisco, any one of whom you might have picked, to mooch off of and fellate. But oh no. You had to pick my husband. Your kind of behavior gave Rimbaud and Verlaine a bad name, and they at least had talent. Splendor, actually. But you two!

KEVIN KILLIAN: My trademark smirk and rope burns devastate you, lady.

JANE: Kevin, don't you ever think about what your poor mom and dad are going through right now? I saw them on the late news last night. They're so depressed I thought I was watching a Werner Herzog movie.

PAUL: Do you really find Herzog depressing? I don't: I find him incredibly filled with energy, expenditure, zip.

JANE: Maybe I'm think of Wim Wenders . . . Anyhow it's all male energy, which in any case is so abysmal it's like tortoises. I wouldn't even call it energy except in deference to my marriage vows.

KEVIN KILLIAN: Who are you to watch me hatch, to touch, to fell, a stumbling adolescent, to tear my own flesh, hate, hate . . .

JANE [*to PAUL*]: Life is really a cake taker this week. First you take up with this male Anne Rice and then a day later I fall in love with a woman who reminds me of a— [*lights match*] —lit match, and I remind myself of the moth—the beautiful white moth—that's not careful with its life . . .

KEVIN KILLIAN: With slow screams your mouth pries wide . . . If you would like, I will tell you the story of how and why I ran away from home.

PAUL: Jane, you might be interested in this. Remember: critics are always accusing your work of an excess of cerebrality. They want to see more of the streets in your writing.

KEVIN KILLIAN (*stiffly*): Actually, the streets play little or no part in my tale.

PAUL: Even better! Pull up a chair, no, sit on your heels, your marvelous heels and insteps.

KEVIN KILLIAN: My story is much too sad to be told. But practically everything leaves me suddenly bold. At twelve, in the barrio near my parents' home, I became a pickpocket. At night I slipped from tienda to tienda, cantina to Cala, like a silent rag, too small to be seen over the counter. Asian immigrants spat on me without knowing I was there.

JANE: I think what they do isn't considered spitting. It's some form of ritual cleansing.

PAUL: I have to run, but you two keep talking. I want you to love each other. You're these important figures in my wife.

[*Exit PAUL BOWLES.*]

KEVIN KILLIAN: Don't count on it. I'm the king of the world!

JANE: When I was young my parents were involved in stopping the deportation of Brecht. Then it was sending Care Packages to Brecht in his new home in East Berlin. Then hawking Berliner Ensemble t-shirts at rock concerts.

KEVIN KILLIAN (*can't believe his ears*): Rock concerts! What cacophony! I know it's unusual in a boy my age to dislike rock,. But I prefer the sophisticated sounds of Mabel Mercer, Bobby Short, Leonard Cohen and Shania Twain . . .

[*Enter HAROLD SEARS, carrying some towels, to show his new tenant her room. She—Cheryl WILSON—is a street person with several large bags full of trash. JANE and KEVIN KILLIAN turn their backs but do not leave the stage.*]

MR. SEARS: So as you can see the room isn't much but if you're not an artist you're welcome to it just as sure as my name is Harold Sears. Just sign here, Ms. Wilson is it? "Cheryl Wilson"—an unusual, mundane, name, I like it by gum. Right here, on the dotted line.

CHERYL WILSON (*pointing to dots*): The dots say my name. "Hannah—Hannah!" Do not call me by my rightful Cheryl Wilson. This room drips alphabet voices in dots: settle on "Hannah." "Hannah Weiner," the wall drop residue.

MR. SEARS: So the dots say your name! Ha ha! I can tell by your outfit you're practically a schizophrenic—fine by me! SSI's a good provider. Go ahead—call yourself "Hannah" if it makes you more comfy. As long as you're not an artist, Sears Manor shall be your home. Got any family, Miss Wilson or Wiener?

CHERYL WILSON (*brightly*): No—wish I did! [*Aside: enraged*]: My little boy—of the future! I see him now, like a midget in a plate of soup!

MR. SEARS: Charming!

CHERYL WILSON: In a dream I had, three cats with duck feet told me to come to Sears Building, steal a child, find a new life. "Hannah, you're bad." "No, Hannah, you're good." "Hannah, steal that purse." "Hannah, don't." "Too late, I done it good." I'm a mess I suppose but a cooing bassinet might cure me of what ails me.

[*HAROLD SEARS and CHERYL WILSON turn their backs, while JANE and KEVIN KILLIAN face audience.*]

JANE: So then I discovered language-centered writing in a funny kind of way. I was teaching ordinary writing in the Tenderloin when a strange woman joined my group, set it on its ear. Her name was Wilson, Cheryl Wilson, but she called herself Hannah, the word that spelled backward spells itself, spells disjunction. If she wasn't schizophrenic she was the next best thing. What a writer! I mean she couldn't write, but every word was a revelation!

KEVIN KILLIAN: That's what people say about me.

JANE: I ditched my old, cold ways of composition, and inched up her bandwagon tout de suite. Then one day two policemen knocked on my door asking questions about Hannah. Seems like she was wanted for questioning in the Baby M case.

[*Enter WAYNE SMITH and LT. KEITEL in a flashback.*]

WAYNE SMITH: Jane Bowles? You are under the dictates of Mayor Willie Brown to tell what you know about the vagabond poet, Cheryl Wilson. Though she may strike you as the female Artaud, she's under suspicion of strong tampering with rabbit results, contraband ova.

LT. KEITEL: She's like any other fugitive, hasty, misty and naught. I fucked her good, till she coughed up the crack in her sleep.

WAYNE SMITH: By day apparently as level-headed at Oprah, Wilson by night stalks back alleys South of Market for test tube babies, turkey basters and other fallopian miracles. Don't conflate her language politesse with the right to stolen motherhood. Cheryl or Hannah, Subject Alias is wanted for abrupt nature, crimes so numerous you need not remember. If you are sheltering this known felon, surrender her now, Jane. The hour is nigh!

LT. KEITEL: Give her to me, I'll sell her, buy crack!

WAYNE SMITH: The hour is nigh!

LT. KEITEL: The piglet is mine!

[*Exit WAYNE SMITH and LT. KEITEL.*]

KEVIN KILLIAN: Hope I don't run into her! A boy alone on the streets can't be too careful these days. I have grief enough to fill my satchel, I don't need implication in a mother-son relation.

MR. SEARS (*facing audience*): If you need anything my wife and I are just down the hall. Ignore if you can the caterwauling sycophants who call themselves artists. My granddaughter, Sara Sears, will destroy them shortly. Only a temporary inconvenience, Miss Weiner Wilson, one you can live with for several days till you find your feet and help us stamp them out like roaches.

JANE: I'd love to meet her again and tell her of my passion for Sara Sears. I used to go to Tenderloin bars, dressed as a man, but no.

CHERYL WILSON (*facing audience*): My shoes are talking—"Hannah! Hannah! The room is larger than your mind!"

KEVIN KILLIAN: Go now, and find peace in your own disgusting way. I'm a boy with promise, who are you to me but mere recrimination.

JANE: If Paul's involved with you he must have more sex drive than I supposed.

KEVIN KILLIAN: I'm no Matt Damon but I'm available.

MR. SEARS (*slamming on door of JANE and PAUL's room*): Pipe down in there you loudmouths. Ah, what have we here, my new janitor playing the fool. Back to work, you slavey, and bring some coal to my new tenant in 304.

JANE (*to KEVIN*): Your kind of attitude got Bertolt Brecht in hot water. I'll go—I'll do the graceful thing. I'll find Sara Sears, with gloves on!

[*Exit JANE.*]

MR. SEARS: I don't suppose you'll be needing these towels, you bring your own soap and water with you every time you speak. Others may cringe from the homeless but at the Sears Building your fragrance is welcome. [*Places towels under chair.*] Say thank you.

CHERYL WILSON: Thank is not you! You are the thank! My shoes say your name—"Hannah! Hannah." Are thank you Hannah, this was the little thank note, are not you the thank, Hannah waves in field of marble, through the notes, when you are the thank!

MR. SEARS (*to heaven*): Thank you, Jesus, for bringing me a tenant unaffiliated with the arts. Now I know how people must feel in, say, Fremont.

[*Exit HAROLD SEARS. CHERYL remains seated throughout, just pressing her fingers to her forehead waiting for messages. KEVIN KILLIAN walks upstage.*]

KEVIN KILLIAN: There's Dad in the shrubs. OK, Kevin, stay cool, it's not like you've never been exploited and maimed.

[*Enter KEVIN KILLIAN.*]

Hi, there, my American friend, you look down in the dumphopper, yes?

KEVIN SENIOR: A friendly Swiss face. I'm looking for my boy, an American lad with rope burns, comprendez-vous? Me—him—tied together from birth?

KEVIN KILLIAN. I saw him at Cal Trans, fleeing a man he hated.

KEVIN SENIOR: Couldn't have been me! I loved him and liked to get in his pockets. We slept together in the same bed, and now he's fourteen. See? Here's his photo, he looks a bit like you, only less Alpine.

KEVIN KILLIAN. Sorry, can't help you.

[*Enter WAYNE SMITH.*]

WAYNE SMITH: OK, break it up. You—coal guy—back to the cellar. You—creepy father guy—take your transference elsewhere.

KEVIN KILLIAN. I dig. See you, Daddy-O.

[*Exit KEVIN KILLIAN.*]

WAYNE SMITH: I've had enough heat for one day—my wedding to Barbara Hutton, the search for Cheryl Wilson, the in-depth profile in Focus magazine—I don't need a sodomy beef on my paperwork. You two were loitering for immoral perps.

KEVIN SENIOR: I resent that. All my love, pure and profane, I spent on my boy Kevin Killian. Long nights together on the Sealycrest. Mornings hot and sunny, only a rope's length apart. Afternoons we'd go to Candlestick and watch the Giants whip the challengers' asses. Nights were ours—sacred to us.

WAYNE SMITH: Don't fuck with me. Whatever "it" is, get over it.

[*Enter JANE and PAUL.*]

PAUL: Jane, Jane, she's all wrong for you. She cares only about herself. She's not even a Lesbian.

JANE: You're confusing my need with identity politics. I exist, now, only as a causal thing. I'm leaving the Sears Building, leaving you, running off to Marin with Sara, if I can find her. We are off to found our new island—Sarasota. Who is? A native woman, tall as a maypole, bearing the fruits of a corn-fed planet, and I, the abyss, the crawlspace beneath her heart. Sarasota, in the Bay, off Marin, hills black with blood flies, swarming round the juice of her navel.

PAUL: "If" you can talk her into it. That's a big if, Jane Bowles.

JANE: Well, I'm a big if type girl, I guess.

[*Exit JANE, enter BARBARA HUTTON.*]

BARBARA HUTTON: Paul, dear, I'm in a pickle. That nice Lieutenant has persuaded me to invest some money in the Dodgers. We're renaming them the Tangier Dodgers after our dear native people and their wooden sticks and balls.

PAUL: Sounds like a done deal.

BARBARA HUTTON: Has a woman like I another chance of love? This blue man I married has strong, almost pernicious vibrations. When I see him I quiver. Yet I'm too smart to fall in love, especially with Nurse Smitty. Or don't you agree? I thought the world of your famous book *The Sheltering Sky*. I learned how to live from touching its pages with my jewels.

[Enter HAROLD SEARS.]

Oh, dear, there's that sinister Mahmoudi. Just this morning he set fire to my sheet music. I'll fly for my blue boy because, after all, sometimes a halo hides the horns.

[Exit BARBARA HUTTON.]

MR. SEARS: Run like the wind, Barbara Hutton! Artistic pretensions!

PAUL: Why is it you don't like us much, Mr. Sears? We're a colorful bunch, unpredictable, like to party . . . I would have thought that at your age you'd have seen enough—corporate real estate, vice presidents, big business types. That we artists would be a sight for sore eyes. Evidently not. But why? Clue me, Harold Sears.

MR. SEARS: For one thing, Paul, your wife is a sexual pervert.

PAUL: She is a Language poet. There's a difference.

MR. SEARS: And you—you're making a name for yourself—and the name isn't *[points upward to Heaven]* HIS.

PAUL: I'm a photographer of the human brain at work.

MR SEARS. Headed for the darkroom of Hell.

PAUL: Actually, come to think of it, your wife's kind of a sex pervert too. So we have something in common.

MR. SEARS: To the acid baths with you, you sodomite!

PAUL: Every word you speak's like a picture, but you'll have to excuse me now, I have a date with a bike messenger . . . Spoke by spoke I aim to make him mine.

[Exits. Left alone, Mr. Sears addresses a picture of his building that hangs from one wall in the classic soliloquy.]

MR. SEARS: Where did we do wrong? I remember the good old days—only the most respectable people in San Francisco rented rooms in this building. The real Falcon Maltese. And now, nothing but those darn artists! What was my mistake? How did this entropic slide begin?

—I know: it was that Mrs. Van Ness in 201. Said she played the piano, would I mind a little piano music now and again . . . Only the masters—Brahms, Chopin, Liszt—I said, "Sure, why not?" I figured, "What the hey, she's in society." I should have known better. That was henna in her hair! First thing I knew, no more Brahms or Liszt. Instead: Stravinsky. Schoenberg. The twelve-tone scale. Notes like pesky stinging hornets rather than the honey of a well-kept beehive. But I kept my temper against my better judgment.

Next came a visit from a lady with a cello—The elevator was too small. Then the cello grew a couple piccolos walked around with her. One thing leads to another. You give them an inch, you start hearing John Cage and Laurie Anderson . . . Meredith Monk . . .

[*Enter ALFRED CHESTER.*]

Yoko Ono . . . RuPaul . . . . Brian Eno—ambient music, Gol-dangit!

ALFRED CHESTER: I have a little jukebox in my head, Liza, it never stops spinning your duet with the Pet Shop Boys. It's like I'm losing my mind, here in Tangier where all the lights are bright.

HAROLD SEARS: Mrs. Sears, come here at once!

[*Enter MRS. SEARS, phone in hand.*]

MRS. SEARS: Harold, you're making a ruckus.

MR. SEARS: I'm having tenant problems.

ALFRED CHESTER: Neil Tennant? Neil Tennant from the Pet Shop Boys? I knew the way your voices blend there was more going down than just vinyl, Liza. You're amazing.

HAROLD SEARS: Gladys, get me the number of the police. I'm reporting a felony. Know that boy who run off from the corner of Haight and Presidio? Paul is lodging him in the boiler room disguised as a porter.

MRS. SEARS: You mean that little Swiss tyke who keeps yodeling Yo-de-lay-hee-hoo?

ALFRED CHESTER: Actually, Liza, I liked you better in your *Arthur* phase, with those funky dog-eared factory gowns. [*Soothingly.*] I know, I know, since the death of Halston there's just nobody left in fashion. That's why we're here, in Tangier, taking all the drugs he would have wanted us to, and thinking of him every time we sodomize a native.

MRS. SEARS: That boy's from Basel or Lausanne or some other Swiss location.

MR. SEARS: If he's from Switzerland, I'll eat every briquette of coal in that cellar. Ten to one that boy is Kevin Killian, the 100,000 dollar kid. Gladys, my eyes, my hawklike, piercing eyes may make us rich yet!

MRS. SEARS:(*sniffs*): "Hawklike"? "Piercing"? Hmmph! Sounds like *M*A*S*H* or I'm not Gladys Sears.

[*Nevertheless she hands him the phone.*]

MR. SEARS: Police?

ALFRED CHESTER: Okay, okay, I get the message, Liza dear. Au revoir, or as we say when we poison our intimates, Allah-ben-azzam.

[*Exit ALFRED CHESTER.*]

MR. SEARS: This is Harold Sears. Yes, the Harold Sears, of the Sears Building. Listen up. Does the name Kevin Killian ring any bells in your flat-footed ears?

[*SARA enters, unseen, followed by her CONSCIENCE.*]

MRS. SEARS: That's right. I heard that Mayor Willie Brown is offering one hundred thousand dollars out of her own pocket for information. Land o Laken! What I could do with that money! Where's my Sears Catalogue? First thing I'll do with that cash is order some curtains to brighten up the place. No. That will be the second thing I do. [*Flings away catalogue.*] I will dial Artists Extermination and rid my home of pests! Harold, finish your business on my Princess phone and let me call for relief. Nancy Reagan said, "Just Say No"—and I'm saying "No" to deadbeats, "no" to painters. No performance, no linguistics. No Poets Theater, no THIS and no [*makes horrible strangled face*] THAT!

CONSCIENCE (*to SARA*): You've made a mess of things, haven't you, Sara Sears?

MR. SEARS (*on the phone to the police*): He's wearing a baseball cap rolled backward, Alp style, and carries a large milk pail and a hunk of chard. Yes, officer. I checked his palms and his penis—he is definitely not Swiss.

SARA (*unheard by her grandparents*): Last night I left my room to fetch a glass of water from the cellar pump. Descending the rickety wooden steps, pushing holes through the webs of the ornate spider family, I dropped my flashlight.

CONSCIENCE: Down the steps it bashed, bang, bang, bang, like the gunshots that killed Marvin Gaye.

SARA: Finally it came to rest with its lighted end wavering across the dusty basement floor, pointing like a weathervane to what wasn't a man or boy, but rather a whole climate of erotic opinion.

CONSCIENCE: The missing boy, Kevin Killian? Or the ghosts of those two teens you drowned at Spirit Lake?

SARA: I was caught—captured—by a pair of blue eyes so vivid and so sleepy they seemed those of Loretta Lynn . . . but they belonged to a sleeping boy—a boy who sleeps with his eyes open, and his mouth open, and his clothes open.

CONSCIENCE: Was there a medal round his neck? Or do I hear the squeamish sounds of animal attraction?

MR. SEARS: "How did he get here?" Officer, this is Harold Sears not Nostradamus. It's too long a story to tell, but I will say this much: it's worse than you think.

[Hangs up; hands phone to MRS. SEARS.]

[CHERYL WILSON sits alone in her room. She opens her shopping bag and puts a series of hats on her head.]

CHERYL WILSON: Hannah lives for child, the hunger in her arms, the sentences creeping like whispers on her back, the back of the four-backed beast. Appease the Master! Shotgun, loaded gun, empty my purse! Bring me the soft nudgable head of my baby boy.

MR. SEARS: Mrs. Sears, it's time to man our stations. I want an APB on that boiler room pronto. Police are on their way and I don't want any Patty Hearst shoot-out. Bring along that cell phone and meet me in the tasteful foyer.

[*Mr. and MRS. SEARS exit with phone.*]

SARA: And only his sense of self seemed closed to me in that—intolerably close room. The cave walls were slimy and covered with graffiti, big pictures of big cocks and big words.

CONSCIENCE: Give back the jewel of the plains to the mom and dad of the dead drowned teens! And stop flirting with Jane, it behooves you to cease!

CHERYL WILSON: This is the hat of the woman who looked at me funny. These ribbons and things were her property.

[*Enter KEVIN SENIOR.*]

KEVIN SENIOR: I've paid 30K to that blonde cop for info leading to my son's arrest and got zero. What does he think, I'm made of obsession?

CHERYL WILSON: Master, I crawled into your youth for a reason. The pipes beneath the sink did scratch my gray brain matter.

SARA: I began to see the connection. The attraction, the allure—of a language.

CONSCIENCE: I feel like I'm wasting my time here. I feel as though I should go back to conscience school.

[*Exit CONSCIENCE.*]

CHERYL WILSON: When Hannah feels blue the roof of the sky did turn with snow. They took my husband and made him suck the big root. In the hour of counterfeit bliss, oh Master, find me my young little precious seed back.

KEVIN SENIOR: Lt. Keitel, find my young little precious seed back.

SARA: I give myself into the world, I lure myself to your mystery chain. He's right under my nose if only I know it.

[*Exit KEVIN SENIOR; SARA and CHERYL remain onstage.*]

CHERYL WILSON: Black whistle in the dead of night, when you come to my
door with coal, have your bags packed. [*Breaking into verse, as follows:*]

on the laughable street, a foot on the curb,
in the gutter a glaze, rain you can taste
but it's pleasant, I don't worry about you

SARA: Awkward salsa music on Noe Street
and a salesman of fringes and tassels
I think he's an eaglet

CHERYL: in the hospital in the crush ward
a visitor in white approached my bed
with an armful of violets

greetings from Robin Blaser's Idaho
as if behind the screen
a patient is groaning, not in pain

SARA: Pretzels and hot Spanish coffee
walls of stone, like dripping honey
Julia Roberts to wed

CHERYL: she's so romantic and exquisite
and this is so tasteful, like
all of Noe Valley from Diamond to

[*Enter KEVIN KILLIAN, bringing a bucket of coal.*]

SARA: Church, old pulp thrillers like
Phenomena Creepers, down to the
corner of Mission and Capp, the galleys

[*CHERYL WILSON pours chloroform into a handkerchief and lavishly douses KEVIN
KILLIAN'S mouth with it.*]

CHERYL: of a new book, paper and purple
wafting up one's nostrils assault
it's not amazing

BOTH: I want him, I want him and I don't care
who knows it

[CHERYL WILSON exultantly drags KEVIN offstage]

[as JANE enters through the audience.]

JANE: I come from a great height with a great love. Sara, I don't know what you think of me, nor of my writing school, I just need your affection—no—not even that. I need to know—that's it!—you exist in the world.

SARA: Unfortunately, I can't guarantee even that much.

JANE: Since I met you a year ago Viagra's taken our town by storm and I finished my masterpiece, *In the Summer House.* But it all seems so insignificant now. You're dangerous, Sara, the lesbian Gloria Grahame.

SARA: Whereas within there is no "I," there's only one man, a boy or guy with black sooty hands and a catch in his throat. We're a pretty pair, you and I.

JANE (*seeing her dreams crumble into ashes; angry*): "Pretty," you say? "Pair," you say? Don't matronize me, Miss Sears! What happens now to my dream of Sarasota? Mo-cho vamoso, and all because, you've taken male energy into your blockhead? Do I just go back to Paul and say retreat cancelled, no black island of heat and syntax?

SARA: And what of my dream? The boy I flew from Kansas to admire has been abducted by your great mentor Hannah! Granny and Gramps are pretty cut up: they weep in sackcloth for my destination. But they're like two glad kittens next to my desolate pup. How can a person bear it? What shall I do?

JANE (*moved to pity*): We're in the same fit of angst, looks like. What are our chances? Fate holds up a vowel to our Wheel of Fortune, behind these curtains loom great prize rooms of possibility:—Careerism's one. Or charity work's been a fatal attraction for many: an hour with Jerry's kids is a month in the country. Or writing projects? Translations of the Russian futurists—[*Hastily*]—or the Kansas City futurists, of course. I imagine they're copious.

SARA (*eagerly*): L. Frank Baum—wrote *The Wizard of Oz*. And Mariette Hartley—who did all those classic Polaroid commercials with James Garner—? They're both from Kansas City;—and now we've got Anne Boyer.

[*To herself, conscience-stricken.*] And so were those two teens . . . crying when I stepped on their fingers with my sling blades . . . at Spirit Lake . . .

JANE: I know, I know . . . Yes, charity might be your donnee: recently I've helped elderly people cross the streets. I have to—it distracts me from my coma of lovelorn. We must put our minds into work like Rube Goldberg clavier inventions. Just say to yourself, today, "Sara, one night with a grinning bag Hannah Wilson did run to steal my boy," and something good will come of this I know.

SARA: Unfortunately I can't guarantee even that much. Which I already told you, Jane! I'm not rad on guarantees like your precious Laura Riding . . . Yet your accommodation had made me twinkle. What's a grin or two, Jane, in this sea of deplenitude? You'd be a regular Vanna White with a few more inches and a tube of peroxide.

MR. SEARS (*hollering offstage*): Gone! What do you mean, gone? Flown the coop, blown the hatch! Dispersed like Baby Lindbergh? With what ladder out which window?

SARA: He's heard.

JANE: So? Why should he be exempt from weltschmerz? Because he owns property? Humbug!

SARA: Someday all that's his will be mine. Blood's thicker than water, ether's thicker than either.

JANE (*cupping her ear*): Cheese it, the cops. Paul says Vanna White's real name's Savannah White, she hails from Belle Reve without illusions. I could do that faded Southern gentility with both hands tied behind your back.

[*Enter HAROLD and GLADYS SEARS, supporting him.*]

MR. SEARS: Never, never, never, never, never!

SARA: He's kind of like Lear in that famous play. But I've enough grief for a whole escutcheon, I don't do Cordelia like Debbie does Dallas.

JANE: Bury your head in tears, my dear. I'll subdue my nature to what it works in, the dyer's hand of discredited Shakespeare.

[*Exit JANE.*]

MRS. SEARS: Thank goodness you're still here, Sara! We had a beast in our cellar you might have eloped with.

SARA (*aside*): Would that I had . . . [*Sunk in grief she collapses in a chair.*]

MRS. SEARS: And now look at my beloved Harold! Before my very eyes he's been aging since we learned the bitter truth of loss. And spouting the gibberish of outer space radio, I've tried pep pills, pacemakers, Viagra but nothing seems to trick him. Says he's hearing voices now coming out of the walls from Mars the Red Planet.

[*Enter LT. KEITEL, with notebook.*]

LT. KEITEL: Are you the party who reported the recovery of the missing boy, Kevin Killian?

MR. SEARS: Hello, this is Judge Wapner
and this is Harold Sears

run by me
this is the famous
belonging of who
is what to decide
run it by me
Bailiff, the oil painting
Bailiff and THE FACT

THIS ACTRESS doing to me
bigger than real

actual size, so Judge,
every one of my factors

So I want you to
vote for me, in my favor
and that's your decision
in my apartment

MRS. SEARS: Harold has taken a turn for the worse since our tenant, Hannah, ran off with the Million Dollar Kid. Are you really a policeman?

LT. KEITEL: I represent Willie Brown to the streets of San Francisco. The man you used to run to when things went wrong, Frank Jordan, no longer has jurisdiction.

MR. SEARS: This is a conspiracy.

LT. KEITEL: If so, it has the emphatic weight of a mandate. Spread em, Sears. No, higher and deeper, give it to me in 3-D.

[*Enter PAUL BOWLES, WAYNE SMITH, BARBARA HUTTON.*]

PAUL: People got tired of Frank Jordan. If it wasn't one thing it was another.

OFFICER SMITH: His program to keep the homeless off the streets backfired badly, and his constant foreign travel gave him the sinister rep of a Colombian coke kingpin.

LT. KEITEL (*to HAROLD SEARS*): Now where is the boy, and where is the woman? You say they're gone? Produce them like acorns. You say the one took the other?

HAROLD SEARS: This is harassment, a broomstick in the scrotum! Which I still have!

PAUL: I read about Willie Brown, he made big promises to the City's artists.

ALFRED CHESTER: I met him on Mt. Tanganyika, he leaned out his howdah, shook my tassel, and signed me his autograph. "Alfred," he said, "my name is Mayor Willie Brown." "Oh, Liza, you're so mistaken," I told him. "Even a broken clock's right twice a day."

PAUL: So we want to know is he gonna keep those promises, or is he like all the other politicians, all meat and no potatoes.

LT. KEITEL: Absolutely. I have here the warrant that once signed will turn this, the Sears Building, into the annex of the Hotel Tax Fund. We'll call it "Small Press Traffic."

ALFRED CHESTER: Silly name, but a great idea. Three cheers for Liza! I feel like all my years baking honey ganoush tea cookies for our pot parties haven't gone to waste. Now where is Neil Tennant? We'll make this a two-way.

MR. SEARS: This must be some kind of nightmare, the kind you get after eating Dagwood's sandwich. My building a Literary Arts Center?

BARBARA HUTTON: Funded by the Barbara Hutton Foundation: a big square box filled with silver, money, copper and gold.

MR. SEARS: A place where people read poetry?

MRS. SEARS: Harold, hush. Sara will help us, I know she will. She's Mayor Brown's goddaughter, his personal pet. Sara, do something. Your grandfather's no longer young, and with his temper eviction's no option.

SARA (*purposely ignoring her grandmother*): Officer, why is it whenever I come to Canessa Park [*SARA may use the name of whatever theatrical space is actually showing THAT in*] it's so sterile in the building—like the inside of an igloo?.

MR. SEARS (*aghast*): She's turned against us like everyone else. Her enigmatic smile belongs on a Cheshire cat, not on the daughter of my youngest whippersnapper.

SARA: And always these poets like Susan Howe, the trendy lack representation.

PAUL (*to police*): And like, I only moved to San Francisco in the first place to see Whoopi Goldberg here, because like I really loved *The Color Purple* and she's so bodacious and you put her in your commercials, but not a sign of her anywhere. Can't the City do something about this? I'm a citizen, I have rights.

[*Enter JANE.*]

JANE: So I apply for the Writer in Residence program, and they take a look at my work—

PAUL: And Robin Williams.

JANE: They read my work and they tell me, sorry, Jane, our quota's filled up for Language writing, we've been in touch with—wow—William T. Vollman and he'll be here a year from September—shooting off pistols, quashing competition—And so I say to them, "William T. Vollman! How long do the knowing have to put up with the wishful!"

PAUL: And all this brouhaha about Cole Slaw Milosz, who's actually been dead for 55 years, still they think he's going to come back from the grave and devour half the world's population. Meanwhile Jane here is blazing with talent and the San Francisco Arts Commission is giving their money to white hula dancers and people who turn concrete into cement!

OFFICER SMITH: We're jotting down as fast as I can, your complaints and roasts.

LT. KEITEL: Mayor Brown will hear about these in the morning. My advice is, give him a call and jog his memory. [*Earnestly.*] He's sweet.

BARBARA HUTTON (*to PAUL*): He's feisty like you—and he's empathetic.

WAYNE SMITH: Meanwhile, I'd like a further description of your tenant, Cheryl Wilson, Mr. Sears, and perhaps we can trace her erratic progress through America's welfare hotels.

[*All but SARA huddle nearby chair that represents CHERYL's apartment*]

SARA: How can a person bear it? "Though nothing remains of the hour/ Of splendor in the grass, or glory in the flower"—

CONSCIENCE: You still have your skating medal to console you.

SARA (*produces medal from around her neck, disgusted*): This?

CONSCIENCE: Two Kansas teens drowned so you could keep that medal, which you didn't deserve.

SARA: I guess I didn't. Is this my pay back? I'll throw the Jewel of the Plains into the ocean. Maybe I was calculating, maybe I was headstrong, and oh yes, I was a killer, but this heartache is unbearable, conscience!

CONSCIENCE (*moved to pity*): Rest your weary head on mine. I'm your shadow and do everything you do, under protest.

SARA: Two into three, or cloves versus garlic . . . I guess eventually you learn to bear everything Life dishes out, like a monkey's paw, or else, where are you?

PAUL: Dreams are a code in writing like punctuation!!!
Largely unexamined or missing like KEVIN COLLINS!!!
Every time the writer tells his or her dream it is an excuse!!!
Let alone being a fact it is not a fact, only a buoy!!!

CONSCIENCE: On the corner of Haight and Presidio there he stood!!!
It was not talking to a dog that made him do it!!!
Naturally this gives rise to apprehension only the wrong sort!!!
Only a dog and only a boy on apparently cool white ocean!!!

MRS. SEARS: After all, we are both human and both need our sleep!!!
Thornton Wilder said the strain is so great, the strain!!!

BARBARA HUTTON: Is so great every sixteen hours we pass out and dream!!!
To stay alive and to try to change like Body Works!!!
But in the car with a cheesecloth stuffed down his throat!!!
And the dog's rough tongue licking his face all the way down!!!

SARA: Bobbing to and fro and almost wholly etiolated!!!

LT. KEITEL: Restive as any other hidden or tortured thing or wife!!!

SARA: Besides this relation is a little like a stepbrother to look at!!!

LT. KEITEL: Even in despite I do not go down to the works like glue, you son
of a bitch!

CHERYL WILSON (*from rear of audience*): Up unto the mountains the car
steadily progresses!!!
And that pressure doesn't ruin the tires, but leaves evidence!!!
Over a rut. Under the branch of a low-lying scrub pine!!!
It is more a threat like home movie of an operation with scars!!!

SARA (*from rear of audience*): This is completely different than the orphic that
I like!!!
So do not confute me while you can with the parallel signs!!!
Nobody gets impressed while all there is to see is a space!!!
and a blazer like a uniform thrown out on the muddy track!!!

JANE: So what is there to write about to really write home!!!
even if it is only a postcard from somebody else all over again!!!
or even a note built out of yesterday's grocery meat sales!!!
that says I want a million dollars and no one will get hurt!!!

ALL. Wake up! Let's go see!!!
Bava's final masterpiece!!!
Red High Heels of Death!!!

[*Music comes up, "We Built this City on Rock and Roll"*]

END

Originally staged at Intersection for the Arts (San Francisco), April 4 and 5, 1988, with the following cast: Lori Lubeski, John Norton, Eileen Corder, Kevin Killian, Camille Roy, Tom Mandel, Dodie Bellamy, Chris Custer, and Cheryl Wilson

Revived at Canessa Park (San Francisco), November 21, 1993, with the following cast: Laurie Amat, Todd Baker, Nayland Blake, Norma Cole, Margaret Crane, Phoebe Gloeckner, Jonathan Hammer, Andrea Juno, Kevin Killian, Kevin Radley, Eleni Sikelianos and Wayne Smith

Island of Lost Souls

characters

GABRIELLE KEROUAC
struggling Lesbian single mother

JACK KEROUAC
failed beat novelist and alcoholic

JEFF
agent with William Morris

JOEY BUTTAFUOCO
teenage paperboy

WILLIAM S BURROUGHS
sinister novelist, wife murderer

SUNNY VON BULOW
heiress, diabetic

CLAUS VON BULOW
suspicious husband

CLARICE
countess von Bulow his sister

JULIE ANDREWS
restless British superstar

YMA SUMAC
peruvian soprano and hasbeen

ANAIS NIN
international gadabout and diarist

[SCENE, Long Island home of Gabrielle Kerouac and her son, Jack. Gabrielle is an elegant, haggard woman of advancing years. Her son is about 35, a drunken wreck of a man who spends all his time staring out of a big armchair, a bottle by his side.]

[As the curtain goes up GABRIELLE is fiddling with an umbrella, while Jack sits drunk in his armchair.]

GABRIELLE: Heavy rains are dashing my hopes for a picnic but it's still a fine day here at the Kerouac home, in Northport, Long Island. The first fine day in a long, long time. Jack!

JACK: A squat room—in a wet house.

GABRIELLE: [*To audience*] That's my son, the beat genius. He's been in kind of a fug for ten years. Wake up, Jack! It's a new dawn—a new day for us both.

JACK: My name is . . . Jack.

GABRIELLE: You can sit there like a bump on a log, but not me—me, Gabrielle. [*Music plays.*] I'm elegant, soignée, a swan indeed, mired in this oil slick we call life. For years I've dreamed for both me and Jack, and today our dreams come true. Now do you need anything before I start breakfast?

JACK: A drink.

GABRIELLE: Zut alors! I ask you one day, not to drink, not to mope, forget your troubled past and think only the happy thoughts of a mother and son, tragically transplanted from Quebec to this [*snarl*] island of lost souls.

JACK: Are you my mother?

GABRIELLE: One day, you 'n' me will share a bungalow on Miami Beach, in the sun. We'll let the sun bake away our cares. But dreams cost money, this I know! And I plan to get it, by all the powers that live within a woman. Me go down to the pay phone on the corner—[*sympathetically*] Okay, I'll pick up a bottle at Liquor Mart. It's 1964 and "co-dependency" isn't even a word yet.

[She steps out of the house and goes to the pay phone at the corner, where a spruce young man, JEFF, is hogging the phone.]

JEFF: Hi, this is Jeff—I can't talk long, I'm at a public phone. And I'm in Public Relations, so that's so droll! Nervous? Oh, just a tad.

GABRIELLE [*approaching phone, annoyed to see someone using it*]: Is your name Tad?

JEFF: No, Jeff.

GABRIELLE: Boy, you're tying up my line. I'm expecting an important phone call from Peru.

JEFF: Beg pardon, but this is a public phone.

GABRIELLE: Oh, I didn't know. [*Makes face as if to indicate how obvious this is.*] I'll stand here and eavesdrop on your conversation then, if it's that public.

[*To audience*]: This boy Tad's a lad, he doesn't realize the urgency of my dime.

JEFF: There's a crazy woman here trying to filibuster, but she won't succeed—what is it about me that makes everyone think I'm timid? Is it the sheen of my face or my downward, glancing eyes?

GABRIELLE: It's because you're weak, Jeff! (*To audience: He's not really, but my call is vital.*) Because you're a pushover for a beautiful lesbian mother! Where are you from, New York? Tell New York I eat boys like you and spit them out like toothpicks! Now get off the fershlugginer phone!

JEFF: Okay, okay. [*He hangs up the phone.*]

GABRIELLE: Never mind.

JEFF: Now you tell me!

GABRIELLE: I was moved to pity by your resemblance to my poor dear son. You can share my umbrella, or, as we say in Peru—[*quickly*] Quebec, mon parapluie.

JEFF: To weather I'm impervious—because I'm young. But dear me, I'm late. I have a terribly important meeting with Jack Kerouac—who's supposed to live somewhere around here.

GABRIELLE: Oh?

JEFF: I'm with the William Morris Agency. My clients include many of the great personalities of the 60s, including Julie Andrews.

GABRIELLE (*eagerly*): Fresh from *My Fair Lady* and *Mary Poppins*.

JEFF: She's been looking for a challenge, she doesn't want to be a governess all her life. She wants to push the Julie Andrews envelope.

GABRIELLE: I've always adored her, like a dainty rose.

JEFF: She now plans to star in the musical version of *On the Road*.

GABRIELLE (*carefully*): Oh? Really?

JEFF: Yes, so she's here in Northport to meet its author, Jack Kerouac. People say he's a terrible drunk. Locals. The hicks you meet at the gas pumps. They say he's pickled morning noon and night.

GABRIELLE: That's a shoddy lie, a common canard.

JEFF: Hope so. Miss Andrews hates a drunk!

GABRIELLE: Has Miss Andrews actually read *On the Road*?

JEFF: No, but she's heard it's hip, and she needs that for the remainder of the 60s. She's only a girl but the young of today have her pegged as a stodge.

GABRIELLE: I'm sure there's a great part for a woman! It's all about Neal Cassady, *ne c'est pas*—we'll just call it, "NEALIE"! With a point d'exclamation! It will be ze hippest. Oh, there's my cab. Have fun in Northport.

JEFF: I'm too nervous for fun. My heebies have jeebies, I'm knotted like a face card, my body starts at the waist and goes up and down, king, queen, jack.

[*exit JEFF*]

GABRIELLE: Poor thing! Driver, take me to Liquor Barn *immediatement*.

[*Frowns.*]

There's a moving van in front of the old Gatsby mansion across the lane. Hmm. One thing I don't want is intrusive strangers bothering my Jack. Oh, Joey!

[Enter paperboy, JOEY, on a bike if possible.]

JOEY: Yes, Ma Kerouac.

GABRIELLE: What's the word on the street about those newcomers to Shady Lane? You're the paper boy, you know it all.

JOEY: They're rich society types from Denmark or Manhattan. The von Bulows, we call them, husband and wife. He's a creepy lounge lizard with long red hair like Chopin. She's a fading yellow primrose, half asleep, looks like. That'll be a nickel, Miss Kerouac, or my name's not Joey—Joey Buttafuoco—as a teenager.

GABRIELLE: You'll go far, Joey, and here's your nickel.

JOEY: And there's the sister of Count Von Bulow. She, like you, is a woman with a secret.

GABRIELLE: Tell you what, bike off to Liquor Mart and tell em to send me a case of J & B. Deliver it to the back door, Joey, tell em that.

JOEY *(pedaling off)*: Extra, extra, read all about it. Von Bulows Move to Shady Lane, details at 11.

[exit JOEY. GABRIELLE *returns to living room, where she fails to see* JEFF *or* WILLIAM BURROUGHS.*]*

GABRIELLE: Jack, remember when you were a paper boy, plowing through the streets of Lowell in search of a scoop? Every time I see little Joey I whisk back a sigh for the days of yore, the *neiges d'antan* as you might say if you spoke a word of French. Oh! Visitors?

JEFF: Why—you're the crazy woman at the pay phone! I thought this was the Kerouac residence, not Grey Gardens.

GABRIELLE: You're right on both counts, Tad.

JEFF: Jeff—*[coming forward to shake hands]*—from the William Morris Agency. I'm representing Julie Andrews in delicate peace talks. I'm supposed to meet Jack Kerouac, and his agent.

GABRIELLE: I act as his agent, *monsieur*. I gave birth to him, now I represent him. In fact I am the history, the histoire, of representation all wrapped up in one still-fetching package, with a Lesbian twist. Is there someone with you, someone in the shadows—the twilight of perversion?

JEFF: This is America's greatest writer, master of the cut-up, a man who needs no introduction.

GABRIELLE: It's William S. Burroughs [*grimaces*], and the "S" stands for "scat"—"skedaddle." Begone!

WILLIAM BURROUGHS: I asked Jeff here to bring me along, because I wanted the pleasure of a private visit with my old beat pal, Jack. How nice to see you after all these years. Years after all these nice how see.

JEFF: He even cuts up his own sentences, he's the recycler we've dreamed of.

WILLIAM BURROUGHS: Jack pal old my beat private?

GABRIELLE: Scram! Even when you were young you were the oldest of the vultures that would swoop around picking at the talents of my boy! Now that you're old, I want none of you or less.

JEFF: But Mrs. Kerouac, you can't talk to a distinguished man like that!

GABRIELLE: Watch me, Tad. Distinguished! A needle in his arm and a scissors in his brain makes a person distinguished! He cut up everything I said and made best sellers from it. And besides that, he killed one of the only fourteen women I have ever, ever loved—Joan. Out, out!

WILLIAM BURROUGHS: I will step into the mansion across the lane. First I will stop in my tracks to buy a paper. There must be a young paper boy between here and the curb.

[*Exit BURROUGHS.*]

JEFF: Now where's Mr. Kerouac?

JACK: I see things unseen by man or dog.

GABRIELLE: He's lying down, writing and typing.

[*GABRIELLE presses a button in a prominent tape recorder that plays a recording of rapid-fire typing.*]

Truman Capote once said, Kerouac doesn't write, he types.

JACK: The cold breath of the dog on the snow.

GABRIELLE: Well clever *moi* got on TV and said, Truman Capote doesn't write, he snipes. Wasn't that a funny little pun? I top myself constantly.

JEFF: What beautiful flowers.

GABRIELLE [*lowers volume on tape recorder*]: Do you like them? They're Peruvian— Peruvian mums. Many say, "Why you, a *Quebeçoise*, like-a Peruvian flowers? Why you not like the French Canadian bouquets?"

JEFF: Oh, I would never ask that. That would be presumptuous.

GABRIELLE: Now let's talk business. You're from William Morris?

JEFF: We envision *On the Road* as a big film musical, perfect for the 60s. Julie Andrews will play the lead. Julie's a peach. We're waiting for her limo right now.

[*Enter JOEY, on bike if possible.*]

JOEY: Extra, extra, read all about it! The hills are alive with the sound of Julie Andrews—heading this way—in Northport's worst rainstorm in years!

GABRIELLE: Joey, come here, let me read that paper, without paying for it. This is Joey Buttafuoco, our paper boy. See the baseball cards attached by clothespins to the spokes of his bicyclette? Cute—*non?*

JOEY: Ma Kerouac, the Von Bulows are out on your doorstep.

JEFF: I'll run out to the curb and wait for Miss Andrews.

JOEY: Say, Mister, you're from New York, you know Roberto Clemente? Can you get me his autograph?

JEFF: Is he like, the cousin, of Francesco Clemente?

[*As JEFF and PAPER BOY exit, doorbell rings.*]

GABRIELLE (*to JACK*): I don't like this news. You have always been Northport's pet. Why should you take a back seat to a pair of rich dilettantes who know nothing of culture.

JACK: White snow on the grave of my mother. Dogs [*makes fucking signals with hands*] on grave. I like that. I'm amused.

[*Enter SUNNY von BULOW.*]

SUNNY: May we come in? We are the von Bulow family, man and wife.

GABRIELLE: Aha! Yes, step this way. Avoid leaving mud on my newly washed floor *s'il vous plait.*

SUNNY: Oh, mud won't be a problem. My maid polished the soles of my shoes on arrival. Are you French? All my life I've hankered for such a *baguette.*

GABRIELLE: Welcome, cherie, or as we say in Quebec, *bienvenue*! However leave your husband on the mat. This is a house which recognizes the beauty of women, a house which hates the smell of men. Except for my poor son. *Mais oui, ma chere*! When a man's musky scent invades its wooden nostrils, my house buckles a bit Your name?

SUNNY: Sunny.

GABRIELLE: Actually it's raining—*chattes and chiennes*. Your name?

SUNNY: [*Tinkling laugh.*] I can't leave my husband on the mat, he's my reason for living. I was a spoiled heiress on the slopes of Berchtsgarden and he came along and swept me off my skiis. You'll like him, all women do. Claus!

[*Enter CLAUS VON BULOW.*]

CLAUS: I track mud, I care not a fig, but—[*Double-take when he sees GABRIELLE*] you, my Canadian swan, you are a delectable pull of taffy. I am Claus von Bulow at your heel-clicking service.

GABRIELLE: If this beautiful woman brings you, welcome to Kerouac House. Otherwise I kick you out with no regret.

CLAUS [*to himself*]. She's a feisty wiener schnitzel, well worth my inquiry. [*To GABRI-ELLE.*] Have the maids come in and offer Sunny some plum tarts and sugar plums. Sweets for the sweet.

SUNNY: Oh, Claus, how charming. But maybe Mrs. Kerouac can't afford a maid.

CLAUS: Oh, how foolish is my little bumblebee. Next you'll be saying she can't afford sugary treats to bring up your glucose.

GABRIELLE: I can't disguise my low poverty, but I offer you my penny candy, Sunny von Bulow.

CLAUS: Yes, give her candy. She likes that.

[*To audience:*] If she hasn't a sou, my charms are wasted here.

SUNNY: Isn't he a doll? And he knows I have diabetes.

CLAUS: Yes, pour candy into her clothes and let us leave your shack with pockets bursting. Goodbye, you distinguished greyhound of a woman.

GABRIELLE [*ignoring CLAUS*]: Goodbye, my darling Sunny. Let us meet again, soon, and live together like two serious ladies, poised carelessly between passion and grief like rag dolls flung from a shelf.

SUNNY: I don't understand everything you say, but you warm me strangely.

GABRIELLE: I'll be the fire to your burning bush.

CLAUS: We'll be right across the street—fabulous, rich, talented, and young. My sister, the Countess, will bring over a spare maid later. When you need a man, plead for me.

[*Exit SUNNY and CLAUS.*]

GABRIELLE: I've lived through two world wars, through Jack's meteoric rise to fame and his sudden burnout. I've lived through De Gaulle and JFK, and a hundred Peruvian twists of fate. But can I live without my sunny valentine? She moves me. Reminding me of a—lovely pineapple or yellow guava, enriched with Tang. I must think of a way to save her from that—[*fluffs hair*] Medusa Moderne. Jack, I'll be back *toute suite*, I'll put your drink in your lap where Neal and Allen used to bob for apples.

[*Exit GABRIELLE.*]

JACK: If I could write my name, I'd die with a grin on my twisted puss. But right now I need a drink.

[*Enter CLARICE, COUNTESS VON BULOW.*]

CLARICE, COUNTESS VON BULOW. Hello! Mrs. Kerouac?

JACK: She's in the cemetery, are you from Heaven?

CLARICE. Have you seen my brother, Claus? I am Clarice, Countess von Bulow. My brother and his silly wife left a road map here. Not that you're not right across the lane.

JACK: I'm in this flat box with a recessed filter. Tell me the truth, am I a cigarette?

CLARICE. He didn't mention me, did he? He's sly, wants to keep "us" under wraps.

JACK: Burnt to the nub like a flat embargo, and embers only. Stub me out in the ashtray of your heart!

CLARICE. I'll sit right here, and wait. Had you ever a sister you loved and loved, when the two of you were tots in Austria, and the snow of the Alps made your red bed a valentine of children? And ever since, I've trailed him around the globe like lederhosen up the legs of a well-made man, or boy.

JACK: Until never.

CLARICE. I've been impetuous.

JACK: You are more like a kitten.

CLARICE. When a man marries, should he leave his sister behind? Ruth and Naomi hadn't a patch on me, so whither do I wander? I know your condition, Jack: you can't think of what to say, or write, since you don't know who or where you are.

JACK: Has MTV been invented yet?

[*JOEY enters, on bike.*]

JOEY: Extra, Extra—Julie Andrews pulls up in Lincoln Town Car!

[*JOEY exits, on bike.*]

CLARICE. I wish I had your world amnesia, could blot out like sealing wax my magnificent Clausession.

[*Enter JEFF with JULIE ANDREWS—carrying basket of fruit.*]

JEFF: Right this way, Miss Andrews. Or can I call you Julie like your other fans?

CLARICE. But I can't, it's the elephant in me.

JULIE ANDREWS: Of course, darling, but where's Mr. Kerouac? I've been in dreary burbs before but never one as—soulless.

COUNTESS: Are you Julie Andrews? My dear, I'm sure you have a brother too. We women of spirit fill Viennese nights with sighs, the two of us should lieder a deux, shame Leonie Rysanek under the table.

JULIE ANDREWS and JEFF: We don't know you.

CLARICE. Where is that red-headed scamp! It's me he loves, you see, not Sunny. You'll see.

[*Exit CLARICE, COUNTESS VON BULOW.*]

JEFF: You're at the top of the heap, for this is still 1964, and your triumphs in *Thoroughly Modern Millie* and *The Sound of Music* are still ringing in your ears! And now you've chosen for your next star vehicle, the musical version of *On the Road*!

JULIE ANDREWS: Yes, well, it's only a natural, don't you think? I can't go play governesses forever. I do want to play a beat soprano—and the buzz is on about *On The Road*. Sue Mengers says that Neely O'Hara's the best part since *Mary Poppins*.

JEFF: I'm so glad you could come to Northport and sing for your supper.

JULIE ANDREWS: Is Yma with us? Oh good.

[*Enter YMA SUMAC, downcast, staring at the floor like a poor relation.*]

She'll do the singing, because my throat's a little sore from the lightning.

YMA SUMAC: Yes, Hoolie.

JEFF: Don't I recognize your stooge?

JULIE ANDREWS: Maybe from the old Ed Sullivan shows she did—ages ago, before I was born. She was Yma Sumac, the legendary songbird of the Andes, with a ten octave range and an imperious, aloof—I don't know—*way* about her I do continue to find annoying. Well—that was then. Now's now. She was down on her luck when I stumbled across her corpse at some party. A hasbeen never goes down for the count. My old voice died and then—a little bird said, "Why not ask Yma?" I pay her thirty pezeitos a month and she sings like an angel. Let's try! First—me.

[*JULIE ANDREWS tries singing "Climb Every Mountain."*]

JEFF: You mean the voice I heard in *Mary Poppins* wasn't yours?

JULIE ANDREWS: Yes it was—I paid for it, didn't I? Yma? Ready, dear?

YMA: Yes, Hoolie.

[*JULIE ANDREWS mouths the words and YMA SUMAC sings "Climb Every Mountain."*]

[*Enter GABRIELLE.*]

GABRIELLE: I am Madame Kerouac. *C'est bien*! Mlle. Andre, you say? *Enchantee.*

JULIE ANDREWS [*to JEFF*]: You didn't tell me she's from [*makes disgusted face*] Quebec. It's like—everyone's a foreigner, even me I suppose, though that doesn't count. [*To GABRIELLE.*] I've brought you a basket of fruit for being so sweet.

JEFF: I don't suppose Jack Kerouac has finished typing yet.

GABRIELLE [*turns on volume of typing tape.*]: No, Tad, he's writing another *chef d'oeuvre* of a masterpiece, without a doubt. But let's conduct our business in my den—it's nicely furnished with thrift store flair.

JULIE ANDREWS: Well, it can't be worse than Barbra Streisand's Village [*makes face*] pad. Is it this way? It must be, there's no other way.

GABRIELLE: You are a sweet girl, no mistake, and I'd like to tell you something of my *mise-en-scene.*

[*Exit JEFF, GABRIELLE, and JULIE ANDREWS.*]

JACK: Clarice! Clarice! Memory . . . sauterne . . . regret . . . fiber-optics.

[*Scene changes to VON BULOW mansion, where WILLIAM BURROUGHS and CLAUS VON BULOW talk.*]

WILLIAM. Let's talk man-to-man for a scene, shall we, Count von Bulow?

CLAUS: Yes, let's. My sister's been telling me the latest trends in technology. He says I should buy this new stock. Did you ever hear of "Nintendo," Mr. Burroughs? In 20 years I'll reap a bundle, true, but till then, I'll have only Sunny to support me, and my own Teutonic airs.

WILLIAM. I see you have an eye on Ma Kerouac. Don't blame you myself. She comes drenched in the dramatic ooze of maple sap. But Clausy, you're on the spot. You've got a wife already. Sap spot wife, already Clausy got. Why not do what I did?

CLAUS [*frostily*]: Tips—from a junkie?

WILLIAM BURROUGHS [*shrugs*]: Joan and I played the William Tell game. It hurt her more than it hurt me.

CLAUS: You mean?

WILLIAM. Yes, I killed Joan, but she was hardly a person to me, in Mexico. I believe Gabrielle had a soft spot for her, but that's the problem with women, one soft spot after another, made of mushy rot. Joan no weasel arrow fly fall concrete. Rush of endorphin, barrel crack high dead. I'll get you an apple.

[*BURROUGHS enters Kerouac place and unwraps basket of fruit.*]

[*SUNNY enters.*]

SUNNY [*over her shoulder to someone offstage*]: Hairdressers, leave me be—my blonde patrician hair needs no lily gilding—thank you!

CLAUS [*on phone to broker*]: "Buy Nintendo." "Buy Nintendo." My good man, you sound like a broken record. I'd buy it in an instant, but I don't have two francs to rub together. I'm just an overworked gigolo.

SUNNY: I never understood much about money, except that everybody wants it from me. Claus, put down the phone, talk to me about my beauty. Your words pamper me, like adoring powder puffs. Tell me I'm a glass of lemonade with the pasty sweetness of eclair stuffing. I'll give you—oh, who's the president on the money?

[*WILLIAM BURROUGHS enters with basket of fruit.*]

Why, hi! Who are you, you look —sinister; as though your left hand was doing your bidding by Satan. Well, names aren't important, except mine.

[*BURROUGHS hands CLAUS the apple, nudges him.*]

CLAUS: How about an apple for my little pet?

SUNNY: Mash it into sauce for me, Claus? I know Clarice would eat it skin and all, but I'm not one of the vulgar toothy Eve types.

CLAUS: No, a smooth apple with its skin on it. Shining red like the rubies you gave me for Midsummer. In Copenhagen, all the smartest cuties are wearing them as hats these days. Come on, put it on your head.

SUNNY: I hate to be petulant. My tiny foot gets sore when I stamp it. And you know I'm diabetic, why push a sweet thing?

WILLIAM BURROUGHS: Insulin! That's the answer.

SUNNY: It's time for my shot—who'll give it to me?

CLAUS: Hope a nurse is free, I'll check. [*On his way out:*] Now tell me more about Nintendo, my good man.

WILLIAM BURROUGHS: On a screen black as squid ink, mad virus mutants flash silver needles into the rectal canals of smooth-skinned Guatemalan mijos . . .

[*exit CLAUS and WILLIAM BURROUGHS*]

SUNNY: Madame Kerouac will shoot me up, I'm sure. I know I've won her over the invisible line between friend and icon. She's Canadian, too, so that means she's passive. [*On telephone.*] Ring-ring!

[*JACK answers phone while GABRIELLE enters.*]

GABRIELLE: Is that the phone?

JACK: Hello?

SUNNY: Hello, Gabrielle? This is Sunny.

[JACK hands phone to GABRIELLE.]

I've a tiny problem you can help me with, I bet. I want to insert something into my skin. Be tender with me—I might leave you something in my will.

GABRIELLE: I'm afraid of hard drugs, they made my boy a, how do you say, rhubarb. *[Eagerly.]* It's great to hear from you—but I have Julie Andrews in my den, we're talking great wads of dollars.

[Enter JULIE ANDREWS into Kerouac House]

JULIE ANDREWS: My mixture of sass and spunk took me far, from underground Blitz to Broadway neon. At heart I do remain this smoke-covered urchin with a grin warm enough to melt a London pea-soup fog, and America eats me up like vittles. I'm Julie with a capital J, so why am I insecure, who do I blame? I'm at the threshold of a great career, but maybe it's death's door: who'll pull me through? At the top, and only "Nealie!" to save me.

[Exit JULIE ANDREWS]

SUNNY *(bares an arm)*: Here's an arm of satin. Will I have to go to another woman, one who'll treat me like cork dartboard? I thought you might help me reduce a glucose level so high I'll never get over it, so deep, I can't get around it. Don't withhold, not from me, Gabrielle, and I'll give you money.

GABRIELLE: I'll be right over, shot in hand. Don't ever change, Sunny. Except in the direction of loving me more each day. *[Hangs up phone.]* Jack, I'm going for two reasons. *Uno*, I love her, and *dos*, she'll help us build our retirement home in Florida.

SUNNY: I'm kind of hypoglycemic, both in blood and breeding. *[Examines mirror.]* Does it show?

JACK: So thirsty. Is this death? Mother death, like the dogs laughing on snow grave island?

GABRIELLE: I'll just make my excuses to Tad, Julie and Yma. Now remember—don't let on to anyone that I've written all your books for you, poor boy. I'll wheel *(or walk)* you into the garden where you can sip from the birdbath.

JACK: Okay.

[Exit JACK and GABRIELLE.]

[*In VON BULOW mansion SUNNY sits admiring herself in mirror.*]

SUNNY: I'm fading, but I'm still stunning, like a loud clap of hands in a forest. —Maybe I shouldn't have eaten all that candy. I feel my blood sugar rising, turning my blue blood white, like the blue frost that makes snow flake. It was chocolate done me in, a victim of Whitman and Godiva. Come, Gabrielle, bring your Canadian freshness to this overheated place of fat!

[*Enter CLARICE, COUNTESS VON BULOW.*]

CLARICE (*matter-of-factly*): Claus von Bulow was mine, you know, till you came along, like a vapid Milly Theale on the wings of a dove.

SUNNY: Clarice, did anyone Danish ever tell you, you've got a one-track mind? I am not the enemy!

CLARICE. You're his wife, and so, yes you are! As we say in Denmark, in the castle of incest, only the reindeer's hoofs break the stillness of the love between brother and sister. I'll track him down with the help of Debrett.

[*Exit CLARICE, COUNTESS VON BULOW.*]

SUNNY (*resignedly*): In-laws! But halt! What horrid perfume's in the air? I know that queasy smell from yore. Mother of money, what is its name? [*Ruefully:*] I need Memorex as much as my insulin. [*Snaps fingers.*] "Anais Anais," that's it! And I know only one dame who dares wear that signature scent in my exalted presence.

[*Enter ANAIS NIN.*]

ANAIS NIN: Sunny von Bulow!

SUNNY: Who would have guessed it—Anais Nin! Still your ninny self, Anais?

ANAIS NIN: Oh, it's wet out there! I'll come in and give you a kiss, if you dare me.

SUNNY: I'm under the weather and would prefer it if you stood where you are, on an Aubusson.

ANAIS NIN [*steps forward, writes in diary.*] Dear Diary, first sight of Sunny von Bulow in fifteen years. One beautiful woman turns yellow with age! But I've changed so little.

[*To SUNNY.*] My dear, you look faultless. A little peaked, perhaps? Have you been stuffing yourself with sugar? It's white death, my dear.

SUNNY: You were always smug, Anais.

ANAIS NIN: "Smug"? A curious choice of words. Better suited to one without my genius. —Dear Diary, she wants me still.

SUNNY: What brings you to Long Island, Anais?

ANAIS NIN: I've never stopped sleeping with the men who pursue me—you remember Henry Miller? Artaud? Gore Vidal? Men drawn to my wistful air of charm, my Lillian Gish [*French word for "girlishness"*], my macabre bag of total sex device. —I hear you're married, Sunny?

SUNNY: To a wonderful man, Claus von Bulow. He's a count in Denmark.

ANAIS NIN [*writing in diary*]: He's of no account till he's a notch in my belt. [*To SUNNY.*] Take me to his bed!

SUNNY: Look, Anais, you're barking up the wrong tree.

ANAIS NIN: Why are plain women so bitchy? If I knew a fact I'd look it up, but who in this island of dreams needs a fact?

SUNNY: Claus is mine: all mine. Except for Clarice, and she has the excuse of early molestation. Stay away, I'm warning you. Yes: you and I knew each other once, in Paris. I gave you a fortune to omit my name from your famous diary of blackmail. Leave me and mine alone, that's all I ask. Oh, mother of cash, where is my insulin, I feel faint from disgust!

ANAIS NIN: Her every word is saying, "Anais, make me a woman again in your delta of Venus."

[*Enter GABRIELLE, panting.*]

GABRIELLE: Came as quick as I could, you comely yellow kitten. Here's your prick of steel, enjoy the rapture.

SUNNY: Thank you, thank you . . .

[*SUNNY collapses into stupor.*]

GABRIELLE: That's right, rest awhile. You'll be right as rain.—I'll sing you a Peruvian lullaby from my childhood I used to sing to Jack:

Hush little llama, don't make a scene,
Mama's gonna buy you a Lima bean . . .

—I shouldn't, I know, but I'll rifle her dear pockets for spare change. Should anyone ask I'll say I was destroying the candy that's killing her. Ah, a thousand pound note—that will dig a cellar in Miami. Raise high the roofbeams, carpenter! Ah, what incendiary thighs, Sunny—they're long pogo sticks of love, I'll jump up and down on them all the way to my Florida paradise.

ANAIS NIN [*clears throat*]: Hello there, magpie.

[*GABRIELLE leaps up, startled.*]

I was in the neighborhood, and I thought I'd drop by to enchant you.

GABRIELLE: Try your sex tricks elsewhere, Miss Nin. I was once your handmaiden—no longer.

ANAIS NIN: Dear Diary, She dotes on me still, and why not? Is Jack next door? I'd like to renew our "acquaintance."

GABRIELLE: Jack's busy.

ANAIS NIN: Jack was panting to tear off my clothes, but jealous Gabrielle barred my way. I am beautiful, talented, fearless—why can't other women love me as a model? [*Spouts some French, which confuses GABRIELLE.*]

GABRIELLE: I can't read lips. Not lips like yours, that wriggle like lies.

ANAIS NIN: Why, you told me once you spoke perfect French.

GABRIELLE: I'm not in the mood for discussing my speech with strangers.

ANAIS NIN [*spouts some more French to test GABRIELLE*].

GABRIELLE (*tentatively*): *Bon ami, vedette.* I've scrubbed miles of floors to avoid this confrontation.

ANAIS NIN: You are a *Quebeçoise?*

GABRIELLE: Of course! *Bien sur!*

[*Music plays.*]

GABRIELLE: I know its streets, its little houses! I know Quebec quite well! I'm great pals *du jour* with Genevieve Bujold, Nicole Brossard, the whole, uh, *femmes de* [*waves hand*]—Quebec!

ANAIS NIN: Or could you be lying? Everyone thinks the Kerouacs come from French Canadian stock. Dear Diary: she weakened, then ran to my arms, a child, thirsty, aching for honey. I change from a woman to a tiger, always seeking my own essential *selfruchenstang*.

[*Enter CLAUS VON BULOW.*]

GABRIELLE [*relieved at the distraction*]: Oh! Mr. Von Bulow! Have you met Anais Nin?

CLAUS VON BULOW (*coldly*): It's Count von Bulow to you. No, I've never met this black-haired hussy, I can only suppose she's poor as you, a negligible zero in spades. Maybe I've seen her in some documentary about—huddled masses.

ANAIS NIN: Already he has divined the essential divinity of Anais.

GABRIELLE (*inspired*): No, Count, she's richer than Croesus—She's the one who invented Nintendo.

CLAUS VON BULOW: Nintendo! Are you now! And you're so stunning—a black and white study, like a late Whistler.

ANAIS NIN: Yes, I invented Nintendo! Dear Diary, I love deceit, Garbo said I would have made a great actress.

CLAUS VON BULOW: Your little brain has made you a very lucky girl, my continental vulva.

GABRIELLE: I met her in Quebec.

ANAIS NIN (*to GABRIELLE*): He's dreamy and sensual. Goody.

[*To audience.*] This wild ogre with the long red hair turns my sugar into crème brulee. [*To CLAUS.*] Take me, take me, whisper my name into the ear of an ass.

CLAUS VON BULOW [*points to SUNNY*]: My wife's asleep, yellow and flat, like a pool of urine. My sister seems to have flown the coupe. Let's take this chance and flee into the rain. There's a palace of mirrors at the Northport Motel. Pay the man at the desk, Anais.

ANAIS NIN: Dear Diary, he thinks I'm an heiress, well, who cares—must ask Henry, what's Nintendo? [*To GABRIELLE:*] Naughty girl, revealing my secret about Nintendo. Just because I put my name into it doesn't mean I wanted the whole world to know.

CLAUS VON BULOW [*to ANAIS NIN*]: In Copenhagen we call women like you "Verhoevenstagen," the flower of the tundra. I had a reindeer once with a little of your gypsy look, large throbbing eyes, exquisite fur like peat moss, horns of ivory.

GABRIELLE [*to ANAIS NIN*]: He's despicable as you are, how dare you hurt Sunny?

ANAIS NIN: Look at her sleeping! What she doesn't know won't hurt her! [*Whispers:*] What the fuck is Nintendo?

GABRIELLE: A new soft drink—like Tab.

ANAIS NIN [*to CLAUS*]: Take me to said love nest, down your Danish gullet I'll pour glass after glass of Nintendo.

CLAUS: What a rich way of talking!

ANAIS NIN: All the better to enslave you, Count. Gabrielle, I'll fill you in later. *Au revoir*—or should I say, *hasta la vista?*

[*Exit ANAIS NIN and CLAUS VON BULOW.*]

GABRIELLE: I think she's on to me, in a big way. Oh dear, I feel specious and bum. If only I had a confidante! A *mujer* to tell my troubles to, confess my wrongs. Despite my French ways and chic looks, I'm no *Quebeçoise*, I just pretended I was for Jack's sake. I'm really a Peruvian woman from the wrong side of the *tracquas*. [*Opens eyes wide as she remembers.*] Back in Peru I had a friend—a nun at the convent I reckoned my oracle. Haven't spoken to her in years—long distance costs so much for a mother like myself! Oh, but here in Sunny's mansion everything's free! Her golden phone gleams like amber, inviting me in. [*Picks up phone.*] Operator—get me San Tanco. Hello, convent, this is—well, never you mind. I'm calling for Sister Bertrille.

[*Enter SISTER BERTRILLE.*]

SR. BERTRILLE [*singing*]: Dominique-calique-calique—*Ola*! This is Bertrille! Who calls from Long Island?

GABRIELLE: Sister, Sister, it's me—Gabrielle Kerouac! Or as I used to be known, Gabrielle of the Mums! I'm in Northport!

SR. BERTRILLE: In Peru we call your land the "Island of Lost Souls." You were wise to call me, my child. In your voice I hear the pain of a sinner *con mucho*.

GABRIELLE: Damaged people are dangerous—we know we can survive. For twenty-five years I've been playing the part of a French native speaker. You see, Sister, back then it wasn't considered safe for a *Peruvista* like myself to get involved in American affairs. I had to tell them something, so I said I was from Montreal. Nobody asked me any questions. I passed as a Canadian.

SR. BERTRILLE: You had a son?

GABRIELLE: Yes, Juan—I mean Jack. I kept Jack with me as others might keep Polaroids. As a souvenir of happier days.

SR. BERTRILLE: And yet you gave away your baby girl?

GABRIELLE [*after a pause*]: What baby girl?

SR. BERTRILLE: Oh, there's Carlos knocking on the convent door, I have to fly off and bring some orphans tacos. Gabrielle, let's talk again soon. I'll say a nice rosary for you, pray for the best. Click.

[*SISTER BERTRILLE fades away, as GABRIELLE bangs phone in frustration.*]

GABRIELLE: What baby girl!

SUNNY [*awakening*]: You have a baby girl, Gabrielle? But you're poor! I'll set up a trust fund for her—what's her name?

GABRIELLE: I don't know.

SUNNY: And people call me vacant, just because I don't know much. Life's unfair, isn't it, darling? I'll tell you my tips, because I too have two children, and to remember their names here's what you do. Get Matisse or someone to set them in diamonds along the wall of your foyer. Then when someone asks you can always say, oh there's someone in the foyer—you slip away and read the diamonds, then you come back and tell proudly.

[*Enter JEFF.*]

JEFF: Oh, there you are, Mrs. Kerouac. Sorry to intrude.

GABRIELLE: I must get back to negotiations.

JEFF: Jack's been typing steadily, but we're a bit uneasy because he seems to be snoring too.

GABRIELLE: There's magic, Tad, in those snores and fingers.

JEFF Jeff.

GABRIELLE [*to SUNNY*]: Will you be hokay, little yellow bird?

SUNNY: Oh yes, today's my makeover, jewelers of all nations arrive in droves to shower my beauty in topaz. Kiss me, Gabrielle. You make me forget my strong bonds with Count von Bulow.

GABRIELLE: I'll make you forget that cheat—once I sort out my progeny, my future, my Lesbian subjectivity and my bankbook. It will be as though no Claus existed.

JEFF: Nice meeting you!

[*Exit JEFF and GABRIELLE.*]

SUNNY: Although I take a lot of drugs, I still can't get used to that "nice meeting you." [*Pause.*] These creatures seem sincere, yet they don't seem to realize I haven't actually really met anyone since 1949.

[*Enter WILLIAM S. BURROUGHS*]

WILLIAM BURROUGHS: Why aren't there better divorce laws where a man could just leave his wife out in the desert with a bowl of figs? Meanwhile the CIA's a vast government octopus, eight slimy members writhing madly along the ocean floor of our synapses. "Not poppy, nor mandragora,/ Nor all the drowsy syrups of the world,/ Shall ever medicine thee to that sweet sleep/ Which thou owedst yesterday." A boy wakes up in a hayloft, dick hard and a cow's horn up his ass.

SUNNY: You must be that friend of Claus, the health expert who advises those apples. Thank you for your every act on my behalf, but no thank you, Mr. Burroughs.

WILLIAM BURROUGHS: In your case omit the figs. A young boy, a boy from Omaha, fresh and pink, waking in golden hay, first dawn, his prostate crawling with bugs.

SUNNY: Are you the gardener? If so let me show you the shed and spray. Right this way, Mr. Burroughs, appropriate name.

[*Exit SUNNY and BURROUGHS.*]

GABRIELLE: I'm ready to sign all forms on behalf of my son.

JEFF: It's a heavenly ointment, but a fly's in it, a fly called Julie. She's balking at signing. She's not sure her role's big enough.

GABRIELLE: I'll write that role big as the sun—if I need to. Across the sky, in letters that will soar a thousand feet high! I need her to sign me my little pad in Miami Beach where Jack and Sunny and I can grow old in peace. [*to herself:*] — What baby girl?

JEFF: Julie went out for a walk in the rain—she's delightfully British that way.

GABRIELLE [*grimly*]: Won't it hurt her voice?

[*Enter YMA SUMAC.*]

YMA SUMAC: I'm her voice, she keeps me under wraps but tight.

GABRIELLE: Oh, yes, Miss Sumac. I was rushed before, didn't get a chance to tell you how strong I am, yes, *ma bonne fille,* I am Gabrielle Kerouac. Did I ever meet you—in Quebec, where every year we hold a winter carnival?

YMA SUMAC: Ola, lady. Years ago, I rode with your son across this land on back of a bike once, in the fifties, when he and I burned bright as two meteors aflame.

GABRIELLE [*forbiddingly*]: He had a lot of *senoritas*—once. Those days are gone.

JEFF [*to audience*]: I always wanted to become an agent, just for moments like these. I live in the agentual field, a pasture of daisies and chow. But—I don't know. Some days you get mud and you gotta make mud pies. I don't know.

GABRIELLE (*to YMA*): Are we speaking of the same Jack, it's not Jack LaLanne by any chance you did your sexy cartwheels for?

YMA SUMAC [*more to audience than anyone else*]: Jack, Jack, you spoke to me from out of a book, and blew smoke rings of dismay through my maculated uvula.

[*enter JACK KEROUAC.*]

JACK: Yma! Get me a drink, will ya?

YMA SUMAC: Jack, you're alive!

JACK: Yah, yeah, ix-nay. What of it?

YMA SUMAC: I'm not joshing with you, Jack. I've got a solid Jones on you, Jack. Know what did it, long ago? When I realized you were the only celebrity in the world whose last name ends in "A-C."

—Beside myself. Oh, and Brainiac too, but he's only a comic strip character.

GABRIELLE: *Ma déesse*, a rival for Jackie's love.

JEFF [*urging GABRIELLE to leave room*]: Come, Mrs. Kerouac, this is our one window of opportunity.

YMA SUMAC: Our names brought us close, this weird coincidence of nomenclature, but who's to say, are you supposed to love someone for his looks, his soul, his name or what? Jack, remember all those nights we cried?

JACK: There were these two dogs, pups really, carousing on a gravestone.

GABRIELLE: Jeff, leave this room with me at once. I have to console with my spiritual mother, Bertrille.

JEFF: It's time to sign!

[Exit JEFF and GABRIELLE.]

YMA SUMAC: I never learned to temper my octaves or my autonomy. I'm yours, hand and foot, and now as my career fades the AC factor's blooming. Tell me what you want.

JACK: And one of them says to the other, or really barks, I guess, being that they're dogs . . . really more like pups . . . .

YMA: For auld lang syne? I'll sing you a song of my own invention, I, the princess of the Incas.

[YMA sings ANDEAN SONG.]

[Enter SUNNY, draped with jewels.]

SUNNY: How do you do. Couldn't help overhearing. Claus and I went to Peru for the Festival of Dollars. I was Marie Antoinette, cute, in a blue marquise wig, shepherdess staff in the hand of Givenchy. Claus, of course, was Hamlet—something rotten from Denmark he joked. What were you?

YMA: An orphan. My mother left me on the church steps with a note, scrawled in maté, across my face, "Call me Yma, teach me to sing."

SUNNY: Maybe I was in the ladies' room, I don't remember that. Claus was Hamlet—did I mention that? Is anyone here good with a needle? I'm feeling tweaky, low and nervous. My gold all spun like Rapunzel's hair or mine. Gabrielle! Gabrielle!

[Enter GABRIELLE.]

GABRIELLE: I'm here, dear. *[Preparing needle. Lovingly:]* Clever moi will call you "Ivy," instead of "Sunny." *[Light little laugh.]* I top myself constantly, never stop. *[To YMA SUMAC]* Did I hear you say—Peru? *Ecouter?*

YMA SUMAC: I was born there thirty years ago in a rainstorm yust like this one. Oh, look at Jack, he's sleeping—lightly, gently, as he used to sleep in North Beach after one of his tremendous orgasms atop my ecstatic bones. *[GABRIELLE winces.]* In the Andes we have an old proverb, it never rains, we say, but it squeezes the neck of the dead goose.

GABRIELLE *[with rising excitement]*: Who taught you that lovely saying, *ma cherie?*

YMA SUMAC: My mother, who I barely remember—not from the drugs, it's just that she threw me off Lake Titicaca during a rainstorm when I was a small girl, and a single tear caught in my throat, making my voice an amazing calliope of sound.

GABRIELLE [*to audience*]: My daughter? *Que tal?*

YMA SUMAC: Okay, there I was, in a coracle like Moses in the bulrushes—then all of a sudden I'm singing like Kiri Te Kanawa, only more spacily, because, I am, after all, only two or three.

SUNNY: Gabrielle, is that needle good and burnt yet? There's a pain behind my eyes, like diamond croquettes.

GABRIELLE: I'll kiss it, make it better.

SUNNY: I feel faint . . . That's good, there's nothing better than a faint . . .

[*SUNNY collapses langorously on JACK's lap.*]

GABRIELLE: Just like the Pieta we used to visit: in Quebec. [*To YMA SUMAC.*] Yma, *mon chou*, was your mother tall and haggard, like a French poodle?

YMA SUMAC: I only remember the strawberry mark on her chest. When she threw me into the lake that mark grew, round the noble map of her breasts, until it grew into a giant letter "G" which stands for: GAVE BABY AWAY.

[*GABRIELLE clutches her chest.*]

SUNNY [*in her sleep*]: What a warm lap. it must belong to a man without a mind.

GABRIELLE [*to herself*]: ¡Incabronada!

YMA SUMAC: I will return to Yack's life, try to produce the passion of a bull in his flaked, bloated body—the body I once adored in club after club, car after car, all the indigenous route 'cross these sad. blue, floating States.

GABRIELLE: Are you saying you once had an affair with Jack?

YMA SUMAC: I know—and look at me now. Last week our baby was born—a baby girl—and I gave it away to a nice couple.

[Enter JOEY BUTTAFUOCO.]

JOEY: Extra—extra! Nintendo stock goes through the roof in Motel 6!

GABRIELLE: Not now, Joey.

SUNNY [*in her sleep*]: If men had minds their laps would be so cold, like aspirins.

YMA SUMAC: I don't mind if a mere paperboy knows my shame. I guess I'll have that scarlet "G" tattooed on my chest too. I named the baby "Amy"—"Yma" spelled backwards.

GABRIELLE [*to audience*]: My granddaughter?

YMA SUMAC: And I left her with the "Fisher" family.

JOEY BUTTAFUOCO: "Amy Fisher," what a pretty name for a baby girl. Wait till I tell Mary Jo. [*Boastfully.*] That's my girlfriend.

GABRIELLE: Run along, now, Joey. This is mother-daughter stuff here. Heavy abandonment issues.

JACK (*to SUNNY*): We don't even know what our names are. Parachutes, my love, could take us no higher.

JOEY: Extra! Extra! William S. Burroughs, Prowling in Gardeners' Shed.

[Exit JOEY.]

GABRIELLE [*rallying*]: Yma Sumac, do me a favor? Sunny needs some sugar, Jack needs a little *je ne sais quoi*. Would you run across to the Gatsby mansion and get us some cash out of the *potpourri*?

YMA SUMAC (*mournfully*): I'll rip apart my icy heart and gash a "G" there.

[Exit YMA SUMAC, singing doleful Andean number.]

GABRIELLE (*to JACK and SUNNY*): Sleep, my dear ones, while I think of my next move. I'm in a fix of discovery, I've got to make a motion. Oh, Sister Bertrille, advise me! I'm no Catholic—I don't believe in repression and torture—but how I valued your womanly words above Eva Peron's, when I was a carefree girl pregnant with twins, and I forgot!

[Enter SISTER BERTRILLE.]

SR. BERTRILLE: I'll give you one last piece of advice: you can't hold on to the past.

GABRIELLE: But I haven't been—that's my problem! How could I have blanked out half of my life?

SR. BERTRILLE: Let it go, like the winds of Macchu Picchu. So you made a few mistakes. "Take what you want, and pay for it," says God.

GABRIELLE: Is Yma Sumac my daughter?

SR. BERTRILLE: We raised her in the convent, taught her a few art songs, and let her fly away, pardon my pun, hee hee. She keeps in touch with us from time to time, always begging us to release the name of her birth mother. I shake my head, great tears in my eyes and wimple, nodding, "No." "Sorry." "No, Yma."

GABRIELLE: And I was too busy to notice or remember! I'm making a new law, against God and man! "Take the woman you want," says Gabrielle. "Make men pay."

SR. BERTRILLE: When I first learned to fly, the skies of San Tanco seemed like blue and white wafers. Long spaces, bursting with seagulls and light. But then I had to come down to the here and now. God is in little people like you and me, not in the heavens. Even in people you distrust, like Count von Bulow.

GABRIELLE: I had hopes for Jack—he wrote a few books, then drink got the better of him. I've written every word ever since, like all women do, taking up the nap and woof of their sons and afterwords. Well I say the Hell with it. I've worked in a rectory, I've seen the worst of humanity. I know all there is to know about the crying game.

SR. BERTRILLE: Cheer up, Gabrielle. As God has often told me, when one door shuts, another opens in your face. Goodbye now, Gabrielle. Your sweet, haggard face of ashen grace, used to be my playground—this used to be my childhood friend.

[Exit SISTER BERTRILLE.]

GABRIELLE: Some friend, I suppose, but we must take our *tapas* with lumps in 'em.

SUNNY (*stirring*): Was it a nun I saw? *[Shakes head.]* I just made a palindrome without even thinking—

GABRIELLE: Like "Amy" and "Yma," a palindrome—

SUNNY: —but then, that's my life isn't it.

GABRIELLE: There was no nun, darling, you were dreaming. I was entertaining some former friends, from Quebec of course—hockey players with big sticks.

SUNNY (*dreamily*): Like Claus. Why is it you've never kissed me?

GABRIELLE: I will if you ask me to.

[*Enter CLAUS and CLARICE, COUNTESS VON BULOW.*]

CLAUS VON BULOW: Tally-ho, what? Clarice and I've come to fetch Sunny.

SUNNY (*warmly*): Ah, speak of the devil!

GABRIELLE: Reeking of Anais. Wonder where he's been—you cad!

CLARICE. He's not a cad, he's a cadaver. But a sister loves the corpse as well as the person, if she has character.

SUNNY: Gabrielle, I came to love you a little late. I was attracted to your depths—here's a woman, thought I, who don't put everything in the shop window. But oh, I'm so tired—I think I'll wheel myself, or Jack, back to the mansion across the lane.

JACK: Okay.

SUNNY: I'll rest awhile in my bed of birds. Claus, dear, I love you less so I'm shaving your allowance.

[*Exit JACK and SUNNY.*]

CLAUS: Your fault, I fear. Oh well, I have bigger sprats in my skillet. If I lose Sunny, Anais waits bangled on the hook. I could have offered you my hand, but you were poor. No, worse than poor. [*To himself:*] But how?

GABRIELLE: You and I, we're a lot alike, really.

CLAUS VON BULOW: Only we couldn't be more different.

GABRIELLE: We both love the same woman—only you don't love her.

CLARICE: Come, Claus, play the Merton Densher to my Madame Merle. I, a great black crow on two wings, and you, the devil in disguise of a child. To Europe, where incest is one of those things—just one of those fabulous things.

[*Enter JOEY.*]

JOEY: Extra! Extra! Read all about it! Worst rainstorm in fifty years!

[*Enter WILLIAM BURROUGHS.*]

WILLIAM BURROUGHS: Boy! Boy! How much for a paper?

JOEY: You from St. Louis? You got any Stan Musial? Dick Groat?

WILLIAM BURROUGHS: Indeed I do, boy. But it'll cost you.

CLARICE. Like fog on the moors, a fact of life. Where a wife is this extra little hood a naughty brother might hang in his closet.

JOEY: Gee, Mister, I guess I'd do just about anything for a rookie Stan Musial.

GABRIELLE: I always pictured myself as a fugitive, running for life against a raging tide.

JOEY: Or Tim McCarver, Bob Gibson?

CLAUS VON BULOW: My activities in the Resistance are well known to the OSS.

GABRIELLE: Sunny means as much to me as Jack himself. [*To Audience:*] But what about Yma?

WILLIAM BURROUGHS: Know anything about the—blue haze, paper boy?

JOEY: You make me squirm with your direction.

WILLIAM BURROUGHS: I'd fit a noose round your throat and pay good money for your scrotal sac.

[*Enter JULIE ANDREWS and YMA SUMAC.*]

JULIE ANDREWS: My patience is worn, thin as my waistline. I'm tearing at the walls of this suburban hell, and I scorch my own hands. Let's rehearse for the big scene in "NEALIE." I'll play Nealie, and you be me.

YMA SUMAC: Yes, Hoolie.

[*JULIE and YMA sing, "Do, a Deer, a Female Deer, etc." and exit*]

CLAUS VON BULOW: My resistance—to working, ha ha ha! Yes, I was born Baroness Blixen in Gotsdottendorf, my age is a secret, candles like torches announced my debut.

GABRIELLE: Your privilege is showing.

CLAUS VON BULOW: Anna, my nurse, liked to take indecent frieze with my royal *urgungenbleggen*. And then where was I? At university Gustaf told me, "Claus, this is no life for a man, a man of action, a man of the sea. Women are attracted to you, Claus, so am I."

WILLIAM BURROUGHS. I nicked this steel dildo from a clapped-out transvestite whore in Yokohama. It comes scummy, you'll lap it up and cheer.

CLAUS VON BULOW: He steered me to Berlin where at the Bluebonnet Grill met I Helga von Thyssen, Peggy Guggenheim and Krauss—the rest is history. Yes, I was a ski instructor. But I fought duels to get there! And my powder blue sweater compliments my face and hair—but everything does, dear lady, is it a crime ? I was assistant to Horst—the Horst.

GABRIELLE: So you haven't been trying to poison Sunny . . . ?

CLAUS VON BULOW: You make me giggle! Me? Horst's mastery of lens and craft focused my drill on a tense, eerie *Gobelinangelin*.

[*Exit CLAUS VON BULOW.*]

JOEY: You want me to do what, Mr. Burroughs?

WILLIAM BURROUGHS. Naive don't play, me not with, I've been raw round the block of punk. Dip your little pink eggs right here in the pump hole.

[*Enter ANAIS NIN.*]

ANAIS NIN: How much is your secret worth, Madame Kerouac? Dear Diary, I watch her squirm before my beauty.

GABRIELLE: Nothing. Don't try to get money out of me, Miss Nin, I'm tighter than a watch wound tight.

ANAIS NIN: Was not money I was thinking of, *mon pauvre turnip*.

JOEY: I'd like to help you out, Mr. Burroughs, my little thing is hard as a thimble, but Mary Jo's waiting.

ANAIS NIN: You've been writing Jack's books for years, and I want you to write mine.

GABRIELLE: That would be prostitution.

WILLIAM BURROUGHS: Meet me at midnight in the gardening shed. I'll shoot your body full of gism nation.

JOEY (*amiably*): Okay.

[*Enter JEFF.*]

JEFF: Mr. Burroughs! Great news!

JOEY: You won't forget my Tim McCarver?

WILLIAM BURROUGHS: Midnight at the shed!

[*Exit JOEY.*]

ANAIS NIN: Don't confuse prostitution with common sense. Or I'll add another charge to my bill of appeal. For example—you're not a Quebeçoise at all, are you? [*Mean little laugh.*] Does Jack know?

GABRIELLE: No, and don't dare you tell him. You'll ruin what's left of his talent.

WILLIAM BURROUGHS: What's news the so great?

JEFF: I just got off the phone with London, and Peggy Ramsay says there's huge interest in a musical of *Naked Lunch*!

GABRIELLE: You see, Miss Nin, I'm all Jack has—and I, like many other women, have been compromised by my attachments to men. I'm sick of the lies and deceit. How often have I stood in this kitchen worried sick someone French might come in, try to *parlez-vous*.

WILLIAM BURROUGHS: Let's go down to the swamp, you 'n' me, try to work on some—numbers.

[*Exit JEFF and WILLIAM BURROUGHS.*]

GABRIELLE: I've turned away so many Francophiles. One time Jackie Kennedy herself—stood on my threshold, begged to come in, and I had to break my own heart—and hers—and say, "Out."

ANAIS NIN: She told me.

GABRIELLE: You're such a liar! Why did I ever tell Claus von Bulow you were rich, I must have been mad!

ANAIS NIN: It might have put Sunny's life in danger—who's the ninny now?

GABRIELLE (*aghast*): You don't think . . .!

ANAIS NIN (*shrugging*): My eyelids flutter. I'm all turns and ladders, how would I know?

GABRIELLE: Have I given him motive to harm her hair? If so, I'll never forgive him or myself. Like we do in Quebec, Miss Nin, if you've ever been there, liar. Where's my good cloth coat! I'm rushing to save her.

ANAIS NIN: Russian! What will you be next? Nationality's not a trousseau you pick and choose from. I'm brooding now, a white hen on a nest of glass eggs.—And I do know Jackie!

GABRIELLE: This is one hen doesn't need no cock! Goodbye and good riddance, Miss Nin. (*At telephone.*) Ring-ring. Sunny, I'm coming.

[*Exit GABRIELLE.*]

ANAIS NIN: Dear Diary, what will my future as Countess von Bulow bring me? All I'm asking for is a little respect. My new agent, Jeff, or Tad, has promised me a "date" with William Morris. I want my diaries published, so the world will know, as much as this silver cube allows. I stand on it—I jump on it—I grow strength from my heels, and my cats'eye glasses point accusing fingers at [*one finger juts in air along the angle of her glasses*] patriarchy [*other finger*] squared.

[*Enter JULIE ANDREWS.*]

JULIE ANDREWS: What's this—another foreigner? What country are you from—Afghanistan? Why can't there just be me, here, from England, and a whole bunch of fans over there, shouting my name.

ANAIS NIN [*To Diary*]: Her peaches and cream looks mashed, rotten, but she cries to me, "Anais, you woman you!" [*To JULIE.*] Come my dear, walk with me in the rain and let me tell you about life, art, and Accustatin. We're both so thin we're like bamboo slivers under your nails.

[*Exit ANAIS NIN, unaware that JULIE ANDREWS is not following her.*]

The night I invented Nintendo, Charles Olson held me in his big burly arms, him a great oak, me an acorn, whispering to me, "You are genius disguised as mundi, passion disguised as mystery, a Sphinx among Penthesilea."

JULIE ANDREWS: No rain for me, thanks just the same. They loved me as Liza Doolittle, as Guinevere in *Camelot*. I was Maria von Trapp and *Mary Poppins*, Millie, too, in a flapper bob with Carol Channing, a perfect cat. But will they love me as "*Nealie*," I can't decide. I'm at the zenith and it's scary. Especially if my "voice," Miss Sumac, decides to take a powder. I'm sure I treated her well, encouraging her to keep her welfare. Giving her my bouquets once I'd smelled them enough—she'd scurry off and crush each bud to make some queer Peruvian penance dust she'd eat with a grimace. Wonder why? I call her "Poison Sumac," to get a rise out of her, but that's just British fun.

[*Enter WILLIAM BURROUGHS.*]

WILLIAM BURROUGHS: Psss—Miss Andrews. Why waste your time and Fox's money doing a bomb like "Nealie," can't I tempt you into the musical version of *Naked Lunch*?

JULIE ANDREWS: "*Naked Lunch*"! Sounds fab! Who do I play?

WILLIAM BURROUGHS: Let me think.

JULIE ANDREWS: See, Mr. Burroughs, I'm tired of being sweet, I want to show my abandon. "*Naked Lunch!*" Is it anything like *Breakfast at Tiffany's?*

WILLIAM BURROUGHS: *Naked lunch* is the frozen moment—when everybody can see what it is at the end of the fork.

JULIE ANDREWS: Maybe we'll call it, *The House of Forks*. I'm a little dubious about "Nealie" at the moment. I haven't seen Jack Kerouac yet. I'm beginning to think he doesn't exist.

WILLIAM BURROUGHS: Everyone knows that his mother writes all his work.

JULIE ANDREWS: Oh really? I wonder if Jeff knows this! In London we say, not every shut eye's sleeping, nor every frappe a tart.

WILLIAM BURROUGHS: I saw you in *My Fair Lady*, but wouldn't it have been better if Prof. Higgins had injected Liza Doolittle with bug juice?

JULIE ANDREWS: Dreamy, Bill—Can you get us some from the gardener's shed?

WILLIAM BURROUGHS: And in *Mary Poppins*, I kept waiting for you to take that umbrella and sodomize those tots. Arm out your hold.

[injects Julie's arm with bug juice]

JULIE ANDREWS: Action! Thanks ever so much, Bill, for your tip. I'm going to march into that house and demand proof Jack Kerouac's alive! Something fishy's going on or my name's not—*[clutches arm]* *Ooga Looga Rentas, naj key lor ranga.*

[collapses onto floor]

WILLIAM BURROUGHS: Out for a while, she. I'll throw this mackintosh over her and fetch bow and apple.

[Exit BURROUGHS.]

JULIE ANDREWS *[stirring]*: What was in that bug juice? I can sing again! My nodes have come to life. Or died or whatever *[Sings scales]*: I'll run by and cheer up some sick folks with my singing. What have we here?

[Enter SUNNY, staggering.]

Did you try that bug juice too? Powerful, no?

SUNNY: Gabrielle—Gabrielle!

JULIE ANDREWS: No, it's me—Julie Andrews! First time I've been mistaken for Canadian, or am I being dense?

[*GABRIELLE rushes in.*]

SUNNY: I'm sinking—a golden nugget dropped in a glass of beer. Save me, Gabrielle, Claus gave me too much of what ails me.

GABRIELLE: Insulin shock! I read about this in—[*eyes JULIE ANDREWS*] in Quebec, of course. But what can I do? I'm not trained as a nurse!

JULIE ANDREWS: Shall I help by singing? "Just a spoonful of sugar helps the medicine go down, in the most delightful way."

[*Enter CLAUS VON BULOW and ANAIS NIN.*]

ANAIS NIN: Sunny was always ineffectual, and look at her now.

CLAUS VON BULOW: The simplest things, she had others do for her.

JULIE ANDREWS: "These are a few of my favorite things."

ANAIS NIN: But dying is difficult in that one must do it for oneself.

CLAUS VON BULOW: That's clever, Anais, almost as clever as having invented Nintendo and made all that lovely money.

[*Enter JEFF.*]

JEFF: Has anyone seen Mr. Burroughs? London is hyperventilating—in a stately grown-up way of course. [*Sees SUNNY.*] Hope that's not one of my clients.

GABRIELLE: We have to do something! Let's make her throw up. Jack—talk about the time you went down on Gregory Corso. No, Jack's not here—he must be typing!—and emetics won't work. Only action will.

[*GABRIELLE rubs mouth.*]

CLAUS: What are you doing with your mouth?

GABRIELLE: Preparing to suck out the insulin, why?

CLAUS: Madame Kerouac—think a moment! Just before she died she made out her will, leaving you her entire fortune.

JULIE ANDREWS: Congratulations!

CLAUS: She knew I'd be amply taken care of due to the Nintendo fortune of my bride-to-be.

GABRIELLE: No, actually, she just wanted to leave you in the cold. She knew as well as I that Anais Nin never invented anything but her life and loves. She didn't invent Nintendo—did you, Anais?

ANAIS NIN: Well, I—[*spouts French.*]

GABRIELLE: Sunny's estate includes huge homes in Florida—if I let her die, I'll inherit?

JEFF: What a great opportunity for you.

JULIE ANDREWS: Oh, and Jeff, please fire Yma for me. With my voice restored, I won't need her any more.

JEFF: I'll see if I can find her.

[*Exit JEFF.*]

SUNNY: It's so nice in a coma, like a featherbed of a princess, oh, but Gabrielle, there's a pea under my millions of mattresses . . .

GABRIELLE: She's in pain!

[*Enter WILLIAM BURROUGHS.*]

WILLIAM BURROUGHS (*politely*): A woman in pain? Come I may in? [*to GABRIELLE:*] Her misery put out of her, as you would a [*coughs*] horse.

GABRIELLE: Let Sunny die? No decent woman would consider doing such a thing. [*Pauses.*] But am I decent? I left my baby girl to die on the banks of Titicaca! I told the whole world I came from Quebec! I wrote all the books of Jack and Burroughs, thereby mothering the beat movement! Having committed these crimes, can I still call myself decent?

WILLIAM BURROUGHS: No, but you're spunky, which I hate in a woman.

[*Enter KEROUAC and YMA SUMAC.*]

Hello, Jack.

JACK: Hi.

GABRIELLE: Here I hesitate when I should be acting! But my golden dreams of Florida are so tempting, so vivid! Sister Bertrille, help me! Operator, get me San Tanco. [*Pauses.*] Make it person to person, if she's not at home well, *que sera sera* I guess.

[*Enter SISTER BERTRILLE.*]

SR. BERTRILLE: Gabrielle, you were always the naughtiest girl on the convent floor—a madcap of cuts and patches, but a mighty spirit shone through the dirt. I hitched up my scapular, taught you to pitch and catch, a nun worth scrapping.

GABRIELLE: You were always so distant from me, flying in the sun like a speck in my eye. The red letter "G" on my breast moans and rumbles, like a thing undone.

SR. BERTRILLE: So now you're faced with a momentous choice—the right thing or the wrong. Well, Gabrielle?

WILLIAM BURROUGHS: Well?

JULIE ANDREWS: Well?

CLAUS VON BULOW: Well?

JACK: Well?

GABRIELLE: I'm afraid of myself, afraid of my anger once I find out I've defrauded my dreams! But I'll do it—I'll save Sunny's life!

[*Sucks insulin out of Sunny.*]

ANAIS NIN: *Mon Dieu*, she's doing it!

WILLIAM BURROUGHS: Flesh oozing flesh, mutating hideous spores of science fiction pus bang. I have a weak stomach, this Lazarus trick is not my scene.

GABRIELLE: Now it's in me, and I'm feeling proud—but pretty dry, like a sponge in reverse.

SR. BERTRILLE: God will bless you—your will and mine, *corazon*.

[*Exit SISTER BERTRILLE.*]

GABRIELLE: Oooh, do I feel *inferma*—that's sick in Spanish, I always meant to tell all of you, I'm not from Quebec, I'm a Peruvista.

CLAUS VON BULOW: Not Canadian!

JACK: No more Canadian Club?

SUNNY (*stirring*): Where am I?

GABRIELLE: Not too disappointed, I hope—I tried to love you as a good woman should, loving even the love you gave to another. You've come back to life just as I push off into the Hell of personal relations. Bye!

WILLIAM BURROUGHS: Just like Romeo and Juliet, only without Romeo, his fresh pink cock salved in the ointment of old curds and whey off some rackety whore's.

SUNNY: It's just too, too romantic.

CLAUS VON BULOW: Only one thing can save Madame Kerouac now, steady application of alcohol, its high sugar content will re-negate the insulin.

WILLIAM BURROUGHS: Maybe apples will help? I'll ask that paperboy to help me find an arboretum, red house of bombs, legs in air, scum seeping from his plums and cherries . . . a mad tyrannical laugh, a shout of ecstasy, curare, asshole sauce.

[*Exit WILLIAM BURROUGHS.*]

ANAIS NIN: Alcohol! Are you a medical doctor?

CLAUS VON BULOW: Why don't you look it up in Nintendo, Miss Dictionary?

GABRIELLE: I've spent my life cleaning liquor out of my home, and flushed Jack's system like a septic tank. Now I'd give my kingdom for a drink.

YMA SUMAC: Oh, Jack, release her from these bonds of love, let us live anew, like two separate peaks in Darien.

JACK: Okay. [*Produces bottle from behind back.*] Here, Ma.

JULIE ANDREWS: I like a play where all the loose ends tie up together like niglets, the children's game of London. Oh, Miss Sumac, can I see you in my office?

YMA SUMAC: She'll hand me my walking papers, I'll be out of a job again. But I've thought of an option, campaigning for the rain forests of Peru.

[*Exit JULIE ANDREWS and YMA SUMAC.*]

ANAIS NIN [*to GABRIELLE*]: Don't you think you've had too much, as I used to say to—uhhh, Georges Bataille?

GABRIELLE: If I drink enough I'll be able to tell you how I feel.

SUNNY: She's braver than sin, tall, too, like some elegant Canadian pine.

GABRIELLE: I'm drunk enough to confess my lies. Sunny, I'm not Canadian, I'm from Peru, and I have two children, Jack and Yma. Not only that but they're lovers.

JACK: We are? Let's celebrate—with a drink.

[*Exit JACK KEROUAC.*]

GABRIELLE: I also wrote all of Jack's books and those of William S. Burroughs. And I flirted with letting you die to secure my inheritance.

SUNNY: You are truly a woman whose price is above rubies, or in my case, oh what are those little yellow things?

CLAUS VON BULOW: I return to Elsinore in the morning. It's homecoming weekend. The peasants are throwing a triumphal march, blowing kisses like smooch confetti, all in our honor.

ANAIS NIN: Oh, yes, I've been invited too, I'm the guest of honor. I must pack my Dior Givenchy ensemble.

GABRIELLE: How can you lie so much, didn't your quota run out, sometime way back in the thirties?

ANAIS NIN: The spring collections are all about me, in Rome and Milan. *No lo entiendo*, Gabrielle [*kisses her hand.*]

CLAUS VON BULOW (*to SUNNY*): I suppose after what's happened you won't be coming with me to Denmark?

SUNNY: I've a forgiving nature, I'm pliant, taffy melting on the curb. However, Claus dear, stay away a little longer, come back for my decision, in the 70s, the era of disco, polyester, then punk, Deborah Harry, Johnny Lydon, Star Wars . . . Watergate, Abscam, Elizabeth Taylor gets really fat . . .

GABRIELLE: She can't make up her mind. She never will. I can face my own reality now, and that of the nation.

ANAIS NIN: Vraiment, Claus? [*offers him her arm. He takes it.*] *Au revoir, mes enfants!* [*To CLAUS.*] I have been longing to revisit Copenhagen, where once Danny Kaye paid court to my langorous body with his sixteen-inch long tongue, *incroyable* . . .

CLAUS VON BULOW: Danny Kaye, Danny Kaye, refresh my memory, you puzzling *schwepperhunhagen.*

[*Exit ANAIS NIN and CLAUS VON BULOW.*]

GABRIELLE: One day soon I'm gonna ask the moon about my love for Sunny— and if he knows, maybe he'll explain.

SUNNY: Gabrielle, if Jack and Yma are really brother and sister, shouldn't you tell them?

GABRIELLE: I often wonder, does candor ever help? You decide, Sunny. Look at them, playing like kittens out in the garden, in the rain, in the shadow of the shed: pouring Johnny Walker down each other's throats like two twin gas pumps— innocent, untouched by the shame and scars that have left us like whales beached on this [*snarls*] Island of Lost Souls.

SUNNY [*after thinking a minute*]: Well, then, don't, then.

[*Enter JULIE ANDREWS and JEFF.*]

JULIE ANDREWS: Grand news, everyone! I've abandoned plans to make *Nealie!* Instead I'm going to play Holly Golightly in the musical film of *Naked Lunch!*

JEFF: It's called—*Lunch!*

JULIE ANDREWS: I get to sing a dozen songs—with my own voice, thank you very much; I'm going to sodomize tots, with my hair up in this cute French twist, and also sport this long, long cigarette holder—smashing!

SUNNY: Have we met?

[*Exit JULIE ANDREWS, singing "Moon River."*]

Gabrielle, you must be disappointed indeed. I remember the name of those yellow things, opals.

JEFF: Sorry things had to work out this way, Madame Kerouac.

GABRIELLE: That's okay, Tad.

JEFF: Jeff.

[*Exit JEFF.*]

SUNNY: You saved my life, so I owe you something.

GABRIELLE: You made me the hero of my own life, a tragic drama suspended by age and time.

SUNNY: Well, let's go shopping to start with. It wouldn't be life without shopping.

[*Enter JOEY BUTTAFUOCO.*]

JOEY BUTTAFUOCO: I waited all night, till dawn, for Mr. Burroughs in the tin shed, but he never came and I never got my Musial.

GABRIELLE: I'd like to re-do my kitchen in traditional Peruvian mate.

SUNNY: Burn this shack and move with me to Florida, where I live in the Trump mansion years before the Trumps.

JOEY: Gabrielle and Sunny lived happily for many years, although Gabrielle eventually left the room for a minute and when she came back, Sunny was in a coma. When Claus was acquitted, Gabrielle died.

GABRIELLE: OK, Sunny, whatever you say. I'm ready to kick this island where I lost my own soul.

SUNNY: But can we stop at the store first? I'd like to buy some Rudi Gernreich—mmm—things. And some diamonds and ice cream.

[Exit SUNNY and GABRIELLE.]

JOEY: Jack died too, after a barroom brawl in a black Miami bar. Though Julie Andrews regained her voice, her career suffered a long decline. Jeff and other disciples continue to piece together old scraps of Gabrielle's writing and continue to publish them as novels under Burroughs' name. He lives in Lawrence, Kansas. Yma Sumac lives quietly in Peru, singing her Peruvian songs of regret and loss. She returned to Long Island last year for the trial of her daughter, Amy Fisher, seated quietly at the back of the courtroom, shrouded in black maté. Her scarlet "G" burning in her chest. Mary Jo and I got married, and I didn't have anything to do with that Amy Fisher. Except I told Mary Jo that nowadays all the prettiest girls on Long Island answer the front doorbell wearing apples on their heads.

Now here I am on this silver stage preaching how to build my body. What I should be doing is placating the imps in my soul, wretched cats that keep clawing my memory, feed me, they seem to say—Feed our brain cells with good Marcel Mauss. I used to ride up street after street, full of my news, the good, the bad and indifferent, oh, don't I wish it was then now. I didn't know that many people—just the neighbors. "Joey, Joey Buttafuoco," they said. "We can always count on Joey, thank God." Didn't I wish it was now back then? I just might believe it if you asked me to.

[Music plays.]

END

In San Francisco the poets, filmmakers, painters, artists and writers love to amuse ourselves by writing and staging these plays under the rubric of the "San Francisco Poets Theater," a name I more or less stole from the departing Language Poets. "Island of Lost Souls" was my third or fourth play, produced by Intersection the non-profit artists' space in San Francisco on April 7, 1993, with the following cast:

GABRIELLE KEROUAC, struggling Lesbian single mother ....Leslie Singer
JACK KEROUAC, failed beat novelist and alcoholic .... Kevin Radley
JEFF, agent with William Morris... Glen Helfand
JOEY BUTTAFUOCO, teenage paperboy..Kevin Killian
WILLIAM S BURROUGHS, sinister novelist, wife murderer .... Philip Horvitz
SUNNY VON BULOW, heiress, diabetic ....Margaret Crane
CLAUS VON BULOW, suspicious husband............................Jonathan Hammer
JULIE ANDREWS, restless British superstar.....................................Andrea Juno
YMA SUMAC, Peruvian soprano and hasbeen................................. Laurie Amat
ANAIS NIN, international gadabout and diarist...................................Norma Cole
SISTER BERTRILLE, Mother Confessor of San Tanco .... Mary Fitzgerald

Years later when we revived this play, I created the part of Clarice for Barbara Guest to play. Thanks to Ms. Guest for allowing me to appropriate so many lines from her own famous poetry into this play—in her honor, and for her amusement. We premiered this version at The Lab, yet another non-profit artists' run space in San Francisco, on March 28, 1996.

GABRIELLE KEROUAC, struggling Lesbian single mother ....Michelle Rollman
JACK KEROUAC, failed beat novelist and alcoholic ....Kevin Killian
JEFF, agent with William Morris... Glen Helfand
JOEY BUTTAFUOCO, teenage paperboy..................................... Scott Hewicker
WILLIAM S BURROUGHS, sinister novelist, wife murderer .... Philip Horvitz
SUNNY VON BULOW, heiress, diabetic .... Alicia Wing
CLAUS VON BULOW, suspicious husband...Rex Ray
CLARICE, Countess von Bulow...Barbara Guest
JULIE ANDREWS, restless British superstar................................Leslie Scalapino
YMA SUMAC, Peruvian soprano and hasbeen............................. Clifford Hengst
ANAIS NIN, international gadabout and diarist....................... Phoebe Gloeckner
SISTER BERTRILLE, Mother Confessor of San Tanco ....Hoa Nguyen

On September 19, 1997 I staged this play at the Kelly Writers House on the Penn Campus in Philadelphia. I didn't write down everyone's names and now I can only recall that Kristen Gallagher was a splendid Gabrielle, Joshua Schuster was super-sinister as William Burroughs, and Rachel Blau DuPlessis jumped in and played Sr. Bertrille to a "T." My dream one day is to stage this play in Northport, Long Island, the town where, as a young boy, I roamed around on my bicycle with baseball cards flapping in the spokes, dreaming of poetry but distracted by everything that was going on around me.

Three on a Match

characters

STEVE POITRINE
San Francisco private eye

LISA
his secretary

LEAF STEELE
Hollywood wild child

RIVER PHOENIX

FEDERICO FELLINI

GIULETTA MASINA

BARBARA STEELE
as a young girl

VINCENT PRICE

GUS VAN SANT

BARBARA STEELE

JEFF GILLOOLY

[*Play begins in San Francisco at the storefront office of STEVE POITRINE and LISA.*]

LISA: You have reached the office of Steve Poitrine, San Francisco private eye. This is Lisa speaking. His Gal Friday. Yes, we do bodyguard work. Our rates aren't cheap, but we are discreet. Oh, hi, Miss Harding—[*To STEVE.*] It's Tonya Harding.

STEVE POITRINE (*to audience*): The night was dim and filled with sudden bursts of gunfire. From out back you could hear the sounds of woman screaming, you could smell the crack burning in the pipes of the oppressed.

LISA: Tonya? You were recommended by whom? Didn't you used to have that other bodyguard service, Tonya dear?

STEVE POITRINE: It was October 1993 and I was about to embark on the biggest case of my career. That's my secretary, Lisa. Lisa Tarantino. She's a peach.

LISA: Yes—that security guard with the bald head and the fat face, looked like Oddjob in *Goldfinger*. I used to be an ice skater, too, Miss Harding. You don't have to tell me how difficult Nancy Kerrigan can be when she doesn't get her way.

[*A knock at the door.*]

STEVE POITRINE: Lisa, buzz in our client.

LISA: But we don't do knee work. [*Looking sidelong at STEVE.*] Well, Steve does, but not on, uh, Olympic femme hopefuls. [*Hangs up phone and presses buzzer.*] Come in! [*To STEVE.*] Here's your client, Mr. Poitrine.

[*Enter LEAF STEELE.*]

LEAF STEELE: I've come to this seedy storefront to seek your help.

STEVE POITRINE: Help?

LEAF STEELE: On behalf of my mother.

STEVE POITRINE: And who's your mother, young lady?

LEAF STEELE: Have you ever heard of the actress, Barbara Steele?

STEVE POITRINE: Barbara Steele . . . hm, the name sounds familiar, does she write romance novels?

LEAF STEELE: No, that's Danielle Steel, mother's younger sister, who enters this story only sidelentually. Barbara Steele, my mother, is a retired movie star who made her debut in 1960 in Mario Bava's *Black Sunday*. She's weird and horrible, but utterly beautiful and inhuman. Many have called her the "Anti-Garbo."

STEVE POITRINE: That's pretty strong. What does it mean?

LISA: Chief, the word is out about Barbara Steele.

LEAF STEELE: Fellini gave her an odd, non-horror role in *8 1/2*. She's terribly worried. Fellini's in a coma and she's afraid he'll whisper some of her damaging secrets to the world press. You know how old men gossip.

STEVE POITRINE: I do indeed. My long affair with Walter Matthau left bruised feelings on both sides. When the blood starts to thin, the mouth starts to flap.

LEAF STEELE: In addiction—I mean, addition, she's worried about the gossipy tongue of her male alter ego, Vincent Price, with whom she starred in Roger Corman's *The Cult of the Crimson Altar*.

LISA: Her masterpiece. Extraordinary. Her eyes are metaphysical, unreal, impossible, like the eyes of a di Chirico. There are times, in certain conditions of light and color, when her face assumes a cast that doesn't appear to be quite human, which would be impossible for any other actress.

STEVE POITRINE: I see. At any rate, I begin to see the strange beauty in your sweet little face, your nostrils, wider than the Nile, your leaf-like complexion. What's your name, dearie?

LEAF STEELE (*blushing*): Leaf.

STEVE POITRINE: No, you leaf. It's my office. It may be Valencia Street, but I'm at home here. I have a bottle in my drawer, a gun in my crotch, a blonde secretary with eighty pounds of pep. I'm crossing you in style, some day.

LISA: Chief, the girl's name is Leaf. She's her mother's daughter all over again, about five foot five, oozing sex appeal, charm, and MasterCard. Take her. Take her to my place, play her lots of Luther Vandross.

LEAF STEELE: Please, Mr. Poitrine, would you come down to Malibu with me to help my mother? She has no one else to turn to, because she burned her bridges long ago. I despise her myself, but steel's in our blood, we stick to each other like my palms around your thing.

STEVE POITRINE: Okay, girls, you've convinced me. Let's lock the door and throw away the key, now, baby.

LEAF STEELE: I'd love to, but my boyfriend's picking me up at noon.

LISA: It's midnight now.

LEAF STEELE: Oh, wow! Okay.

LISA: I'm your average height and weight, I feel like living in a big way.

STEVE POITRINE: Say no more, a little dab'll do ya. I'm wearing Matt Helm cologne and can I count backwards from 100 down the nape of your neck?

[*Enter RIVER PHOENIX.*]

Who's this?

LEAF STEELE: Oh, did we get the time mixed up? This is River Phoenix, the boy I was telling you about, kind of. He's my boyfriend.

LISA: Why, he's cute. And sassy.

LEAF STEELE: And my brother.

STEVE POITRINE: Hey—nobody's perfect—except for [*turns to RIVER*] you, River. Tell me, in real life are you more like the tough, streetwise punk you played in *Stand by Me*, or the narcoleptic hustler of *My Own Private Idaho*?

LISA: Want a hot dog, Mr. Phoenix?

RIVER PHOENIX: Absolutely not.

LEAF STEELE: He and I are vegans. We don't do meat or dairy. I forget what we do eat.

STEVE POITRINE: Whenever I see you in the movies, I get a little chill. You're so attractive.

RIVER: I'm used to your stares . . . I feel them right through the celluloid closet of my heart.

STEVE POITRINE: You're a good-looking couple.

[*LISA inserts herself between LEAF and RIVER.*]

LISA: Three on a match, get it? OK, let's have the kind of sex I learned about from watching Gus Van Sant movies, starring you.

LEAF STEELE: Oh, wow, sure, but first, like, let's go to my mother's house. Like I told you, she's worried sick about her future.

RIVER: Leaf's got this mother thing going big time.

LEAF STEELE: Wouldn't you, if Mother gave a damn about you?

RIVER: Let's do some speedballs first.

LISA: That's a potent mix of heroin and cocaine, Chief. River hates people who wear leather, except for their drugs.

RIVER: I do them, otherwise they'd do them.

STEVE POITRINE: Market economy, I read about it in *Christopher Street*. Okay, grab my hat, we're off to Steele Manor.

[*Blackout. Exit STEVE, LISA, LEAF and RIVER. Enter FELLINI and MASINA.*]

FELLINI: Meanwhile, halfway around the world, in a hospital bed, lie I, the great Fellini, in a coma, while the dancing figures of my films flit through my mind. Fat ladies, clowns, dogs, freaks, paparazzi—I, who created a multicultural world, lie back, in a daze, while they make me miserable. Who was it who said, "Rosebud" while he lay dying? Was it—Fellini? No! I am Fellini!

MASINA: Shut up, you old fool. [*Fondly.*] I am Masina, but I don't run around screaming it to everyone. I, who shun publicity, always your wife, I cook, I stay home and mind the—little children we never had.

FELLINI (*shrugging*): *Que vesta?*

MASINA: And halfway around the world, in a spooky Malibu mansion, Barbara Steele lives on, still ageless and beautiful and demented—still Barbara Steele, the only woman you ever really loved.

FELLINI (*to audience*): Come into my private coma, you, my audience, you who have loved my foibles. Mix me in the great blender of imagination, of memory. I always shared with you my confetti. Picture to yourself me, the great Fellini, meeting the young Barbara Steele at a party in 1963.

[*Enter YOUNG BARBARA STEELE.*]

YOUNG BARBARA STEELE: Are you really going to make me a star, Maestro?

FELLINI: I will, tho' you'll come to rue the day.

YOUNG BARBARA STEELE: Will your wife be in the film? I loved her in *La Strada*. She was so—oh, what's the word—not "deformed"—

FELLINI: "Dwarfish"?

MASINA: "Victimized"? I feel like the Menendez brothers, a puddle of rape on an old Italian tennis court of hate!

YOUNG BARBARA STEELE: Masina is my idol—but I have more ambition. I'd do anything to get away from horror films.

FELLINI (*to himself*): How could you resist her, you, who resisted so little?

YOUNG BARBARA STEELE: Anything, Federico . . .

[*Exit YOUNG BARBARA STEELE.*]

FELLINI: Giuletta, turn up the heat, I feel a draft. I remember when I was a little boy in Siena, the women with the big breasts would taunt me by exposing themselves to each other. The mystery of big life!

MASINA: You are on your death bed! When I met you, I was a circus freak, and you made my oddity globular. Soon the sensitive loved me all over the world. I was like Lucille Ball for the brainy. Always a sad little smirk on my wide rubbery face.

FELLINI: I made the world my mirror, via Veneto, the spectacle of my exuberant nature.

MASINA: And then you met Barbara Steele.

FELLINI: Saw her in *Black Sunday*, called her agento. "I want the thin black English girl."

MASINA: Then she came to Rome.

FELLINI: And then we fell in love! Isn't life marvelous, Masina!

MASINA: Marvelous, Fellini. And now you die! Life comes in through one window like a bird, then flieth out the other window like a fat old man, leaving feathers in the rain, no more, feathers only.

FELLINI: You-a no like-a Barbara Steele? Why you no-a like-a Barbara Steele?

[*Enter STEVE POITRINE.*]

STEVE POITRINE (*in front of STEELE MANOR*): Big fancy place, with kind of a Hitchcock feel to it. Tall crenellated windows, towers of old stone. Ding-dong.

MASINA: Why don't I like her? Because she *bellisima*, me so plain men put soap in me like soap dish? She so full of hot voodoo, while I sit on shelf like plunger in *baño*? No! We go tonight to Malibu. I call the doctor. Doctor! Pack our bags. We leave Rome tonight, you and me.

[*Exit MASINA and FELLINI.*]

STEVE POITRINE: Gee, I hate to repeat myself, haven't done so since Walter Matthau forced me to eat that horseradish, but—ding-dong! I feel nervous, like a young boy asking a horse out on a date.

[*Enter VINCENT PRICE.*]

VINCENT PRICE: You wish to see Miss Steele? What name shall I give her?

STEVE POITRINE: Doesn't she already have a name? Don't they call her the Anti-Garbo? Catchy. Accurate too. I remember when I first saw Bava's final masterpiece, *Red High Heels of Death*, Barbara Steele's lurid, grimacing black eyes pinned my dick to my seat.

VINCENT PRICE: Forgive the suds. I'm washing her delicate underthings by hand.

STEVE POITRINE: I'll eat those suds if they're hers. I'll eat you if you belong to her. She's Barbara Steele—and I'm only a man. You're the butler? Call her down to see me.

VINCENT PRICE: Miss Steele sees no one. It's as though we were all ghosts in the haunted house of her own memory. We're invisible.

STEVE POITRINE: She'll come out to play once she hears it's about Mr. Vincent Price.

VINCENT PRICE: I am Vincent Price. Retired from the screen for years, I have taken the post as her butler. And why?

STEVE POITRINE: Why? Why, Price?

VINCENT PRICE: Because I love her as few women have ever loved a man.

STEVE POITRINE: That is so romantic. I feel like waltzing. "If I loved you, time and again I would try to say . . ."

VINCENT PRICE: And she has something on me, and I don't mean merely the tremendous shadow that hovers over all who would come to Steele Manor.

STEVE POITRINE: You know, Vince, I have something on myself. The radio! Something about you turns my knees to castanets, hear them knocking like crickets all the way to your bedroom door.

VINCENT PRICE: I'd love to oblige you, but the suds are chapping my hands and digits. I haven't stopped slaving for even a moment, like Anthony Hopkins in *Remains of the Day*.

[*Enter LEAF STEELE and RIVER PHOENIX.*]

LEAF STEELE: Price! Get us some scotch and helium, will ya? I'm, like, parched.

VINCENT PRICE: Yes, Miss Leaf. If Miss Barbara Steele asks, you will tell her I'm a good servant?

LEAF STEELE: I'll tell her whatever comes into my mind, which is usually—air.

RIVER PHOENIX: Whose night is it for the genitals? Mine?

LEAF STEELE: No, mine, ha ha.

VINCENT PRICE: Very good, Miss Leaf. Sob.

[*Exit VINCENT PRICE.*]

LEAF STEELE: Now, Steve, what'd you make of him?

STEVE POITRINE: Under his trousers there's a strange bulge which I think might be a gun, or bugle.

LEAF STEELE: A gun!

RIVER PHOENIX: Or a syringe? Jesus H. Christ, in two days I start work on *Interview with a Vampire*, let's go down to the Viper Club, have a drink.

LEAF STEELE: Ohhhh—he wants to see Johnny Depp again.

RIVER PHOENIX: Do not.

LEAF STEELE: You're so transparent, River.

STEVE POITRINE: That's what the critics like about you. Your skin is like freckled glass, and underneath we see the poignant workings of your pure heart. Touching. Hard to believe you're the son of the infamous Barbara Steele.

[*Enter VINCENT PRICE.*]

VINCENT PRICE: There will be no remarks about Miss Steele, or you'll taste the lip of my guillotine.

LEAF STEELE: Cut with the threats and get me my helium now! I'm a spinning top, filled with fizz, but Mother always manages to get these servants who think it's their destiny to thwart me!

VINCENT PRICE: Mr. River, a Gus Van Sant here to see you.

RIVER PHOENIX: Christ, he's always crawling around behind me, wanting to lick my sneakers. And I have to start *Interview with a Vampire* in the morning. If he asks for me tell him it's all over, the mirrors, the three-ways, the nitro inhalers and the Udo Kier syndrome. What he had for me is worn down to a little nub. No, I'll tell him in person.

[*Exit RIVER PHOENIX and VINCENT PRICE.*]

LEAF: Why, that doesn't look like Gus, not unless he's grown a wife. Or is she some kind of clown like that babysitter who shot all those children?

[*Enter FELLINI and MASINA.*]

MASINA: Clown? *Que "clown"?*

FELLINI: In Italian, "camera" means room; so you have to ask yourself, what room? Possibly the parents' bedroom as they lie making love, what Freud called the "primal scene"? And that leads to Michael Powell, *Peeping Tom*, and that leads to Fellini—to me—Fellini's sentence.

MASINA (*to LEAF STEELE*): So—you are Barbara Steele! Foul spider poached on the branch of the cuckold tree.

LEAF STEELE (*after a pause*): Is she talking in English?

STEVE POITRINE: No, Madame Fellini, this is her daughter, Leaf.

MASINA: I will not leaf. Her daughter? [*Assailing FELLINI.*] Your daughter too.

LEAF STEELE: I dropped out of Beverly Hills High when I failed the Tori Spelling bee. Mother says I have no intellect. She'd rather I stayed home all the time, reading Julia Kristeva and Avital Ronell, and I say, "Mother? Who is Julia Kristeva? Did Julia Roberts change her name or something when she married Lyle Lovett? If so I don't want to know. And 'Avital Ronell'? Hello!! Is it some kind of pasta from Spago's?"

FELLINI: Look at Masina, my bulldog screen against the winds of my fame, the fame of me, Fellini. Oh, but she is a jealous bulldog beauty, no? Tickle her under loose floppy ears—

MASINA (*threatening*): Fellini! Shut the mouth! Or I pull plug on big iron lung that keep you alive, bragging and planning next feature film, *I Made Masina Look Stupid*. She your daughter?

FELLINI: No! Hmmm, maybe—I find out! [*To LEAF.*] Carezza, kiss me on my kneecap.

MASINA: If you dare touch Fellini, I, I, Masina, will make you the Lorena Bobbitt of women.

STEVE POITRINE: Now let's not get hasty—

LEAF STEELE: I will so not!

MASINA: Where is the room of oxygen tent? My husband must lie down at once, presto!

LEAF STEELE: With nurses? Around the corner.

FELLINI: Stop right now, before we go any further. Is Barbara Steele here to greet the great Fellini? Will I open that door and see her *mal'occhio*, how you say, evil eye, present me with Oscar, as best director, of all time and space, you, Fellini? With my many films, each one telling a dramatic story of modern life, its beauty, its degradation, why, there's a word for me—Felliniesque.

[*Enter LISA.*]

LISA: Hiya, Chief. I came down from San Francisco to lend a hand.

FELLINI: Are you my daughter? You have my eyes, my twinkle toes, my continental Nebuchadnezzar.

MASINA: Lie down, Fellini! No more daughters—you die soon! And I will be there on your bed of death, looking kooky.

[*Exit FELLINI and MASINA.*]

LEAF: Like I was really going to kiss his disgusting kneecaps . . .

LISA: Chief, that reminds me, Tonya Harding's been calling and calling . . .

LEAF: He's so—self-centered!

LISA: I used to skate myself, so I know what it's like, you get this one Brooke Shields look-alike and all of a sudden judges all over the world are writing 10, 10, 10, it gets a girl down, if she's from Portland and scrappy.

STEVE: Okay, okay! I'll call her!

[*Enter VINCENT PRICE.*]

VINCENT PRICE: Mr. Gus Van Sant.

[*Enter GUS VAN SANT.*]

STEVE POITRINE (*to audience*): And he's from Portland, too! Is this some kind of—conspiracy?

GUS VAN SANT (*to VINCENT PRICE*): Wow, dude, you look so much like Vincent Price!

LEAF: Like who? Is that a person?

STEVE POITRINE (*to audience*): I wasn't always a private eye. Once I was a young aspiring art student, working nights sketching in all the colors Ross Bleckner didn't feel like. I had a steady girl, a bright future as the plaything of aging screen idol Walter Matthau. But then tragedy struck. The art market fell apart, and Walter Matthau turned gamy and sullen, like a cake left out in the rain. I quit art school and moved to San Francisco, joining the parade of slackers that have followed me ever since. I became a private eye, turning my bright inquisitive gaze to the dark corners of crime. Lisa turned up later. I took to her right away—she's hard and cold, like me, I'm the Brian Boitano to her Katarina Witt.

VINCENT PRICE (*coldly*): Excuse me, please, I'm washing delicate stains, fiant blurs, from the pale silk of my mistress's panties. I'm trying to be Bob Flanagan without actually having to feel any pain.

GUS VAN SANT: Have you tried morphine? Ah, of course you have, you're old! When you were young it was legal, like Midol. Whoa! I swear the resemblance threw me off—I'm, like, doing this dude double take. I took the psillocybin like, at dinner time, what time is it now?

LISA: It's about—

GUS VAN SANT: Don't answer that, I don't want to know.

STEVE POITRINE: Lisa, this number for Tonya Harding, who recommended her?

GUS VAN SANT: For me it's always lunar time, the moon, a moon full and red as the night I first pulled my SUV over by the Clackamas Town Center and picked up the young, straight-acting Portland hustler Jeff Gillooly.

STEVE POITRINE: I remember Jeff. For me he took a piece of Wonder Bread and turned it to toast between hairless thighs.

GUS VAN SANT: He was wearing the grunge look, that I invented, he was—whoa! Am I having a flashback or are you really Vincent Price?

VINCENT PRICE (*with disdain*): If you say so.

GUS VAN SANT: Wow, look, Vince, dude, I'm up to my ass in alligators but I'm thinking of doing the Michael Jackson thing and adding a voiceover to *Cowgirls*.

LEAF STEELE: My movie debut. You made River a star, then it was going to be my turn. But I watch the previews week after week and they never say, "Opening Soon." Roger Ebert just sits there and says, two big thumbs down.

GUS VAN SANT: I don't know, Leaf. —Sometimes you run it up the flagpole and no one salutes.

LEAF: I gave you my all, I even went for collagen thumb implants, and people laugh now when I go bowling and have to, you know, push the ball down the alley.

LISA: I enjoyed having sex with you last night, but tell me, Leaf, where were your genitals?

GUS VAN SANT (*shrugging*): But Vincent Price could do this narration and make it all seem like an opium dream.

LEAF: Which it was.

GUS VAN SANT: Whatever.

LEAF STEELE (*to LISA*): That's confidential. I can't really talk about the genital thing right now, I promised my mother.

GUS VAN SANT: Or *Psycho*! We could re-make *Psycho*! With Vincent Price!

LISA: Just like I promised my mother that one day I'd win a gold medal skating—for our country. [*Despairingly.*] And look at me now!

VINCENT PRICE: Excuse me, Van Sant, but I, Vincent Price, accept no film offers. The unexpected success of the discount store I founded, The Price Club, has freed me from financial obligations, allowing me to spend the winter of my life doing what I have always wanted to do, wash the delicate underthings of a great and fairly clean lady, Miss Barbara Steele.

LEAF: I tried to help once, didn't I, Vince?

VINCENT PRICE: Yes, Miss Leaf—but you were all thumbs.

LEAF (*to GUS VAN SANT*): Thanks to you!

VINCENT PRICE: I hear the swish of her lingerie now. She's coming this way, like Simba the White Lion. May I present the one and only Barbara Steele?

[*Enter BARBARA STEELE.*]

BARBARA STEELE: Often I am permitted to return to Santa Monica, where outside my balcony the glazed ocean roars and shrieks, like me in any one of my 47 Italian horror films of the sixties. But I'm retired, have been for a long time.

STEVE POITRINE: Our loss.

LEAF: My mother would be on *Falcon Crest*, but she was too inscrutable. Look at her, she's a legend.

VINCENT PRICE: A legend in hand-washed silk, caressing her tender underparts like *The 5,000 Fingers of Dr. T.*

BARBARA STEELE: I am all those things and more: I am Barbara Steele. Madly unhappy, and you have come, you, Steve Poitrine, to rescue me from the swamps of my own perfidy, and my twins.

LEAF: Mother!

BARBARA STEELE: Children, servants, intellectuals, all leave. I've asked Mr. Poitrine here all the way from San Francisco. Leaf, is it your turn with the genitals tonight? Well, be a good girl, don't let that Heidi Fleiss keep you out too late.

LEAF: Mother!

[*All leave but BARBARA STEELE and STEVE POITRINE.*]

BARBARA STEELE: In the dawn that is nowhere I have seen my willful children clockwise and counter-clockwise turning. Especially that Leaf!

STEVE POITRINE: So what's on your mind, Barbara Steele? You got me up here from the Mission for a reason.

BARBARA STEELE: Won't you sit down?

STEVE POITRINE: I'd prefer to stand, thanks. I've researched your unthinkable career, Ms. Steele, and I find that between 1960 and 1966 you became to Italian horror films what Louise Brooks was for Weimar cinema in the 20s. Then you married and left filmmaking for a decade. In the mid-seventies you returned to the screen, and then the twins were born. Since then you've been living in eerie solitude here at Steele Manor. You used to be big.

BARBARA STEELE: Tell me, Mr. Poitrine, deep down in the center of your mind, haven't you long harbored a secret fantasy to be stripped naked and pelted with stones by a beautiful woman?

STEVE POITRINE: Anti-Garbo, your wicked eyes see far too sharply. Rent them out as can-openers.

BARBARA STEELE: But I don't need the money a can-opener franchise might net me. This face [*touches her face*], rumor'd to have been Sodom, has for many moons been my meal ticket. But now Fellini is here, in this house. I feel my doom drawing round me, close, like a particularly vacant picture by Robert Ryman, all white and pink, like puff pastry. Can you help me, Steve?

STEVE POITRINE: What's your deal with Fellini? I know you're one of his alumnae, but you're no Anita Ekberg, you've kept your sharpei.

BARBARA STEELE: He's in a coma, so to speak. Back when the world was young, we were young in an enchanted world of spaghetti and straps. Now he returns, one foot in the grave, pulling the foul reek of Hell behind him in a mulch bag. And so do my memories. Help me, Steve, return him and his precious Masina to silence blah blah blah.

[*Enter YOUNG BARBARA STEELE.*]

YOUNG BARBARA STEELE: Oh, Maestro, I'd do anything to get out of horror films.

BARBARA STEELE: One film—*8 1/2*—then back on the weary treadmill of Eurotrash. Where did it go?

STEVE POITRINE: There's something you're not telling me.

BARBARA STEELE: Consider the Lilith of the field, I'm glamorous and antino-mistic, but like every other girl with backbone, I've got skeletons in my closet. So? Even you've got a secret, Steve, and you don't even have backbone.

STEVE POITRINE: Who told?

YOUNG BARBARA STEELE: Oh, Mr. Price, imagine me, a girl from the slums of London, acting with the great Vincent Price. I adore you, and your pretensions about modern art.

BARBARA STEELE: I didn't want Vincent Price in my house, but he got it into his head that only he can save me from my fate. He used his knowledge of my twins' medical problem to inject himself, like insulin, into Steele Manor. I wish that boiling water I poured on his face in Corman's *Tomb of Ligeia* had really been hot.

STEVE: 1963. And you're lovelier now—what witchcraft availeth thee, Ligeia?

YOUNG BARBARA STEELE: "Lovelier now"!—don't make me laugh.

BARBARA STEELE: What keeps me young? Possibly my long-standing love affair with Beverly D'Angelo, best known for her turn as Patsy Cline in *Coal Miner's Daughter*, and perhaps for her role as the hapless wife in the *National Lampoon "Vacation"* films with Chevy Chase. She's upstairs now. Waiting for me. So I really should go.

[*To YOUNG BARBARA STEELE.*] Don't taunt me with your fresh allure, ghost! You aren't real, you can't be! Image, begone!

[*Enter LISA.*]

LISA: This is some mansion, Steve! There's even an ice rink down in the base-ment. I'm going to practice again. Practice hard. I know I can win a gold medal for our country.

YOUNG BARBARA STEELE: You're alive, and I'm dead! Isn't that revenge enough for Barbara Steele?

BARBARA STEELE: Excuse me, Steve? Right now Beverly's in a bit of pain—or *pain*, meaning "bread"—, can we cut this a bit short, thanks! *Abbodanza!*

[*Enter VINCENT PRICE.*]

VINCENT PRICE: Can I have a moment, Miss Steele? Barbara?

BARBARA STEELE: You have sapped me of a great deal more than a moment. Pardon me—Sudsy.

[*Exit BARBARA STEELE.*]

STEVE POITRINE: What a femme! Now where's Fellini?

LISA: I was asking him if he thinks I have a future in the movies. Skating films are bound to come back, I want to position myself as the new Sonja Henie.

VINCENT PRICE: When I look at you, I think of the young Barbara Steele, my mistress as I knew her when we were both young and naive.

LISA: Or Lynn-Holly Johnson in *Ice Castles*, from the 70s!

YOUNG BARBARA STEELE: She is not like me! I was suave, evil, fresh! I was poison wrapped in black sugar! She's from the Valley, or Portland!

VINCENT PRICE: Tell me, my dear, what kind of crotchless underwear have you got in your little dresser drawer?

STEVE POITRINE: Bring me Fellini at once!

VINCENT PRICE: Under your flaring skating skirt, your panties must often be stained by ice. Are they cold when you put them to your face? I'll be in the pantry, thinking of you, my arms shoved up to the elbows in Dove.

LISA: I saw you in *Edward Scissorhands*, covered with ice in a cold lonely prison of self. You must have plenty to say about skating. Chief, don't do anything stupid. You let your gonads think for you, not that that's a plus or minus.

[*Exit LISA and VINCENT PRICE.*]

STEVE POITRINE: Okay, so what do we know so far? Barbara Steele, the anti-Garbo—her two twins, Leaf and River—a strange situation about their genitals—hmm—female circumcision? Remind me to call Alice Walker and Pratibha Parmar.

YOUNG BARBARA STEELE: They can't help you! You're beyond assistance!

STEVE POITRINE: Here in this house of long hair, I get the shivers with every step I take. If I strain I can hear the thin silver whisper of a voice, but Dr. Dean Edell says straining's so bad for the testicles, and I'm not dialing for dollars.

[*Enter RIVER PHOENIX.*]

RIVER PHOENIX: I'm tough on the outside, but cut up here. I'm like a copy of *Spin* magazine ripped in shreds.

STEVE: Oh—my—God, it's River Phoenix.

RIVER PHOENIX: Oh, Johnny, Johnny, Johnny! I pretend I don't care about him, but I do. I want to turn my love into reality. But he doesn't let me. He's Johnny Depp, and who am I?

YOUNG BARBARA STEELE: My little boy—of the future! I always knew that I, the young Barbara Steele, would bear a child precious as topaz. But you're far away in the future—only a prospect. I beat the walls of this white air I walk among like a mad mime on Union Square, searching for you, I'd beat the rain out of the sky to make you mine but time stands between us like a traffic cop with wings.

[*Exit YOUNG BARBARA STEELE.*]

RIVER PHOENIX: My mother told me, don't take that part on *Jump Street*, hold out for big screen stardom. But if I had, maybe Johnny and I would be friends. Close friends. The kind of friends who do everything together, naked.

STEVE: I know, I know. I felt the same way about Walter Matthau. Poor boy, come live with me in San Francisco, we'll put you in Delancey Street for a year and by the time you're selling your first Christmas tree, you'll be clean. You'll be the angel we put on top of the tree, and you will be mine.

RIVER PHOENIX: That's nice of you, Mr. Poitrine, but no thanks. I find the older I get, and I'm almost 20 now, the more I need the consolations crank and Ritalin bring to a boy.

STEVE (*bitterly*): I should take my own advice! Here I am advising you to drop your foolish crush on a film star, and I'm tumbling head over heels for one. For one damaged as a drainpipe, but sweet as a little gingerbread boy I could put in my oven, then bake till golden brown and chewy.

RIVER PHOENIX: A gingerbread figure without genitals to call his own. Hope Johnny isn't a—what do you call it?

STEVE: I'm drawing a blank.

RIVER PHOENIX: Just like Mother Nature did, long ago, around my industrial area. Goodbye, Steve.

[*Exit RIVER PHOENIX.*]

STEVE (*still bitter*): And it was Ross Bleckner who introduced me to Rachel Marron, the "Queen of the Night," played by Whitney Houston in *The Bodyguard*—the docudrama of our doomed love affair. She told me, "I will always love you," but she lied, like every other client I've ever had. She's skiing down the slopes of Aspen, while I nestle a broken heart in my pint-size flask of gin. Waiter!

[*Enter FELLINI.*]

STEVE (*sourly*): Oh! Look who's here.

FELLINI: Fellini, the great maker of worlds, me. Born in circus of crazy, fighting Fascists in brown shirts—colorful. The War, the Depresion, and always Fellini, making the little man a Little Big, and the little woman, Masina, America's meatball hero princess, the shy Arlecchina no man would touch.

STEVE: I'm not familiar with Masina. While all the other art students were watching foreign films, I was busting my balls for Ross Bleckner with the one hand, while sucking Walter Matthau's cock with the other.

FELLINI: Others try to imitate Giuletta and me—One big man, one slow woman. Jackson Pollock, Lee Krasner. Me outlive them, me and Masina. In the 60s there was John and Yoko—in the 70s Archie and Edith. We outlive them. In the 80s there was Raymond Carver and Tess Gallagher—or Blake and Krystle Carrington. But Fellini and Masina, I've seen 'em all and my dear, we're still here.

STEVE: So, how's the coma?

FELLINI: How I talk to you when me in coma? I use sophisticated sign language, oversized gestures, the gestures created by me, me, Fellini, in *La Dolce Vita* and other films. People come to me, daily, young college boys, say, we bow down to you, Maestro. We genuine humble *Satyricon* love slave harem. But there is the problem of genius! Positively Felliniesque!

STEVE POITRINE (*intrigued*): Young college boys? Come again?

[*Enter GUS VAN SANT.*]

GUS VAN SANT: So you're Fellini. Hey—fuck you.

FELLINI (*oblivious*): Everybody love the man with the big lens, the big smile, the Roman schwing of Mrs. Stone.

GUS VAN SANT: Guess he doesn't hear me. Hey! Fellini!

FELLINI: Always a crowd when Fellini make appearance. They come hungry for tell me, Fellini, why you so much talent when we, the nobody people of world, look so downcast with our mediocrasia?

STEVE: Gus, why aren't you making that Harvey Milk film? I knew Harvey, my first case involved tenderly separating him from then-cute teen star Johnny Whitaker of TV's *Family Affair*.

GUS VAN SANT: I tried, man. I tried, but the studio wasn't anywhere near ready to let me cast it my way. We had a meeting of the minds, and mine was fried, like an egg ready to sizzle in the snow. [*Pounds head.*]

FELLINI: I invent the movies, make Roma film center, give Masina big break as ugly duckling, then at crowded cocktail party guests part like Red Sea, and in the distance Barbara Steele make her way, her confident way, toward Fellini, say to Fellini, "Maestro, make me ready for you to touch me there."

STEVE: I thought Robin Williams was gonna to star in it?

GUS VAN SANT: But do people really want to see Robin Williams have sex? I don't think so, my friend. I wanted Angie Dickinson, possibly Andre Agassi, hey, don't laugh.

FELLINI: After that my life grow, and grow old, I climb into coma on soft biscotti bed, curl up. What is life, after all? Is it a big plate of pasta fongool, or the defiant face of freak self, a bucket of worms, curling, alive? She gave me long liquid look, she close my eyes, say, "Arrivederci," I fade away into black hole gaze of Barbara Steele—La Stupenda.

[*Exit FELLINI.*]

GUS VAN SANT: Yeah, take your spaghettios with you, fuck you!

STEVE: And who'll play Dan White?

GUS VAN SANT: I wanted William Burroughs. His whole gun career leading up to this moment. I last saw Bill propped up against a storm fence in Lawrence, Kansas, shooting blanks and downing Twinkies as though his whole life depended on it. The studio wants Daniel Day Lewis who is such a bullshit actor, man. Anyway, I've washed my hands clean. I'm doing *Sunset Boulevard* next.

STEVE: Quite a stretch?

GUS VAN SANT: Not with Angie Dickison and about ten pounds of psychedelics. We're using this old house, Steele Manor, manned with street hustlers, to represent the beauty of life. Then we're going to try to get Burt Bacharach as the butler. "I've got lots of friends in San Jose." You know. Moral gravity.

[*Enter LISA.*]

LISA: Steve! Now Tonya's husband's on the line for you—Jeff Gillooly.

GUS VAN SANT: Now stop right a minute there. Jeff—Gillooly? You know him? He calls you on your Watts Line?

STEVE: Night and day.

GUS VAN SANT (*to LISA*): And you know him too?

LISA: Well, I've met him, of course. I am a skater—whether anyone on Heaven or Earth takes me seriously, I do!

GUS VAN SANT: Lucky ducks. Red moonlight was pouring out of the sky and the roof of my van was loud with rain. Under a streetlight there he stood, thumbs in his pockets, a strange flicker of credit crossing his face. Down by the Clackamas Town Center in a nippy world of appetite on ice. Jeff Gillooly, not only a man, not only a boy, but the central figure of 20th Century myth and hung like Forrest Tucker.

LISA: Hey, I was just in the kitchen and River Phoenix was there, having sex with Vincent Price.

STEVE: And?

LISA: And he died, Steve! In slow motion, like the triple axel I'm planning for Salt Lake. I just have to give everybody in that city a hundred thousand dollars for the Olympics.

STEVE: Who died? Not River Phoenix!

[*Enter RIVER PHOENIX.*]

RIVER: No, Vincent Price. Old man chewed me a new asshole.

GUS VAN SANT: Well, look what the cat dragged in.

RIVER: Gus—I was only doing it with him to try 'n' pique your interest.

GUS VAN SANT: Might as well try to catch the wind, Speedball.

STEVE: Vincent Price—dead? Oh, the calamity! And he was my prime suspect.

RIVER PHOENIX: Don't call me Speedball!

LISA: I'll get you your smelling salts, if that's what you call them on your cellular phone.

[*Exit LISA.*]

RIVER PHOENIX: Gus, Gus, how can you be so cruel?

GUS VAN SANT: I'll take some pictures of the corpse, sell them to Kenneth Anger. Or maybe I'll do an Ed Wood/Tim Burton kind of thing and make the corpse dance around and tell funny stories. Life in Steele Manor must of given Vincent Price a few laughs. And having sex with Speedball is always a chuckle.

RIVER: I don't do those speedballs any more.

GUS VAN SANT: It's like putting oysters in a parking meter.

[*Exit GUS VAN SANT.*]

RIVER: I'm clean! Gus!

STEVE (*to audience*): He was born just plain Gus Sant, but he pulled over so many hustlers into that van with the black windows, the kids soon used to say, you mean Gus "Van" Sant?

RIVER (*broken-hearted*): Soon, they're going to call it Portland Van Oregon.

STEVE: All the windows of the van are painted black, and all the doors are childproof.

RIVER: You check in but you don't check out. And he wears those knitted caps like Mike Nesmith in the Monkees, the truth is, I used to love him but a long time ago he stopped caring for me . . . He said I was a freak only good for a Fellini picture.

STEVE: Poor boy, you've been stun gunned, let me dress you in lace. I'll examine the wounds the late fiend Price left in your anus.

RIVER: Oh . . . I'm not too worried. I'm regularly tested for lockjaw—and besides, it's pretty well coated in Woolite. Kills the germs you know. It's just squishy when I walk and I'm not much of a walker.

[*Enter LEAF and BARBARA STEELE.*]

BARBARA STEELE (*merrily*): The light foot hears me and the brightness begins!

LEAF: River! Mom says you have to let me use the—oh, hi, everybody.

RIVER: Why, Mother, why? You know I'm seeing Johnny tonight.

BARBARA STEELE: After what happened with Vincent Price in the pantry, I think enough is enough. Don't you?

RIVER: That wasn't my fault. I was just standing there when these big soapy hands came behind me and met at my belt buckle. Before I knew what was happening I was bent over the sink with my face floating in your underwear, and I felt this elderly tongue do the thing—the wild thing, the very thing I need Johnny Depp for.

LEAF: Too bad, Speedball! C'mon, swap!

[*RIVER and LEAF exchange genitals.*]

I feel so much better now, my X and Ys all revved up like Meat Loaf, *Bat Out of Hell.* Come on, gang, Charlie Sheen's waiting for us down at the Viper.

RIVER: This isn't fair, as I've said so many times, to so many men.

[Exit RIVER and LEAF]

STEVE: Okay, Miss Steele, it's time to spill the beans. There's some deep secret going on between those twins and you. I can't figure it out but when I do I'm calling *Inside Edition.*

BARBARA STEELE: All right! All right! I'll tell you the whole awful truth. The twins were born with only one set of genitals between them. When either of them wants to use them, they have to switch off!

STEVE POITRINE: Tell me, Miss Steele—are they male or female genitals?

BARBARA STEELE *(dryly)*: You know, I've never known how to answer that question. But who cares? I've lived too long with the secret of my chldren's sex, it lacks interest for me. Tell me, Mr. Poitrine, what do you know about Satan?

STEVE POITRINE: They called him "Jeff" in Portland . . .

BARBARA STEELE: I had a child with Satan once, in Italy, where I was making *Terror Creatures of the Grave.* I remember straddling a waterfall, dressed as the death goddess of the River Po, and suddenly, sharp pangs shot through me, just as Jess Franco was yelling "Action" in that Spanglish/phony French he thought so impressive. Pangs, like arrows tipped with liquid fire. It was my afterbirth. I looked down, down into the Po, and I saw the body of a baby boy gush away down the waterfall, moving its little hands and feet and calling my name. This had also happened to a friend of mine, Gabrielle Kerouac, so I wasn't startled or anything. But Mr. Poitrine, I'm sure that baby was the spawn of Satan!

[Enter LEAF STEELE.]

LEAF: Mother! I was just down at the Viper Club with Lisa and River and Heidi, and River died! Do I get the genitals?

STEVE: And he was my prime suspect! And plus, I loved him!

BARBARA STEELE: Is there a curse on Steele Manor? Did my black eyes and my mysterious, tormented affect cast a pall of gloom and death over the men who adored me most?

STEVE POITRINE: It's a possibility.

BARBARA STEELE: It's a consummation—devoutly to be wished. [*Maniacal laugh.*] But I didn't ask you here to rehash the past. Is Fellini still alive?

STEVE POITRINE: I hope so—he's my new prime suspect. Leaf, show me the body of your brother.

LEAF STEELE: He's all, like, covered in Woolite! I don't want to paw through his pockets, but I do need his, ahem, dog tags. Now that I'm so well-endowed, I feel like doing a little of what comes naturally. I know sexuality's a constructed artifact, I know that statements like "show me the body" only underline how little thought goes into "me"—"me" as a kind of maquette for a perfect me. So, yeah, let's go, the whole *Melrose Place* gang's just hanging around hiding their needles and smiling vacantly for the press.

[*Exit STEVE and LEAF.*]

BARBARA STEELE: Am I alone? I keep telling myself I am, despite my cult status. It gives me comfort knowing there are probably sixteen or seventeen people in the US alone who obsess about me daily. Am I alone? I showed one face to the world—a mask that had lost touch with the real. I'd love to work with Argento— he just hasn't asked me. I'd love to do more sophisticated comedy, Noel Coward. Or Sam Shepard! I'm unlimited, talent-wise, it's just this face has me cast, like a deathmask of Houdon. People seem to think all I can do is scream.

[*Enter MASINA.*]

MASINA: Tragedia! Fellini della morte! As if a coma wasn't enough to keep him quiet, penseroso, someone crept into his hospital room and hit his kneecaps with a piece of lead pipe. [*To BARBARA STEELE.*] Holy Mary, mother of God, it's Barbara Steele, woman who killed Fellini!

BARBARA STEELE: Let's ignore that slur and, Giuletta Masina, may I introduce you to myself, Barbara Steele, since we've never met. I've enjoyed your movies ever since, when I was a tiny girl in London, my grandmother used to take me. You had been her mother's favorite star of the 19th century.

MASINA: We're the same age, you and me.

BARBARA STEELE: Of consent, dear.

MASINA: He would come to your palazzo in a gondola, bring you fine washables from my bureau, out of my vanity.

BARBARA STEELE: How we laughed when we considered the fate of Masina—I, burnt at the stake in film after film, but triumphant; you, urchin with sooty cheeks and wide moon saucer eyes, forever the victim.

MASINA: You—you! Tell me, were those two children Fellini's?

[*Attempts to strangle BARBARA STEELE.*]

BARBARA STEELE: Yes—No! —Yes. [*To herself:*] I thought they were—Louis Malle's. [*To MASINA.*] The truth is I don't remember. Did that ever happen to you, Masina? You wake up, you're eating your wheat germ and listening to lite rock, it's a sunny morning in—[*looks at MASINA*]—Rome, and all of a sudden you realize you don't even know your own name?

MASINA: No. Slut of England, no, a thousand times no. I know who I am. I am widow.

BARBARA STEELE (*touching her bruised neck*): I feel better now. In fact, I feel pretty good. You've got good hands. Long, slender, delicate hands like the lilies of my reputation. I'd like to see them bent and twisted around my waist, holding me high above a crowd of hooded men.

MASINA: How do I live without Fellini?

BARBARA STEELE: You didn't do much living while he was alive. I have lost my son, but I think actually, I had the twins so I'd have one left over. Like sometimes in Rome, don't you leave the house with another pair of pantyhose rolled up in your purse?

MASINA: Me? Heavy socks. Heavy socks of wool.

BARBARA STEELE: I have lost Vincent Price, twice: first as a co-star, then as a butler. And finally, if all you say is true, Fellini is dead. You and I, Masina, have some catching up to do.

MASINA: I get my knitting, be right back. You and me, we sit by the fire and we knit the names of the dead into bright shawls.

[*Exit MASINA.*]

BARBARA STEELE: Well, something like that, I suppose. We have come so far that all the old stories whisper once more *L'Orribile Segreto del Dr. Hitchcock, La Danza*

Macabre (*Castle of Blood*), *I Lunghi Capelli della Morte, Cinque Tombe per un Medium* (*Le Cimitiere des Morts-Vivants*), *Nightmare Castle, The She-Beast, Un Angelo per Satana,* and Bava's final masterpiece, *Red High Heels of Death.* Rise to adore the mystery of Barbara Steele!

[*Enter STEVE.*]

STEVE: You're mad as a hattress!

BARBARA STEELE (*turning*): I am all those hats and more! I am Barbara Steele. Men have longed for me since the days of Keats and Gerald de Nerval, for I am La Belle Dame sans Merci.

STEVE: Uh-hunh, and I'm Patti LaBelle. Cut to the chase, Barbara. Did you commit these murders, or are you innocent?

BARBARA STEELE: No more blood and no more tears—now I'm a crystal chandelier. No honey mango, no woman, no cry: I once was wet and now I'm dry. O Preterite, o ghostly Patriarch, you will not need to fear me after dark . . . Back to San Francisco Mr. Poitrine. You failed to prevent any crimes from occurring. The three men I loved most are dead, one, two, three on a match. I'd say you've done a grand job. Oh, for the maniacal laugh I employed to such effect in The Three Deaths of Dr. Terror's Nurse (*La Lago di Satana*)! But I'm rusty.

[*Exit BARBARA STEELE.*]

STEVE POITRINE (*in his office in San Francisco*): The night was dim and filled with sudden bursts of gunfire. From out back you could hear the sounds of women oppressed, you could smell the crack burning in the pipes of the huddled. I was baffled. A baffled dick.

[*Enter LISA.*]

Oh, there you are, Okay, back to basics. First thing, filing's a mess.

LISA: I've got two words for you, boss—I quit.

STEVE: No! Lisa, why? How can you quit, now, when I've sunk to the very nadir of my detective career? I have no idea who killed Vincent Price, River Phoenix, or Fellini. My chief suspect, Barbara Steele, was proven innocent in court. So who's left? I keep going over every detail in my little mind.

LISA: And all the time, the answer was under your nose.

[*Significant pause.*]

STEVE: You mean—you? You, Lisa Tarantino? You masterminded the bloodbath at Steele Manor? But how? You had an alibi too!

LISA: Yes. I killed them all. It was I who dropped the cold pills in River Phoenix's Mountain Dew. I who felled Fellini. And I slammed the final door in Vincent Price's House on Haunted Hill.

STEVE: But why, Lisa, why?

LISA: You knew I was an ice skater, Steve. You knew my greatest dream was to win the gold medal for my country. Or did you forget? They were all of them—Fellini, Vincent Price, and River Phoenix—all three had been named skating judges at the Olympic Games. And all openly boasted of favoring Nancy Kerrigan. Everybody does. Even I like her, and I hate her.

STEVE: Even I like her, and I think she'll go for the Gold. But you couldn't have killed Fellini—you have an alibi.

LISA: Little man, hear me chuckle. What makes you so sure I was in this alone? Foolish man, you lived at the end of a gun all your days. [*Pulls out gun.*] Tonight I'm in critical form, a woman on the edge of violence.

[*Enter JEFF GILLOOLY.*]

JEFF: Put down the gun, Lisa.

LISA: Here's my silent partner, and the number one skating coach in the country, the young, straight-acting Portland hustler Jeff Gillooly.

JEFF: So, Steve, we meet again.

STEVE: Is it really you? Hate to be a doubting Thomas, but you look different somehow. Older. Christ told Thomas, put your hand into my side.

JEFF (*resigned*): Okay, okay! Put your hand between my thighs.

[*STEVE does so.*]

STEVE: It's him all right! Toast!

JEFF: Want a toast? How about "Skol" as we say in Lillehammer!

STEVE (*to audience*): Maybe a little older . . .

LISA: We're off to Norway in the morning to skate rings around Tonya and Nancy. Skol!

STEVE: What's to prevent me from picking up the phone and dialing the police?

JEFF: Memories, Steve—memories alone. You and me, on a hot summer night. You and me, deceiving Walter Matthau in that Detroit hotel room.

STEVE: You make a strong case.

LISA: Jeff, are my heavy furs packed?

JEFF: Yes, Miss Tarantino?

LISA: Then we're off to Lillehammer. Steve, I'd like to thank you for the many years I slaved for you while you ignored my Olympic dreams. These dreams, these feet, these legs, will win a gold medal for our country, no thanks to you.

STEVE: The nearest you'll get to a gold medal, young lady, will be from good old-fashioned Gold Medal brand flour. Buy a bag at Safeway.

LISA (*to JEFF*): Is the plane ready? [*To STEVE.*] I'll go out the same way you came in, in a burst of glory.

[*Exit LISA and JEFF*]

STEVE: Where did it all go wrong for me? I could blame Ross Bleckner, but that wouldn't be fair, now, would it? As I look back through the yesterday of my years, I see no face within, only a face of freckled glass so finely spun I saw a living heart, and half a brain, built within—like my bedside Baby Ben. The world gave me River Phoenix, but then turned around and threw me a cold cigar, a kick in the ass. They say all missing men eventually turn up in San Francisco. How missing am I? I'll tell you how missing . . .

END

I wrote "Three on a Match" and "Life After Prince" for the same venue, a tiny and short-lived San Francisco art gallery called "Kiki," and it was a dramatic sea change from the big performance spaces I had been used to before. Kiki was a storefront gallery on a terrible street in the Mission, one you might be afraid to walk down, but it was the place where many of the most exciting happened occurred in the art world and the writing world. It has been much eulogized in the decades since, especially by myself, but the facts can still confound me when I see pictures of the space or watch video of its events. The film-maker Leslie Singer suggested that she could film the rehearsals for "Three on a Match" like D.A. Pennebaker had done during the making of the original cast album of Stephen Sondheim's Company" in the 1970 era. This footage still exists, and when I watch it I find myself marveling we ever did such a thing, mainly because the space was so tiny. If you and I stood next to each other and held out our arms and legs spreadeagle, we couldn't fit inside the space side by side. I think you could fit in three rows of four folding chairs into the gallery space, with a little space marked off at the front window, next to the front door, that was our playing area. Half the gallery was further divided by a loft bed, on which an additional 13th, 14th or 15th patron might sprawl or lounge when the show came on. The players had no conventional exit or entrance, so they watched the action from the front door and entered when they thought it might be their cue. You couldn't really have more than a handful of characters on stage at any one time. (I notice today that I wrote a lot more soliloquies then than I do today, and that's one reason why.) And plays had to be short so that you could have another show at 9, and a third at 10, if business dictated.

STEVE POITRINE, San Francisco private eye. Rex Ray
LISA, his secretary. . . . . Mary Margaret Sloan
LEAF STEELE, Hollywood wild child. . . . . Jocelyn Saidenberg
RIVER PHOENIX. . . . . Scott Hewicker
FEDERICO FELLINI . . . . Clifford Hengst
GIULETTA MASINA . . . . Phoebe Gloeckner
BARBARA STEELE, as a young girl. . . . . Yedda Morrison
VINCENT PRICE. . . . . Wayne Smith
GUS VAN SANT. . . . . Craig Goodman
BARBARA STEELE. . . . . Norma Cole
JEFF GILLOOLY. . . . . Cedar Sigo

Original Cast, 3 on a Match, produced at Kiki Gallery (San Francisco), February
21, 1994.

STEVE POITRINE, San Francisco private eye . . . . .Clifford Hengst
LISA, his secretary . . . . Margaret Cran
LEAF STEELE, Hollywood wild child. . . . . Andrea
JunoRIVER PHOENIX . . . . Scott Hewicker
FEDERICO FELLINI. . . . . Jonathan Hammer
GIULETTA MASINA. . . . . Phoebe Gloeckner
BARBARA STEELE, as a young girl. . . . . Erin Courtney
VINCENT PRICE. . . . . Wayne Smith
GUS VAN SANT. . . . . Nayland Blake
BARBARA STEELE. . . . . Norma Cole
JEFF GILLOOLY. . . . . .Kevin Killian

Life After Prince

characters

CLERK

JUDGE WAYNE SMITH
SF Unemployment Court

VANITY
born Denise Matthews, US pop singer

APOLLONIA
her rival

WENDY & LISA
musicians

KIM BASINGER
top Hollywood star of 1994

ALEC BALDWIN
soon to be her husband

SHEENA EASTON
Scottish pop singer

SINEAD O'CONNOR
Irish pop singer

KATE BUSH
English pop singer

MAVIS STAPLES
American gospel singer

SCOTT HEWICKER
artist and Prince fan

[*Play is set in the San Francisco unemployment court with a bailiff and a distinguished judge awaiting the opening of the day's session, in the spring of 1994.*]

CLERK: Hear ye! Hear ye! We're at the unemployment court of Judge Wayne Smith. He's the man with the power, the man with the cards up his sleeves of his robe. He determines who gets what, based not on merit alone.

JUDGE SMITH: What's on my docket today? I'm calling this special session in one of the most distressed parts of Dogpatch, a secret session devoted to Prince.

CLERK: I wonder if Prince will appear in court. I'm just a clerk, but I'm just as star-struck as the next man.

JUDGE SMITH [*to audience*]: I'm a San Franciscan, just like you. I walk around and see chronic victims of recession and abuse, some who pick the refuse from the gutter, others who try to defraud the state I command.

CLERK: Oh, now who would do that?

JUDGE SMITH: It's 1994, and everything's changing.

CLERK: Ten years ago I had never even heard of Prince, and now he's everywhere. He's so popular that they've renamed Skid Row and now they call it Minnesota Street—in honor of Prince.

JUDGE SMITH: And we've been getting all the claims funneled in here like Hurricane Betsy.

CLERK: What claims?

JUDGE SMITH: I mean the endless parade—a veritable blitz—of Prince's female collaborators whom he's let go.

CLERK: Judge Smith, it's going to be a long day. Don't get your back up before noon. Are you favoring your left foot?

JUDGE SMITH: I walked here all the way from Dolores and Market.

CLERK: You say you walked here but I see your limo. Driven by ex-offenders you're trying to put straight.

JUDGE SMITH: My policy in regards to ex-offenders remains putatively firm—mild really, considering. "Why spare the rod?" is my watchword.

CLERK: Your ballot measure to bring back the cane to reduce unemployment is still controversial.

JUDGE SMITH: Okay, get this. Her name is "Vanity"?

CLERK: I call Vanity to the stand.

[*Enter VANITY.*]

VANITY: Thank you, Mr. Clerk. [*To JUDGE*]. Hear my plea, don't turn on me. I once was a verb of sex control; I shook your whip with my guacamole. Listen, Judge, I've got a grudge, gimme my chit or this court won't budge.

JUDGE SMITH: So, your name is Vanity.

VANITY: And I am funky! Can I call you Wayne like the other girls from Prospect Street?

CLERK: Contempt of court.

JUDGE SMITH [*to VANITY*]: I see here that you've been charged with ten years of continuous unemployment, ever since your career highlight—*Purple Rain*, in 1984.

VANITY: Want to hear something?

CLERK (*hopefully*): Something funky?

VANITY: People say that was me in *Purple Rain*, but it wasn't no way, that was Apollonia. Or, as I call her, baloney-face. She looks like me, she talks like me, but she's processed. She took everything I had, including my face and body, and delivered them up to Prince like waiters on wheels.

JUDGE SMITH: Fascinating!

VANITY: I despise a cheat, don't you?

CLERK: Don't get personal with Judge Smith; he's a mortal man beneath those robes.

JUDGE SMITH: No, let her go on. Her strange visuals interest me deeply. You're in fine fettle for a woman without virtual reality.

CLERK: I think he likes you.

VANITY [*touched*]: Well, look at you—even doves have pride! And here some people tell me I should be called "Humility," not "Vanity," and then to hear a lovely compliment like that.

JUDGE SMITH: You've been out of work for nine years? And still you find the soap to keep yourself clean.

VANITY: As I was saying, Judge, help me pack my fudge.

[*Enter APOLLONIA.*]

APOLLONIA: Excuse me, your honor, that woman, Vanity, is trying my patience. I heard her take my name in vain. I, Apollonia—of the Greek National Serk.

JUDGE SMITH: Who is Apollonia?

APOLLONIA: I am the girl Prince truly loves, not her, and I appeal to you, give me back my rights. I come to you from Greece wearing the tragic mask, just like Pagliacci did.

JUDGE SMITH: But—

APOLLONIA: The tears of a clone.

CLERK: Apollonia Kotero has no real connections with either Greece or the Greek National Serk. But what I say is, let her think so, who's it hurting?

VANITY: Have you ever heard of—the truth?

APOLLONIA: I want forty dollars a week for my role in *Purple Rain*. I even sang in that picture. I also went on to star in *Falcon Crest*, based on my own royal crest as Minister of Culture for the Greek National Serk.

VANITY: She may be Greek, but she's a bird-doggin' fruitcake.

JUDGE SMITH: Order in the court! One witness at a time, I'm not a metronome.

CLERK: Maybe I can explain.

JUDGE SMITH: Your explanations make the whole world wince.

VANITY: And it rhymes with Prince! Prince done left me and he ain't been back since! Take my fingerprints, I'm a juicy quince, you put the meat in my mincemeat mince. Hey, baloney-head, go back to your phony bed, I made that pony red. I am Vanity (*pause*)—the original place where the horses run free.

APOLLONIA: Look at her, gone mad with the natural flaw of the second-best. Vanity's a fool who doesn't deserve to be copied by me, but alas, it's like I, an ordinary Grecian goddess-type multicultural girl, stepped into the transport chamber of the Fly, and wound up her clone. So be it, said He, the Purple One, and like Botticelli's Venus I emerged from the surf of his breath.

VANITY: Inject her with meth and put her to death!

[*Enter WENDY AND LISA.*]

WENDY AND LISA: Order in the court! Order in the court!

JUDGE SMITH: And who have we here? Who are these two women approaching my bench like a set of conjoined twins?

APOLLONIA [*to VANITY*]: He wanted to call you "Vagina," but that was too risqué for the 80's!

VANITY: Well, it's the 90s now, and I want my check, Judge Smith!

WENDY AND LISA: Hello. Hello.

CLERK: These two women are Wendy and Lisa, core members of Prince's old band the Revolution.

JUDGE SMITH: Out of work too?

WENDY AND LISA: We have come far and sunk low. Give one of we half of a weekly check, and the other half of we will take the rest. For one is the other in the land we hail from.

APOLLONIA: I recognize them now. Judge, these two drips were hired by Prince for some of that Helmut Newton sideshow sleaze appeal. You couldn't even tell the two of them apart except one had less make-up than the other, which is, all by itself, a crime against Revlon.

WENDY AND LISA: We are mystic Cassandras, often speculated about, never construed.

VANITY: And never been screwed. Tell 'em sayonara, give me stamps for food!

JUDGE SMITH: I find that Apollonia and Vanity are interfering with my brand of justice.

VANITY: Justice? Again I cry, "What about—the truth?"

JUDGE SMITH: This is the surrogate court of the newly named Minnesota Street: go now, and dig if you will, your case is in abeyance.

VANITY (*in a surly mood*): I'll go, with my road to hoe. I am Vanity, stop the insanity.

APOLLONIA: I shall report this indignity to the Greek Consul of Serk.

CLERK: Goodbye, and good riddance, to the both of you. I'm as star-struck as the next man, but those two were never stars, just inventions of Prince.

[*Exit VANITY and APOLLONIA.*]

WENDY AND LISA: Goodbye. Goodbye.

JUDGE SMITH: Wendy and Lisa, say your piece.

WENDY AND LISA: We, involved in art production of lovely sound, do good work, on many instruments of fine design.

CLERK: On second thought, stand silently while a real star approaches the court. Ladies and gentlemen, and Judge Smith, may I present, Miss Kim Basinger.

[*Enter KIM BASINGER.*]

KIM BASINGER: Has the whole world gone ballistic? Not only can I not land a job, people are suing me for backing out of *Boxing Helena*. Show a little common sense and what happens? It backfires.

WENDY AND LISA: We will stay mum out of worship of Kim Basinger. Her immutable sang-froid turns us to rocky stone. Sound-wise.

KIM BASINGER: As if anyone would want to see me amputated, in a box, with odious Julian Sands peering in at me, leering, ugh! He was *Warlock*! It's like there's some kind of vicious—I won't say "backlash,"—but something.—I don't want to dignify what's happened to me with a word. I am innocent of all charges brought against me. And Prince knows I'm innocent—why is he avoiding me?

JUDGE SMITH: Miss Basinger, help this court understand the ways of Hollywood and the music world—come to the point and start again.

KIM BASINGER: —Judge, you look like a handsome man, with a sex drive, correct?

JUDGE SMITH: Sustained.

KIM BASINGER: Is that a yes or a no?

CLERK: Overruled!

KIM BASINGER: Your Honor, Prince aged my predecessors overnight. When Mary Tyler Moore fled Minneapolis, she was no longer vivacious. She had that look, like, "What was that?"

WENDY AND LISA: We agree. We were once two happy scamps.

KIM BASINGER: Prince did write a song about me, "Scandalous," to which I contributed sex noises and grunts—creative contributions on the order of Jane Birkin working with Serge Gainsbourg. I think, in fact, he saw us as the Serge and Jane of the 80's.

WENDY AND LISA: No—like Britt Ekland and Rod Stewart.

KIM BASINGER: I am just an ordinary Oscar-winning star. I don't pretend to know everything that passes through the Purple One's head.

CLERK: It's like you were Kim Kardashian and he was Kanye.

WENDY AND LISA: Oh they are far in the future!

KIM BASINGER: All I know is that, he's rich and famous, while my career has ground to a screeching skid. I come to you, hat in hand, for a measly $234.00 a week, which I could make selling Tupperware. Keep a star off the street, huh?

JUDGE SMITH: How did you meet Prince?

KIM BASINGER: At Swifty Lazar's annual Oscar bash, he sauntered in wearing purple—distinctive shade—past my then husband, whom the Purple One ignored as like invisible air; instead he turned to me, placed his hands on his crotch and said, "U mystify me, Kim." Dig if you will the picture, of him and me engaged in a kiss. But I'm Kim Basinger, I didn't suck six bushels of grapes and shaved ice off Mickey Rourke's chest to become one of Prince's harem of available tarts! I bought my little town in Georgia . . . headed for the Frisco Bay . . .

WENDY AND LISA: He said that to us, he said that to us. To both of we.

KIM BASINGER: He told me you two were lesbians, or intellectuals, like Susan Sontag.

WENDY AND LISA: Half of we is, half of we are not. We're like Susan Sontag, but minus the Sturm und Drang.

KIM BASINGER: Especially ludicrous is the way these two women, who did not work for Prince, or if so not very hard, are somehow entitled to the same sum as me weekly under California law. Judge, have you any idea how hard I work? Worked my tail off, Judge. It was I who had to kiss Jeff Bridges, Jan-Michael Vincent, Michael Keaton. All these mean-spirited men with not half the soul of the Purple One.

[*Enter ALEC BALDWIN.*]

ALEC BALDWIN: I'm Alec Baldwin, the oldest of the four brothers with sad mournful basset hound eyes. I love Kim, she's a trouper. We made a flick together, a Neil Simon laugh riot, *The Marrying Man*—

CLERK: Guilty in the first degree! With Elizabeth Shue, who I used to like!

JUDGE SMITH: Miss Basinger, have you been offered a job within the past six weeks?

KIM BASINGER (*firmly*): No. [*Pause.*] Well—not a job job.

[Enter VANITY and APOLLONIA.]

VANITY (*to WENDY AND LISA*): Hi!

WENDY AND LISA: Hello.

APOLLONIA (*to WENDY AND LISA*): Hi!

WENDY AND LISA: Hello.

VANITY: Kim, we're going down to the Tonga Room later, for a drink, then film an "erotic thriller" for Cinemax. The whole lot of us.

APOLLONIA: Tracy Scoggins, Shannon Tweed, Tanya Roberts, Pam Grier, c'mon, girl, don't get left out.

WENDY AND LISA: We will go. That is our cup of tea. Half of we wears lingerie, half of we do not. Goodbye.

[Exit WENDY AND LISA, VANITY and APOLLONIA.]

KIM BASINGER: Judge, please—release me into my own custody, I won't ask for much. Only lunch money, limo fare, the basics. I see Sheena Easton coming this way, Scottish fire in her mean little eyes. She out of work too?

ALEC BALDWIN: Hon, things are tough all over for former stars with ties to Prince.

KIM BASINGER: Alec, I'm arguing my case!

ALEC BALDWIN: She's fiery, she whines, she talks the talk. I'd walk on coals of fire on my hands and knees for Kim, but [*pause*] does anybody have any cocaine?

KIM BASINGER: It is Sheena Easton, I recognize her limp red hair from here. Poor thing, she was devastated when I entered the scene, with my blonde fox tails and wide cheekbones. Poor little critter, she was spooked, like a mole when you rough up his burrow with your shotgun and pull the trigger, Braselton-style.

ALEC BALDWIN: Braselton. That's the town she bought in Georgia.

KIM BASINGER: Headed for the Frisco Bay.

CLERK: The court recognizes Sheena Easton.

ALEC BALDWIN: A once-booming burg, Braselton's a town now as full of ghosts as Kim's once-thriving career.

CLERK: Sheena Easton!

[*Enter SHEENA EASTON.*]

SHEENA EASTON: I made my name in Scotland. [*As if stricken by uncontrollable memories, bursts into hysterical laughter.*] Singing innocuous pop ditties, like "Morning Train."

JUDGE SMITH (*recalling song*): "My baby takes the morning train"—[*SHEENA EASTON joins him*]—"he takes it every day and then, he comes back waiting for me."

SHEENA EASTON: Yes, that was me. As well as "For Your Eyes Only." I was bright, fresh, a bite of corn on the cob, except, you know, Scottish. Anyhow I came to the States and met Prince. Soon enough he had me out of romper pullovers and into tight fitting lame gowns, singing a song he wrote just for me called "Manic Monday." No, that wasn't me, was it, ha ha ha.

CLERK: That was the Bangles.

SHEENA EASTON: My song was "Sugar Walls." and the NEA withdrew my grant. I said, "Why, why, why, Mr. Frohnmayer?" Later Holly Hughes took me to one side and said, "Sheena, don't you know what you're singing?" Karen Finley goes, like, "Sheena, there are boys around, you shouldn't be singing so loud about—you know."

JUDGE SMITH (*indignantly*): How was a sweet sycophantic girl like you, fresh off a Scots coalminers slag team, supposed to know? How were you ever to know "Sugar Walls" was Prince's sly reference to your p-p-p-private parts?

SHEENA EASTON: Exactly! I didn't even know I had any, I was so naive.

KIM BASINGER: May I say a word? I've been raked over the coals, I've been leaned on, I've had my skirts soiled in public with a big crowd looking on, their faces round like the moon over Georgia on a cold December night.

JUDGE SMITH (*flatly*): Maybe it was Christmas. Next!

CLERK: The Court of Unemployment calls Sinead O'Connor.

JUDGE SMITH: But what's her connection with Prince?

[*Enter SINEAD O'CONNOR.*]

CLERK: We'll let the public tell the tale. Miss O'Connor?

SINEAD O'CONNOR: My name is Sinead O'Connor, and I'm a child trying to learn to love myself.

SHEENA EASTON: I know her from the UK! She's with the IRA and she killed hundreds of miners!

SINEAD O'CONNOR: I did not!

SHEENA EASTON (*to JUDGE SMITH*): Did you ever see *The Crying Game?*

KIM BASINGER: Anyway, there I was, in public, moon faces glaring at me with contempt and lust, their onerous organs grinding like—rhythms of raw heat, me in the middle, always on trial. [*Defiantly*]. And yes, it was Christmas, a merry Christmas for everyone else, a tragic one for Kim Basinger, as usual, the one everyone laughs at and boos.

ALEC BALDWIN: Even I booed—and I love her.

SINEAD O'CONNOR (*raising her arms for silence*): The real enemy is the Pope, and Prince comes a close second. In Minneapolis I was in his house and his bodyguards kidnapped me, for trying to give him a speech about the starving children of the world, children starving, not for food or tins, but for love and self-esteem.

[*Enter VANITY and APOLLONIA.*]

VANITY: We're all looking for self-esteem.

APOLLONIA: And for passion, flowing like the sweet retsina of my native Greece.

SINEAD O'CONNOR: I do not want what I haven't got.

VANITY: And that's a lot, cause you've turned up my G-spot.

APOLLONIA: Take her before the Greek Cultural Hydra Serk, bare her back to the whip!

CLERK: You're not in Greece any longer, Miss Kotero.

VANITY: And she never was. This Greece stuff is pathetic, designed to catch attention of people who always say to her, didn't you used to be somebody?

JUDGE SMITH: I am Wayne Smith, gavel please! Continue, Miss O'Connor.

SINEAD O'CONNOR: Since you been gone I can do whatever I want, I can see whomever I choose. I can eat my dinner in a fancy restaurant, but nothing, I said, nothing, can take away these blues . . .

KIM BASINGER: I was classically trained as a blues singer.

VANITY: People make fun of my name, but what kind of name is "Sinead"?

KIM BASINGER (*to SINEAD O'CONNOR*): Prince tells me that he calls you "Sin Head," since you're always going on about people trying to do you wrong, well, I call it narcissistic.

SINEAD O'CONNOR: Let everybody in the world learn to love me.

KIM BASINGER (*reconsidering*): Or "conceited."

ALEC BALDWIN: She is conceited. Baby, let me rub my face in your hair, sniff out the coke.

SINEAD O'CONNOR: Nothing can stop these lonely tears from falling, tell me baby, where did I go wrong?

SHEENA EASTON: This all sounds so familiar, but she's Irish! In Prince's parade of flora and fauna, she played the shamrock to my Scottish heather.

SINEAD O'CONNOR: I went to the doctor, and guess what he told me, guess what he told me? He said, "Girl you better try to have fun no matter what you do," but he's a fool.

KIM BASINGER: Well, doctors are fools—I had one who told me, "Kim, you're at the top of your profession, even Sam Shepard has a little thing for you"—i.e., respect, which honestly is all I ever wanted, not the money, not the outfits, not the money, not the money, acclaim or money. Certainly not having my limbs severed and placed in a box for ten weeks of filming, in Savannah. I locked at the people who were making *Boxing Helena*, and I told them flat out, maybe Madonna would play this part, but I'm not desperate like Madonna. I'm not Madonna, I'm me, and I reserve the right to go around with all my arms and legs the way Mother Nature intended stars to shine. "Okay," they said, and I went on my merry way till this lawsuit was slapped in my face like I was oh, I don't know—that girl in *Different Strokes*.

VANITY: I was offered that part, and completed it, to raves.

APOLLONIA: Liar! I will trout your will under the cherry moon!

SINEAD O'CONNOR: Let the whole world know the truth that lies buried deep inside the heart of one suffering afflicted girl!

ALEC BALDWIN: Kim, baby, you know that wasn't exactly how it went down. I love you, baby, but you're kind of moody, kind of—

SHEENA EASTON: You ask why I let Prince change my image which was once so sweet? Well, he's little. He's a tad under four feet tall. Ever go to the suburbs, see a birdbath in the garden? About the size of that mythical birdbath. In Scotland we have these things called—scones.

APOLLONIA [*interrupting*]: Don't talk to me about those little biscuit cakes! He is a great Colossus of love, astride the Bosporus.

VANITY: But—

APOLLONIA (*like Maria Montez in Cobra Woman*): I LUFF HIM.

VANITY: You don't "luff" anyone or anything but the sound of your own voice, baloney head.

KIM BASINGER: Alec, I'm sensing a certain, oh, never mind.

APOLLONIA: And in a way, Prince shares much with Diaghilev both men absolute perfectionists, both petite, both kick you out once you finish make him your masterpiece.

SINEAD O'CONNOR: Tell the planet—about me! Me and my loneliness that could melt a hole through the earth's core!

SHEENA EASTON: So I never thought he was dangerous, because, I mean, well, he's only like this little statue, like a troll doll. I collect troll dolls.

KIM BASINGER: A certain cold indifference that's—I don't mind admitting—putting a cold lace of frost across my hot little pot.

ALEC BALDWIN: I'll wait outside, I have to get some cocaine or something to clear my noggin.

[*Exit ALEC BALDWIN.*]

CLERK: Oh, don't go.—I hate to see a star leave the courtroom.

KIM BASINGER: He'll be back. Ain't a man in the world turns his back on a Basinger.

VANITY: Except for Prince, and he ain't been back since. Two thousand zero zero, party over.

APOLLONIA: Oops, out of time, Kim Basinger!

VANITY: Kim, Kim, they're kicking us out like we're Tiny Tim.

[*Exit VANITY and APOLLONIA.*]

SINEAD O'CONNOR: Leave Kim alone, she's a child with the inner urge to heal herself by any means necessary.

SHEENA EASTON: In America, do you have people who collect little things?

JUDGE SMITH: Thank you for your testimony. Who's this woman approaching the bench?

CLERK: That's Kate Bush from England.

JUDGE SMITH: Each one more flamboyant than the one before. She approacheth like a panther, sleek, her limbs like drones.

CLERK: Yes, that's a good description. She worked with Prince on a track for her album *The Red Shoes*. She's my idol, Judge Smith.

JUDGE SMITH: We've seen many of your idols this afternoon, Craig Goodman.

CLERK: But none like Kate Bush.

JUDGE SMITH: Clear the courtroom!

CLERK: Sheena Easton?

SHEENA EASTON: Yes?

CLERK: In America, we do have people who collect little things.

JUDGE SMITH: Goodbye! Sinead O'Connor?

SINEAD O'CONNOR: Am I too, to be booted from unemployment court without even a shilling to buy grog with, like the old fisher laundry women of *Finnegans Wake*?

JUDGE SMITH: In short, yes.

[*Exit SINEAD O'CONNOR and SHEENA EASTON.*]

CLERK: Kim Basinger?

KIM BASINGER: I don't even like saying "yes," any more, it means that you have agreed to cut off your arms and legs and be filmed inside a tacky little box like you're a pecan pie.

JUDGE SMITH: Then say, "No," but go, Kim Basinger.

KIM: I thought you liked me, Judge Smith.

JUDGE SMITH: I can't have you around—you distract me too deeply. Please go, in the name of economic equity.

[*Enter KATE BUSH*]

KATE BUSH (*to exiting WOMEN*): Wait, go not, angry women. We are all in this state of affairs together.

KIM: Maybe you think so, Kate Bush, but in Georgia it's every girl for herself!

KATE BUSH: I never let my love for Prince get in my way.

KIM: I did—Did I make a mistake?

[*Exit KIM BASINGER.*]

JUDGE SMITH: Now you are a British citizen?

KATE BUSH: There are many of us in England, and many called Kate. It's short for educate.

JUDGE SMITH: I beg your pardon?

KATE BUSH: Admit it, your honor, you never even heard of *Wuthering Heights* till I re-wrote it from the point of view of someone fabulous.

CLERK: I will never forget you, coming out of the night. "Out of the wily, windy night, we'd roll and fall in green."

KATE BUSH (*reminiscently*): I was thinking of course, of your American cartoon about Wile E. Coyote and the Road Runner.

JUDGE SMITH: Yes—yes I see. "Out of the wily, windy night, we'd roll and fall in green." Like Wile E. Coyote.

KATE BUSH: How Prince loved my sly allusions to American culture. "What does that even mean, the night is wily? Windy I could see."

JUDGE SMITH: You're a mesmerizing woman, Kate Bush. Come now, adjudicate me.

KATE BUSH: I was a dancer, like that woman Prince eventually married, and yet I was a mime too, so I was special. Oh, he had a temper—like my jealousy, too hot, too greedy. I had the mime's moves. her vocabulary. I could be silent, but I could also use my incredible five octave voice. Watch me mime playing croquet.

Watch me mime opening and closing a window.

Watch me leaning down, picking a flower, and depositing a kiss on the lips of Prince. He's tiny you know.

He could be in this courtroom concealed as a sunbeam.

JUDGE SMITH: What attracted you to Prince?

KATE BUSH: There I was, living in England, discovered by Peter Gabriel—no picnic, believe me. And I was married to what's his name, the creepy one, from *Withnail and I*? Can't think of his name.

JUDGE SMITH: Hugh Grant? But he's not creepy.

CLERK: No—Richard E. Grant, and yes, Judge Smith, even you would think him creepy.

KATE BUSH: So when I met Prince I thought, well, he's not tall and cadaverous—like my husband. He was winsome—I could put him in my red shoes and fly through the skies over the Atlantic and I'd feel that tickle. Like the sunbeam. Judge, deep in your robes are you feeling that tickle? That's Prince, he's here.

JUDGE: I do feel a little itch, not a tickle perhaps—or, damn it, yes, something like a tickle—a tickular feeling—a tickularity.

Tell me, who is that attractive young man out in the corridor looking innocent? Is that Prince?

CLERK: That's Scott Hewicker.

JUDGE SMITH (*agog*): The daughter of Princess Grace?

CLERK: No, he's a local figure, an artist, well known in the Bay Area for unceasing Prince advocacy.

[*Enter SCOTT HEWICKER.*]

SCOTT HEWICKER. Your Honor, I'm an ordinary person, who happens to be a big fan of Prince. The flash is, Prince has changed his name, and we are now to call him Victor. He's thirty-five, and I guess he decided to do what he feels like doing. Fair enough, say I!

JUDGE SMITH: This is Kate Bush, from England.

SCOTT HEWICKER: Hello, Miss Bush. I respect you as an artist and I love the song you recorded with Prince—I mean Victor.

CLERK: Time is speeding up so fast. I just got my very first e-mail just now. It says here that Victor is now to be referred to as unpronounceable symbol.

SCOTT HEWICKER: How wise of the impenetrable artist formerly known as Prince. I'd still like to say a few words in defense of Symbol. He's creative. His music has the power to change the world. He's made Minneapolis hum with excitement. I think he's handsome, too.

KATE BUSH: I agree. Those big eyes in that little head, like a pair of flashlights stuck in a tangerine.

SCOTT HEWICKER: Miss Bush, I know you had high hopes for a hit single with your song with Prince, "Why Should I Love You?" But it was not to be. Tell you the truth, I was afraid you would marry Prince, and change him somehow.

KATE BUSH: Just to make him stable, like me. That was many years ago now. I have stopped recording and I never tour.

CLERK: The years flow quickly now. Prince has turned to Jehovah's Witness and has stopped being so nasty.

[*Enter KIM BASINGER and ALEC BALDWIN.*]

CLERK: Kim is almost entirely forgotten today. But Alec remains my all-time ideal, everything a man should be and more.

ALEC BALDWIN (*snorting*): I feel focused, incredibly sharp. Is this Howard Johnson's? I'll take the fried clams.

SCOTT HEWICKER: Hello, Alec Baldwin.

KIM BASINGER: He's mine, darling. Day after day I get respect from my peers. Don't let this be my Achilles heel, I beg you.

SCOTT HEWICKER: I hope that I'm not in the way. I only came to court to give fan support to a great artiste.

CLERK: Judge Smith, what grade do you give this testimony?

JUDGE SMITH: A perfect 10. Mr. Hewicker, do you seek court compensation too?

SCOTT HEWICKER: I'm just looking for a fair shake for Prince—I mean, Victor.

I guess now we call him Prince again. So often people treat him as some kind of joke, but really, he's the Picasso of our time. I'm an artist myself, with a show coming up at Gallery 16: naturally I think in terms of art.

JUDGE SMITH: Well, it looks as though you are the only witness today who has a job. Well done, Scott Hewicker.

KIM BASINGER: How can you privilege art above ordinary things like check cashing at the A & W? I want my money! Needless to say, I'll give all of it to worthy causes like animal testing.

SCOTT HEWICKER: He's very spiritual, too, always seeking.

JUDGE SMITH: They'll probably bring in Mavis Staples next!

SCOTT HEWICKER: Kim, perhaps Prince was hurt after you backed out of co-starring with him in *Graffiti Bridge*, after promising you would.

KIM BASINGER: What can I say? That's my track record. I'm not consistent, I'm a wind from the swamp.

CLERK: I vote for Kim. She's a thoroughbred.

JUDGE SMITH: I vote for Vanity, she's clean through and through.

KATE BUSH: And me? I suppose I could make erotic thrillers like the rest of the castaways.

KIM BASINGER: It's 2015 and the age of erotic thrillers passed long ago. I couldn't make *9 1/2 Weeks* now even if I wanted to.

JUDGE SMITH: Well, if you do, you do. [*Shrugs.*] I work, you play. Play and complain, it's a travesty. Miss Basinger, you've heard my decision. Run along and let me counsel other witnesses.

KIM BASINGER: Instead I'll concentrate on swinging the vote of this young man. You know, Craig, there's a promising part you'd be right for in my next movie, *The Clerk's Girlfriend*. I'm playing the girlfriend, but we're looking for just the right leading man . . .

CLERK: Well, uh, is Alec going to be in it too?

KIM BASINGER (*smoothly*): Did I say "girlfriend"? It's—*The Clerk's Boyfriend and their Pal, the Star*—that's me—*and their Cook and their Lover*. It's by Peter Greenaway so it'll have that British hauteur and attitude.

ALEC BALDWIN: Kim, did you really tell Prince you'd star in *Graffiti Bridge?* What about professionalism? What about me?

KIM BASINGER: Never mind that. I've never walked out on a role in my life, and I never intend to. But I'm walking out of this courtroom, clerk in tow. We have a meeting at Minnesota Street Projects when it opens. Peter Greenaway, Tilda Swinton, Derek Jarman, and Sally Potter. Eddie Redmayne's making little biscuit cakes.

KATE BUSH: Scones! May I join you too?

CLERK: Thank you, Judge Smith. I won't say it's been a pleasure working for you.

ALEC BALDWIN: Where are we now? This courtroom needs better cocaine, so does Kim's hair. I've had better coke in the scalp of Goldie Hawn.

KIM BASINGER: Craig, Alec, let's go—the New British Cinema needs some glamour. It has everything up here [*indicates head*] but lacks a little Georgia-based petroleum jelly [*rubs abdomen*]. And Prince is doing the music.

[*Exit KIM BASINGER, ALEC BALDWIN, KATE BUSH and CLERK.*]

JUDGE SMITH: I guess I have to do my own hear ye's from now on.

[*Enter SHEENA EASTON.*]

SHEENA EASTON: Just like I had to write all my own records after the Purple One took his inspiration elsewhere.

SCOTT HEWICKER (*tactfully*): You have a wonderful voice, Miss Easton, and I know you'll continue to do well.

JUDGE SMITH: Though I can't see my way clear to giving you any money, Miss Easton, perhaps on our way out you could give me your recipe for those Scottish biscuits everyone was raving about.

SHEENA EASTON: I'd be glad to. Oh, and Scott? May I make a little suggestion?

SCOTT HEWICKER: Sure.

SHEENA EASTON: Next time you do something like this, why don't you lend your advocacy to someone who really needs it? Someone who's really at the bottom of the barrel, someone who's really over. Like Bjork.

JUDGE SMITH: Or Mike Myers from *Saturday Night Live.*

SHEENA EASTON: Now about those scones . . .

[*Exit SHEENA EASTON and JUDGE SMITH.*]

[*Enter SINEAD O'CONNOR.*]

SINEAD O'CONNOR: San Francisco, you've changed a lot since I was here in 1994. I got rid of the Pope, but other popes popped up to take their place.

This neighborhood is different, like, dramatically so. Last time I was here it was actually a dog patch. People came here in the dead of night and tossed their dying dogs onto that patch where they would meet each other and lick each other.

You're Scott Hewicker, aren't you?

SCOTT HEWICKER: I am indeed. Prince's fan from way back when. Though when I was in school and Prince was starting out, you couldn't brag about it, people would think you were a fag.

[*Enter MAVIS STAPLES and APOLLONIA.*]

MAVIS STAPLES: Wait!

APOLLONIA: She's dead! Vanity is dead!

SINEAD O'CONNOR: What?

SCOTT HEWICKER: Dead?

APOLLONIA: It was just on the news. I woke up and I had a funny feeling about that girl. Like she was trying to tell me something.

SCOTT: This is awful. What happened?

APOLLONIA (*to MAVIS STAPLES*): I remember you—you used to work with Prince.

SCOTT: You're Mavis Staples, aren't you?

MAVIS STAPLES: Yes, and I've just come from a meeting with God.

SINEAD O'CONNOR: You were a gospel singer?

[*Enter CLERK.*]

CLERK: She is still one of the rare treasures of gospel.

MAVIS STAPLES: Got to explain my name to you young people. But I'll take you there. Staples used to demand explanation, but once they had a Staples store for office products, everyone knew Staples.

CLERK: The Staples Center is where Michael Jackson held his funeral.

MAVIS: And as God is my witness, that's where I'll take my Vanity.

SINEAD O'CONNOR: In the 20s, women's names ending in "I-S" swept the globe.

MAVIS: And a few of us still have 'em. There's me, Mavis Staples. There's Doris Day. There's Cloris Leachman.

APOLLONIA: My God, they're all of them eighty.

MAVIS: There's Phyllis Diller.

APOLLONIA: No, not any more there's not.

MAVIS: Has she passed on too?

SINEAD O'CONNOR: I'm afraid so.

MAVIS: Then she's safe in the arms of our Lord. We will have the funeral for her at Staples Center.

SCOTT HEWICKER: When he heard she had died, Prince gave a concert in Oakland, and he said, "Can I tell you a story about Vanity?"

APOLLONIA: Then he goes, "Or should I tell you a story about Denise? Her and I used to love each other deeply."

MAVIS: "She loved me for the artist I was, I loved her for the artist she was trying to be."

[*Enter WENDY AND LISA.*]

MAVIS: Wendy and Lisa! You still look the same.

APOLLONIA: They will never change.

WENDY AND LISA: Hello, hello, hello. More bad news, we are afraid to tell you.

[*Enter JUDGE SMITH.*]

JUDGE SMITH: Out on Minnesota Street, people are crying and tearing their outfits. What happened?

SINEAD O'CONNOR: Thought you retired, Judge Smith.

JUDGE SMITH: Indeed I did, moved to Palm Springs.

SINEAD O'CONNOR: Did you know Alanis Morissette is eighty?

WENDY AND LISA: May we break it to you? Prince is dead now.

[*ALL gasp.*]

APOLLONIA: Died of a broken heart when Denise died.

MAVIS STAPLES: God will take them in his arms and love them.

[*Enter SHEENA EASTON.*]

SHEENA EASTON (*to JUDGE SMITH*): Thank you for texting me. I came from Scotland as soon as I could.

JUDGE SMITH: You look lovely, Sheena Easton.

SHEENA EASTON: What a terrible thing! The whole world's changed—I feel it in my sugar walls.

MAVIS STAPLES: Soon we shall hear from Kim and Alec.

WENDY AND LISA: The sky has grown dark in San Francisco. All through the night, we cry for Prince.

APOLLONIA: And Vanity.

[*Enter KATE BUSH.*]

KATE BUSH: "Ooh it gets dark, it gets lonely."

ALL: "On the other side from you."

KATE BUSH: "I pine a lot, I find the lot falls through without you."

SCOTT HEWICKER: Ladies and gentlemen, I'm still afraid you might have gotten a wrong impression about Prince—I mean, Victor. He's really special. When you listen to one of his songs, you'll know. He's no clown, he's one of the top creators of all time.

MAVIS STAPLES: He was born under a magic star.

SCOTT HEWICKER: He was born under a magic star, under a dark sky, and the whole world trembled that night—

WENDY AND LISA: Just like it's trembling now.

SCOTT HEWICKER: And ever since his second record, I've been telling everyone I know, how great he is.

[*Enter KIM BASINGER and ALEC BALDWIN.*]

ALEC BALDWIN: If drugs were involved—are there any left over?

KIM BASINGER: Alec—behave.

SCOTT HEWICKER: Maybe he made mistakes, I don't know, but everyone makes mistakes. He's sensitive and proud—I admire that. I like everything about him—almost. Give him another chance, I know you'll say, he's really great. Thank you and—

[*Enter VANITY, who walks over to SCOTT HEWICKER, takes his hand, and the two of them bow. When they rise, the whole cast bows in unison.*]

SCOTT HEWICKER: Thank you and—

ALL: Good night!

END

Produced at Minnesota Street Projects (San Francisco) on September 17, 2016 in connection with Glen Helfand's memorial exhibition "After Pop Life" (September 14—October 1, 2016)

CLERK...Craig Goodman
JUDGE WAYNE SMITH, S.F. Unemployment Court.......................... Wayne Smith
VANITY, born Denise Matthews, US pop singer ....Jackie Clay
APOLLONIA, her rival..Cliff Hengst
WENDY & LISA, musicians...................................Michele Carlscn & Matt Gordon
KIM BASINGER, top Hollywood star of 1994 ....Juana Berrio
ALEC BALDWIN, soon to be her husband...................................... Randall Mann
SHEENA EASTON, Scottish pop singer ....Patricia Maloney
SINEAD O'CONNOR, Irish pop singer..Karla Milosevich
KATE BUSH, English pop singer...Laurie Reid
MAVIS STAPLES, American gospel singer ....Gerald Corbin
SCOTT HEWICKER, artist and Prince fan .... Himself

This version was an expansion of the original script which was produced by
Rick Jacobsen at Kiki Gallery on San Francisco early in 1994 with the following
cast:

CLERK ....Kevin Killian
JUDGE WAYNE SMITH, San Francisco Unemployment Court......... Wayne Smith
VANITY, born Denise Matthews,US pop singer ....Nayland Blake
APOLLONIA, her rival.. also Nayland Blake
WENDY & LISA, musicians............................ Leslie Singer & Cecilia Dougherty
KIM BASINGER, top Hollywood star of 1994 ....Margaret Crane
ALEC BALDWIN, soon to be her husband...Kevin Radley
SHEENA EASTON, Scottish pop singer ....Andrea Juno
STEPHANIE CANNIZZO, artist and Prince fan...Herself

Cut

for Mary Gaitskill

characters

"ALFRED HITCHCOCK" / STEVE POITRINE
cub reporter for the *Berkeley Times*
BILLY HAMMER
gadabout son of Marcella and Douglas Devlin
MARCELLA DEVLIN
his mother, a discontented faculty wife
CHITA DU SUMATRA
the maid of Tippi Hedren
DOUGLAS DEVLIN
director of the Berkeley Film Archive
STEPHANIE, Princess of Monaco
the daughter of the late Grace Kelly
TIPPI HEDREN
abiding star of *Marnie* and *The Birds*
MELANIE GRIFFITH
her daughter
ANDY GRIFFITH
the legendary "Andy of Mayberry"
ISABELLA ROSSELLINI
Lancome model and daughter of Ingrid Bergman
JAMIE LEE CURTIS
KARL LAGERFELD
top haute couture man from Europe

[*MARCELLA, BILLY, CHITA and STEVE POITRINE onstage during a seance.*]

STEVE (*imitating "ALFRED HITCHCOCK"*): Good evening.

BILLY: Oh, my God, it's Alfred Hitchcock.

MARCELLA (*seated*): Billy, hush, I'm trying to concentrate.

BILLY (*to CHITA*): Mother's been a trance medium for twenty-five years, but never before has she been able to bring anyone over from the other side.

STEVE (*as "ALFRED HITCHCOCK"*): Good evening. [*Steps forward onstage and addresses audience, as himself.*] I'm not really Hitchcock—I'm me . . . Steve Poitrine! But what could I do? I was young—22—cub reporter for the Berkeley Times—helplessly in love with a married woman [*places hands on MARCELLA's shoulders*]—an older woman—Marcella Devlin, who I met at a mixer. At thirty, Marcella Devlin had the complex charm of a hot skillet sizzling with brandy and trout.

CHITA (*regarding STEVE*): He's a big man—with big face.

STEVE (*as "ALFRED HITCHCOCK"*): Good evening.

BILLY: Mother! Does Daddy know? [*To CHITA.*] Daddy is the director of the Berkeley Film Archive, and he's planning this big Hitchcock festival April 2.

MARCELLA (*eyes closed*): No, "Daddy" doesn't know! And don't tell him!

BILLY: I'm his right hand man.

CHITA (*admiringly*): Billy Hammer, you clever, sadistic bastard.

STEVE (*as "ALFRED HITCHCOCK"*): Good evening. [*Again steps forward onstage and addresses audience, as himself.*] What could I do? I went along with her fake seance, since she ordered me to.

MARCELLA (*eyes closed*): Suggested.

STEVE: She told me that if her plans worked, she would be free—free of the cruel husband—Dr. Douglas Devlin—the man who stole her youth. To seal our bargain she gave herself to me on the bearskin rug at the Faculty

Club. "Steve!" she cried. "Steve! All I want is to get my husband to invite Melanie Griffith to the Hitchcock Festival." [*As "ALFRED HITCHCOCK"*] I think it would be a marvelous idea to bring together, in one room, on one April afternoon, the daughters of my greatest stars. Marvelous!

BILLY (*like Macaulay Culkin*): Yes! Yes! [*Struck by an abrupt realization.*] But Daddy won't like it. [*To CHITA.*] Daddy's into theory.

CHITA: In Sumatra, we call "theory" the juice of the rubber bug plant, and squish it out of tapir heads.

ALFRED HITCHCOCK: Cut! Good evening! Bring to the conference Stephanie, daughter of Princess Grace; Isabella Rossellini—daughter of Ingrid Bergman; and Melanie Griffith, the daughter of Tippi Hedren.

BILLY: He'll never go for that. He wants people like Jane Gallop and Julia Kristeva.

CHITA (*pointing at STEVE*): Is that spook or is that man? Me very skeptical, in Sumatra grow up skeptical, like Gulliver.

MARCELLA: Billy, who's your friend and tell her to be quiet! The aura's growing fainter. Mr. Hitchcock! Alfred! Do you have final words for us here in Berkeley?

"ALFRED HITCHCOCK." Every time a director says "Cut," the action stops, and a new action fills the screen. Wouldn't it be nice if life were like that? Good evening.

[*Exit STEVE POITRINE.*]

CHITA: Look—he hide behind curtain.

MARCELLA: How refreshing, a woman from the rubber rooms of the South Pacific! What brings you to Berkeley? Wedding bells, Billy?

BILLY: Mother—

MARCELLA: Don't roll your eyes, I'm trying to be sincere.

BILLY: Mother, this is Chita du Sumatra—of Beverly Hills. Chita, this is Marcella Devlin, repressed, witty, the talk of the campus.

MARCELLA: Charmed.

CHITA: I go now.

[*Exit CHITA.*]

MARCELLA: Lovely idea. Billy, what are we to do!

BILLY: When Dad put me in charge of marketing the Festival, he expressly said, no stars. I said, "Dad! Who do you want to attract, a lot of egg-heads?"

MARCELLA: Here he comes now, try to break it to him gently.

[*Enter DEVLIN.*]

DEVLIN: Marcella! Billy! In one hour theorists from all over the world will descend on Berkeley to try to deal with Hitchcock's work, his delicate negotiation between the rational and the dead. Cultural studies has taken over the University. There's no more this or that, there's only cultural studies. Well, Hitchcock sits, like a fat rock, right in the middle of this swimming stream. You my wife?

MARCELLA: Presently . . . Dear, we've just had an interesting visitor from the spirit world. Alfred Hitchcock. From Heaven.

BILLY: And he wants us to invite stars to your gala!

[*Enter STEPHANIE.*]

DEVLIN (*repelled*): Who are you?

MARCELLA: Dr. Devlin, don't you recognize her? That's Princess Stephanie of Monaco!

DEVLIN: When it comes to cultural studies, actors are cattle.

STEPHANIE: Is this the big party with the pictures?

DEVLIN (*sternly*): This is not "the big party with the pictures"! Who invited you?

BILLY: I did! What's wrong with starpower?

DEVLIN: Billy, we've gone over this again and again. I wanted no stars at this conference, this is serious!

BILLY: I know, I know, you the man, Dad, and I should have respected your orders. But I thought—oh, gee, Princess Grace is dead, and I've been dying to meet the daughter who killed her! I think this cuts to the very core of Hitchcock's universe!

STEPHANIE: The car, the race car, on the steep Riviera slope! And I—filled with a powerful drug that made my foot so heavy on the metal! My mother—screaming! Screaming, "Stephanie! Slow down!"

DEVLIN: Thank you, I suppose, for coming today to be our patron. But Billy—I hope you haven't invited any other so-called "celebrities."

STEPHANIE: And yet my wretched foot got in my way, a foot so heavy it bled the blood of my mother over the hills of our little principality. Which I now own.

BILLY: Stephanie also invented the Wet T-shirt Contest. No, Dad, there are no other stars coming, more's the pity. [*To MARCELLA.*] I'm lying.

MARCELLA: Princess, are you coming to the Hitchcock fete, topless I assume?

STEPHANIE: Decisions!

MARCELLA (*eagerly*): Do you know if by any chance Melanie Griffith is flying in?

STEPHANIE (*shrugging*): Take me to my big chair and the pictures, Devil Man.

DEVLIN (*coldly*): It's Devlin. Billy, if one other celebrity shows up at this conference, you're a dead son.

[*Exit DEVLIN and STEPHANIE.*]

BILLY: Oh dear, and I've asked oodles! Want to hear how I do it? [*On the phone, in a flashback.*] Chita?

[*Enter CHITA.*]

CHITA: Hello?

BILLY: Hi, I'm Billy Hammer from the Berkeley Film Commission? Have I reached the African home of Tippi Hedren and Melanie Griffith?

CHITA: Miss Tippi, Miss Melanie, not home now. You call back I give a goodbye.

BILLY: Is this Chita, by any chance? [*To MARCELLA.*] Chita's their housekeeper. Oh, who knows what she is! [*To CHITA.*] Chita dear, it's Billy! Remember me, Billy, from college? [*To MARCELLA.*] We went to Bard together. You have to use any angle with these servants. Actually, Chita's more of a family friend. I think Tippi picked her up on safari somewhere.

CHITA (*pondering*): Billy—Billy—

BILLY (*to MARCELLA*): Eventually she came to her senses.

MARCELLA: Interesting.

CHITA: I go and fetch my two blonde girls.

[*Enter DEVLIN.*]

DEVLIN: Son, what's this collect call from Isabella Rossellini in Rome?

BILLY (*to CHITA*): I'll come with you! We'll have a class reunion. Of course, we come from different classes.

CHITA: I, from the ruling caste of Cobra Island.

[*Exit BILLY and CHITA.*]

DEVLIN (*to audience.*) According to the theorist Joan-Géane Dumbrowski-Huffington, the classic Hollywood cinema is built upon a word, a word unexpressed on the screen you see before you. When that word is spoken, the director, a white, male, Eurocentric, commits an act of violence on the screen, on the text of the film. It is also used to implied sexual activity (*unseen*) among the actors whose images are thus shredded inside the eyes of the audience.

[*Enter STEVE, who stands to one side.*]

STEVE: Cut!

[*Exit DEVLIN.*]

MARCELLA: Oh, God, please let Melanie Griffith say yes! God, God, I've been everything a bad woman can be, and more . . . but let me have just this one wish, and I'll turn over a new . . . can't say "leaf," that's been said already. I'll be less mischievous, how's that?

[Enter CHITA.]

Chita! In the flesh! Chita dear, you've never looked more radiant! And where are
our two super guests?

CHITA: Miss Tippi, she come soon. Miss Melanie, she at Betty Ford. Tell me,
Mrs. Devlin, who this "Betty Ford"?

MARCELLA: Oh, Chita, let your hair down for once! Look, all the great Hitchcock
stars have the famous daughters, right? I know Stephanie will come, all I have to
do is say there's cocaine. I'm doing my best to get Isabella Rossellini.

CHITA: I hate her.

MARCELLA: She's not the warmest person, dear, but we all get tired of balls of fire.

CHITA: I guess.

STEVE: Cut.

[Enter TIPPI HEDREN. Exit MARCELLA and CHITA.]

TIPPI: And meanwhile halfway around the world, in my African retreat I, Tippi
Hedren, prepare for my comeback. Under a Mercury moon I spin web after web
of mosquito wings, my fragile, exoskeletal grease. Chita? Chita? *[No reply.]* Are the
elephants mating, ivory tusks locked in a kiss? Once upon a time the great Hitchcock
plucked me out of obscurity and cast me in two films, *The Birds* and *Marnie*. I did
him right in return! Yet always there was something strained between us, the feeling
that one of us was married to another, and my name, "Tippi," which he gave me,
saying, "You tippy-toe across my great fat red boulevard of a heart."

[Enter MELANIE GRIFFITH.]

Then Hitchcock died, the screen door slammed and I haven't made a movie in 35
years. This is my daughter, and oh, how it hurts! Melanie, dear, how do I look?

MELANIE: Oh, Mother!

TIPPI: It's so good of you to let me come to the Conference with you. I haven't
had a life lately, not since JFK.

MELANIE: You've had bit parts in my films.

TIPPI: Which nobody goes to see or likes anyhow. It's my birthday, darling, be good to me.

MELANIE: Mother?

TIPPI: Yes, Melanie?

MELANIE: Mother . . . were you ever pretty?

TIPPI: Of course I was!

[*Enter MARCELLA, who stands alone in another part of the world.*]

MARCELLA: Moon, careless moon!

TIPPI HEDREN: And I'm still pretty, if ever you took your nose out of a whiskey bottle long enough to care. Alfred Hitchcock certainly thought so!

MELANIE: Mother, when we get to Berkeley, you won't embarrass me again by claiming that my father was Alfred Hitchcock. Chita!

STEVE: Cut.

[*Enter DEVLIN and STEPHANIE: Exit MELANIE and TIPPI.*]

DEVLIN (*to MARCELLA*): Oh! There you are! Watching the skies when you should be working!

MARCELLA: Moon, moon, gold over Berkeley, are you the same moon that shines over Tippi Hedren's Wild Life Kingdom in Equatorial Africa?

DEVLIN: I have no idea. Come to attention! Avital Ronell just sent a fax on my prodigy line, she's expected at dawn. And Laura Mulvey called, Marcella! Imagine, Marcella—Laura Mulvey!

MARCELLA: I know, I know, she invented the "male gaze." But what work has she done on exposing the many contradictions of Melanie Griffith?

STEPHANIE: Moon, lonely moon, high above the night! Look down at my feet, kiss the blood off my hands!

STEVE: Cut.

[*Exit MARCELLA, DEVLIN and STEVE: Enter MELANIE and CHITA.*]

CHITA: Yes, Miss Melanie?

STEPHANIE: Every time I run a red light, I think of my mother. I run a few fingers through my hair, most of them my own. On water skis I, Stephanie, prowl the beaches seeking redemption.

MELANIE: Now who are these people we're going to meet? Film students?

STEPHANIE: Not really thinking it out, I posed for *Playgirl*—anything to rebel against my mother and my foot.

CHITA: Ah, your hair gives me a bright pain between my two eyes, let me fix it, my banana girl.

[*Exit STEPHANIE: CHITA begins to fix MELANIE's hair.*]

MELANIE: Do you have a drink?

CHITA: I used to nurse you with my two big breasts, now you're almost grown.

MELANIE: I am grown, and I don't want to have to babysit my own mother.

[*Enter TIPPI HEDREN.*]

Hear that, Tippi Hedren! Remember the story we agreed on, all those years ago, when people first started asking, "How come your name is 'Griffith' if your mother's name is 'Hedren'?"

TIPPI: But aren't you tired of the lies, sweetie?

MELANIE (*firmly*): No! As far as the world is concerned, my father is Andy Griffith! I insist, or we're not going to Berkeley or anywhere else on Earth!

TIPPI: All right.

CHITA: Shall you tell me to pack, Miss Melanie?

MELANIE: I'll tell Chita to pack—twenty bags for me, and your knapsack. Chita, pack! Mother, call Berkeley, tell them we're on our way. It's my birthday present to you.

[*Enter STEVE and MARCELLA. Exit MELANIE GRIFFITH.*]

STEVE: When will I see you alone?

MARCELLA: I want you, I need you, but let my plans burn down the sky before I give you a kiss.

STEVE: Marcella, you took advantage of my striking resmblance to Alfred Hitchcock. But your lips—like twin cherries—no! One's a cherry, but the other's a bee, stuffed with wine. I must taste those lips. Cut.

[*MARCELLA and STEVE now are smoking cigarettes, after sex.*]

STEVE: Was that as good for you—drag—as it was for me?

MARCELLA: Not really. I'm a lesbian, you see. Yes, we have sex, but with each other, not with guys like you.

STEVE: A lesbian! Cut!

TIPPI HEDREN (*to CHITA*): Why did she tell me to call Berkeley? Does she hate me—she must! She knows I have trouble with phone booths—not only here in Africa, but everywhere.

[*Exit STEVE and MARCELLA.*]

CHITA: Miss Tippi, you must rest now.

TIPPI HEDREN: I remember—the birds . . . flapping at the booth, while I was trying to call my lover—

CHITA: Hitchcock—

TIPPI HEDREN: No—Andy Griffith—I was pregnant—oh, I can't hide the truth from you, Chita. I'd never even dated Andy Griffith.

CHITA: You poor, restless devil of a ham!

TIPPI: The wings—brightly colored as Richmond Burtons—beating on the glass—my pulse beating—little Melanie, kicking against my ribs, and I couldn't remember the number! I tried the phone book. I tried the operator. Then the glass broke and the birds flew in! And my water broke—and there she was, my little daughter of sin. On the floor of the phone booth.

CHITA: Was there liquor on the floor of the phone booth?

TIPPI: The birds—pecking my face—then a strong man came and kind of—swooshed them away—a strong man with a gentle Southern drawl.

[*Enter ANDY GRIFFITH.*]

ANDY GRIFFITH: Hello, little lady.

TIPPI: Who are you?

ANDY GRIFFITH: Why, I'm Andy—Andy of Mayberry. Mayberry, RFD.

TIPPI: I'm bleeding like a stuffed pig.

ANDY GRIFFITH: So you are! But down South we have a saying, "Have no fear, Andy's here." I cure post-partum trauma by applying loam and dead leaves to the ruptured private pelvic parts.

CHITA: He was a saint.

ANDY GRIFFITH: Let me take this little one home with me to Mayberry. Aunt Bee will make her a big breakfast of whiskey and grits.

[*Enter "ALFRED HITCHCOCK."*]

ALFRED HITCHCOCK: Is there a problem on the set?

TIPPI: Hitchcock! You put steak sauce on my face so those birds would mar my beauty! You've got a camera where most men have a heart.

ALFRED HITCHCOCK: You did not perform the trailer strip tease I demanded!

TIPPI: Mr. Griffith—Sheriff Andy—take this baby away before I scream. Bring her up in the rural pine woods, where coons and skunks shall be her sole companions.

ANDY: And Opie. C'mon, sweet thing.

TIPPI: I don't want her soiled by Hollywood.

ALFRED HITCHCOCK: Meanwhile, dear, the cameras keep rolling! Cut!

[*Enter BILLY and ISABELLA ROSSELLINI. Exit ANDY, TIPPI, and "ALFRED HITCHCOCK."*]

BILLY: Now, Bella dear, welcome to Berkeley!

ISABELLA: I love the little houses and students. I love the hills, even the street, how do you say, people. But where are the trees, the famous pine trees of Berkeley?

BILLY: Mother had the trees cut down. Chita, have you met Isabella Rossellini?

CHITA (*smouldering with hatred*): I hate her. We went to Bard together.

ISABELLA: That's right, and Chita majored in threat. A simple "Hello" would have sufficed.

BILLY: Bella dear, in this film you're playing an American woman, Jane Gallop, come to Berkeley to make new Amazon friends and give your own take on the oeuvre of Alfred Hitchcock. Got that?

ISABELLA: Do I have a script?

BILLY: No, we're doing everything in this really fab Cassavetes mix and match string quartet! You'll be wonderful! Oscar—Oscar! Oh, God, here comes Tippi Hedren—

[*Exit BILLY. An awkward silence.*]

CHITA: Heard Lancome fired you, Bella.

ISABELLA: Oh? It's a jungle in there.

CHITA: Even in Equatorial Africa, where I live with my two blonde ladies, we hear the news on the drums—Isabella Rossellini, too old to wear makeup.

ISABELLA: Shatter my composure? Never! David Lynch tried—Gary Oldman tried, as did Gary Coleman from TV's *Different Strokes*. I was married to Martin

Scorsese for four long years and, always, always, came I out the other end the ethereal Isabella. That's Italian for "lovely," you fiend.

CHITA: It's now Italian for "over." Wake up, Bella, smell the coffee. It's hot.

ISABELLA: Is there coffee? Bella!—that means "lovely," in Italian.

CHITA: I used to bring you flowers and money, every day at Bard. Long, cool roses and lilies of worship, with the *Bard Gazette* propped up on your breakfast tray in bed. And the steam of coffee ringed your face.

ISABELLA: You kept me beautiful, Chita. But you haven't spoken to me in years.

CHITA (*drawn to her*): It's not an exact silence.

ISABELLA: Honestly, Chita, I thought when you gave me the cobra jewel, you gave it to me for keeps. No strings attached. It was your way of saying, "I'm mad about you," without the English.

CHITA: Geef me the cobarah chewel.

[*Enter TIPPI HEDREN.*]

TIPPI: My birds brought me here, my birds, here to Berkeley. My birds, and my Chita!

ISABELLA: We will discuss the cobra jewel, but later.

[*Enter DEVLIN and BILLY.*]

DEVLIN: Ah, here she is—

BILLY (*indicating TIPPI HEDREN*): This is Laura Mulvey, Dad. And this [*pointing at ISABELLA*] is Jane Gallop—

ISABELLA (*shaking hands with DEVLIN*): I know who I am, no matter who fires me from what job! I am a supermodel—

BILLY: A super theorist, one of our best and one of Sweden's best! [*Aside to ISA-BELLA.*] Run now, Bella dear, Gary Coleman is waiting for you upstairs next to the Tchelitchev.

CHITA: Geef me the cobarah chewel!

ISABELLA: Arrivederci, wonderful men!

[*Exit ROSSELLINI.*]

DEVLIN: How long have I wanted to gaze on your refulgent form, Laura Mulvey, and to ask you from this podium, in front of all these people, how you came up with the revolutionary idea of the "male gaze."

TIPPI (*nervously*): Male gays? I don't know—maybe Melanie knows. In my day, most of the gays were in the closet, like Rock Hudson. But Melanie's worked with all of them, she's always on the go, and of course living in Aspen she knows David Geffen and Keanu Reeves.

BILLY (*hastily*): Chita, why don't you take Miss Mulvey down to her trailer and give her some Mandrax and herbal lotion? [*To DEVLIN.*] The great avatars of film theory require special handling.

TIPPI: Tell everyone . . . not to wear red.

CHITA: No red dresses! No red scarves or pins for my little blonde lady!

TIPPI: Thank you, Chita.

[*Exit CHITA and TIPPI.*]

DEVLIN: Why certainly, Ms. Mulvey. Billy, did you hear that? No red!

BILLY: I heard, Dad. At Bard I got straight A's in listening.

DEVLIN: Well, son, you've done a fine job for me. Laura Mulvey's a distinguished thinker, neurotic about red, I suppose, and Jane Gallop's a bit imperious. But I can handle them both. The only thing that bothers me is—where's Julia Kristeva?

BILLY: Mom's picking her up at the airport.

DEVLIN: Oh, good—hope she takes the short cut.

BILLY: You said, "Cut!"

[DEVLIN and BILLY are now smoking cigarettes.]

BILLY: That was great . . . oh, Dad, I had all these unrealized Oedipal longings in me, paralyzed by frost and apathy, but one touch of your hand would have been enough! Instead we had the ultimate father-son je ne sais quoi.

DEVLIN: That precious mousy brown and gray hair—I remember fondling it in your cradle, the last time I thought of family life.

BILLY: Ah, well, let's not make too big a deal out of it, shall we? I'm ready to go on with life, how about you?

DEVLIN: Instead I turned to Godard and his dictum that truth is 24 frames a second. Oh what a fool I was! You're beautiful, Billy.

BILLY: If only I could turn my beauty into respect! Dad—now that we're close, can I confess my ruse to you?

DEVLIN: Billy—Billy—cut—cut—cut, cut, cut!

[Exit DEVLIN and BILLY. Enter MARCELLA and MELANIE.]

MARCELLA: Where are you staying? Don't even answer. You're coming with us. My husband's bungalow, at 2527 College, is a Maybeck, perfect as an ark. Who knows, it may rain; and you and I will start a whole new race of blondes.

The only thing is, you have to pretend that you're Julia Kristeva.

MELANIE: Who?

MARCELLA: I'll tell you later. The important thing, Miss Griffith, is—I love you. Earnestly, honestly, from the time I was a young girl, I've lived my whole life for you. Sweetly, tenderly, I long for you. Take me, Miss Griffith. You with the mind of a CPA and the bod made for sin. Take me away from this humdrum Berkeley Chez Panisse-UAM-David Lance Goines merry go round and make love to me.

MELANIE: But I'm married! To Don Johnson—I think. No! Antonio Banderas!

MARCELLA: I'm married, too—to Douglas Devlin, need I say more?

MELANIE: This is all happening too fast for a girl from Mayberry, RFD.

MARCELLA: I know you want a drink.

MELANIE: I don't drink. [*Panicking*] Wine.

MARCELLA: For you I have cut down all the famous Berkeley pines, and gathered their cones, and made you a heaping jug full of pine cognac.

MELANIE: Oh, my favorite . . . from Mayberry. I took my first drink at age four, with Opie, down in the shadow of the pines, and he turned over a rock and pointed out a little pool of pine cognac. [*Giggles*] We went skinny-dipping. But I don't drink any more. I'm in a twelve-step program.

MARCELLA: Melanie dear, forget about AA and Betty Ford, forget about your endless war with your mother and being born in a phone booth, forget Don and Antonio and just concentrate on cognac, drinking, and me, me, Marcella Devlin. Cut!

[*Enter DEVLIN and STEPHANIE.*]

DEVLIN: Princess, help me. I'm confused. Torn by the irrevocable violence of the text of this film, yet haunted by what lies behind the screen.

MELANIE: I'm confused. You confuse me, Marcella.

MARCELLA: I'll take you to the barrel.

[*Exit MARCELLA and MELANIE.*]

DEVLIN: Is the film experience an allegory for the myth of Abraham and Isaac? Or what's the famous tale where a father makes love to his own son, then wakes up realizing maybe it was all a dream?

STEPHANIE: If you stood where I stand, you would see yourself, Douglas Devlin, alone, a man with no friends, facing a woman with a heart torn apart, formerly a piece of Eurotrash, now a nothing.

[*Enter JAMIE LEE CURTIS (played by two actors).*]

I'm seeing double and I haven't had a drink since the crash.

JAMIE LEE CURTIS: I am Jamie Lee Curtis.

STEPHANIE: Ah, bon jour! *C'est vrai*—you were born in the shower in *Psycho*, and shortly afterwards developed a strong male and strong female side of your character.

JAMIE LEE CURTIS (*male*): There is no "strong male" side to Jamie Lee Curtis.

JAMIE LEE CURTIS (*female*): Am I a strong woman? Hear me roar.

DEVLIN: I told Billy Hammer, no stars at this conference! But you—Miss Curtis— interest me more than I should.

JAMIE LEE (*Male*): We have that effect—

JAMIE LEE (*female*): —On men and women of all sexes. Come to me,—

JAMIE LEE (*male*): —come to me, Douglas Devlin.

JAMIE LEE (*both*): Tell me all your cares and woes.

STEPHANIE (*to audience*): I have been asked to talk about Alfred Hitchcock and the collapse of meaning. The narratological desire of the—steep Riviera slopes—I with my walkman blaring my hit Euro-single "Hurricane"—and my mother's fat drunken face screaming—and my foot, that pesky, heavy foot—

DEVLIN: Oh, get out of here, you're the pesky one. Stop blaming everything on your foot! It's you! You're the problem, not your foot!

STEPHANIE: Welcome! *Bienvenue*! In tears I hereby open this festival.

JAMIE LEE (*both*): You want to talk to a woman so big she inhabits the bodies of all genders.

STEPHANIE: I'll take my foot out of the way. My foot, that you don't like!

[*Exit STEPHANIE.*]

DEVLIN: I'm so afraid of the conference! I'm afraid Avital Ronell won't show up, I'll be laughed out of the MLA.

JAMIE LEE (*female*): I used to be frightened, too. After all,—

JAMIE LEE (*male*): —I was born during the shower scene in *Psycho*.

JAMIE LEE (*female*): My first memories were blood—rushing water—

JAMIE LEE (*male*): And a big knife!

DEVLIN (*shivering*): Mine too.

[*Enter STEVE.*]

STEVE (*to audience*): Shall I?

DEVLIN: Ah, Jamie Lee Curtis . . .

STEVE: Cut.

DEVLIN: I'm sorry.

JAMIE LEE (*female*): Don't worry about it.

JAMIE LEE (*male*): It's the stress. Don't blame yourself.

DEVLIN: No—I'm never like this—ask Marcella.

JAMIE LEE (*both*): We have much to ask Marcella.

STEVE: Cut. [*To audience.*] So what would you do? Marcella Devlin had me pinned down to her wall like a pet in a movie, stuffed with my own lust and deceit.

[*Exit DEVLIN and JAMIE LEE.*]

How could I let her get away with what amounted to murder? I'm an ordinary guy, with ordinary hands and feet. I'm not an angel or a monster. I'm me—me, Steve Poitrine. I'm gonna find Marcella Devlin and tell her—it's Melanie Griffith or me, or your husband!

[*Enter BILLY.*]

BILLY: I wasn't always like this—wasn't always the magnet for fun and excitement. My celullar phone drips numbers like honey, but once I was dull, a Berkeley frump. Then I went to Bard and learned a little bit about computer science and Jheri curls. I realized, "Hey! Language comes in a one and a zero. The world is digital." From then on life assumed a binary purpose and a sense of meaning. Now I'm representing clients.

[Enter KARL LAGERFELD.]

KARL (*claps hands above his head*): I am here!

STEVE: That bozo looks familiar. Isn't he in *Vogue?*

BILLY (*to STEVE*): Actually—you look familiar. Didn't you go to Bard?

KARL: Where are the festival servants?

BILLY: I'm going to check my yearbook. Or did you have a twin, who had sex
with the whole lacrosse team?

[Exit BILLY.]

STEVE: I shouldn't have gone out for lacrosse. I fell asleep in the locker room,
woke up in a sling, my rosy medallions slithered with grease.

KARL (*claps hands above his head*): I am here!

STEVE: He was in *Prêt-à-Porter* . . . and Marcella's hands came up through my
popcorn. It's Oscar de la Renta—no! I, Steve, say no.

KARL: Is no one here to wipe the boots of the great Karl Lagerfeld? No one in all
of Berkeley is fit to remove mud from my fez. Strange mud, as though the bulldozers
had ripped up every pine in the city—perhaps to make pine cognac to celebrate my
arrival. You—young man with the black hair—handsome as Alain Delon or Vincent
Perez. Come and kiss my lips, the torrid lips of the ageless designer of Lancome.

STEVE: I was hungry—and you came with a whole German army of schnitzel.

KARL: After we endure our love, you will help me crown the new Lancome woman
and inaugurate fashion here in Berkeley.

STEVE: New Lancome woman? What's wrong with Isabella Rossellini?

[Enter ANDY GRIFFITH.]

KARL: I shudder when I think of her. No, she has kept the cobra jewel too long,
that one. You—you, Andy Griffith—you are here, good! You will be playing "me"
at this fete. I am too well known to go in public to perform the cobra ritual. Who
knows what Valerie Solanases lurk among the tree stumps of this ugly city by the bay.

ANDY: Well shucks, Karl, I'm straight off the set of *Matlock*, still wearin' my seer-
sucker with mah good luck Hush Puppies.

KARL: Straight? Puppies? I do not care. This [*indicating STEVE*] is my—how
do you say—inspiration. He—Steve Poitrine—cub reporter, acting student, now
supermodel for Lagerfeld, Chloe, Lancome. He—Andy Griffith—father of Melanie
Griffith.

STEVE: Hi.

ANDY: Nice to meet you, son. You know Goober? Goober would like you, I don't.

KARL: Play me to a T, Mr. Andy.

STEVE: But hurry! The conference is about to start!

[*Exit STEVE and KARL.*]

ANDY: It was a cold rainy night in Bodega Bay when I first met Tippi Hedren. She
was covered with birds and I took her into a nearby diner to clean the mud off her.

[*Enter KARL LAGERFELD.*]

KARL (*waving a finger*): Andy, Andy, you are not being me very nicely!

ANDY: Fashion is fun! Fashion is the now! Fashion is excitement, chocolate
bonbons on a cake de la wedding! Fashion is what I mandate for the future and
ze president!

KARL (*mollified*): Better, Andy!

ANDY (*under his breath*): Sprecken zie fuckez-vous, Mr. German know it all. [*Aloud:*]
Fashion makes the man live like ze emperor of cream!

KARL: I thought Andie McDowell was a prettier woman than that. *Zut alors*. No
matter.

[*Exit KARL LAGERFELD. Enter TIPPI HEDREN.*]

ANDY: My, she was a pretty little sight, a dumpling of plenty.

TIPPI: My baby—where's my baby?

ANDY: Remember, sugar plum? Your baby's in Mayberry. I just fed exed the poor, squawling thing to Aunt Bee not thirty minutes ago.

TIPPI: He came to me in the guise of a bird . . . a big bird, horrid . . . pecking away, pecking the tender spots of my scrap. In my trailer. A trailer, the last safe place left in America, that's why I left and set up my wild animal preserve in Africa. If even a trailer isn't safe from your director, why live in the States? A big bird, with black eyes, round in the middle, like a robin fat with worms . . . Robin Redbreast . . .

ANDY GRIFFITH: Shucks, that was no bird, that was just me, Andy of Mayberry.

[*Enter DEVLIN.*]

DEVLIN: Ladies and gentlemen, I'm Douglas Devlin, and welcome to the Berkeley Film Commission and our first annual Hitchcock deconstruction. First, I'd like to introduce you to—my God, Devlin—what have you done? Had sex with your own son, like Mrs. Norman Bates! And with Jamie Lee Curtis, kind of!

[*Enter BILLY.*]

BILLY HAMMER. Dad—Dad—it's all right. Excuse me, audience, my father's had a great shock.

TIPPI: Now he wants me to go on and tell the world I'm Laura Mulvey. Whoever that is. Something to do with gays.

ANDY: Well, you're an actress, hon!

TIPPI: Tell me, Andy, why does Melanie hate me so?

BILLY: What my father's trying to say is—he's signed up a great bill of talent for you this afternoon, so hold on to your hats, because here they come now—Julia Kristeva . . . Laura Mulvey . . . Jane Gallop, ladies and gentlemen.

[*MELANIE and ISABELLA shuffle on stage, disgruntled. MELANIE is drunk and wearing a spectacular red dress. Lastly, JAMIE LEE CURTIS enters the stage.*]

And who's this? I forget.

JAMIE LEE CURTIS: We are Avital Ronell.

BILLY: Give them a great round of applause.

[*ISABELLA, TIPPI and MELANIE take their seats.*]

DEVLIN: In my moment of triumph I feel sick. Up on the mountain of Everest, plunged to hell by my guilt and pain.

BILLY: Well—why don't you lie down?

JAMIE LEE CURTIS (*male*): We will help you—

JAMIE LEE CURTIS (*female*): —drag the exquisite corpse of your father off the stage.

BILLY: Oh my God, it's Karl Lagerfeld. Dad, I tried to get Lacan, but he must be dead or something, and Lagerfeld's right under Lacan in the phone books of Paris, so—shrug!

DEVLIN (*faintly*): Where is Marcella?

JAMIE LEE CURTIS (*both*): She has found her niche.

DEVLIN: While I have found the awful nothing in the eye of narratology.

JAMIE LEE CURTIS (*male*): Come—

JAMIE LEE CURTIS (*female*): —Come with us, Douglas Devlin.

[*They lift an arm over their shoulders and carry DEVLIN off stage.*]

ANDY GRIFFITH (*as "KARL LAGERFELD"*): I am Karl Lagerfeld, come to Berkeley to crown new Lancome frau—I mean, woman. First, I must strip the crown off tired, selfish frau who has held it too long—Isabella Rossellini?

ISABELLA ROSSELLINI: I'm listening, but I am Jane Gallop, playing the part of a woman, listening, suspiciously, thinking to herself, that man's a snake!

ANDY GRIFFITH (*as "KARL LAGERFELD"*): Give me the cobra jewel.

ISABELLA ROSSELLINI: Karl, Karl, how cruel. Jane Gallop, calling Karl Lagerfeld cruel, calling the man playing Lagerfeld cruel. None of this is real, none sinks into the bewildered mind of Jane Gallop, which twitches with every word like snakes writhing in one of those metal baskets, poised above the sizzling grease, in the McDonalds of Berkeley, where they make the french fries.

[Enter CHITA.]

CHITA: Geef me the cobarah chewel!

ISABELLA: I would, but I don't have it!

BILLY: I love you both, but let's not get sticky about it.

CHITA: Two things I can smell within a hundred feet—burning hamburger, and the lies of Rossellini.

ISABELLA: I was napping atop Gary Coleman, when I felt a sharp tug at my neck.

MELANIE (*after a beat*): Mother!

TIPPI HEDREN: You wore that red dress!

MELANIE: You're wearing one too! I'm not the only "co" here.

TIPPI HEDREN: Okay, okay. I took the cobra jewel. I left it in my trailer, next to the bird cage.

CHITA: I will fetch it and return it to print ads and Sumatra.

ISABELLA: I go with you.

CHITA: You know I have loved you since Bard. Will you take from me the symbol of my only advantage, my beauty?

ISABELLA: I haven't decided. You're going to find it easy to take back my tray. Oh, Chita, I love your hair.

CHITA: But do you like its—cut?

[Exit CHITA and ISABELLA.]

BILLY: Now—the showdown! Melanie Griffith?

MELANIE: Am I still supposed to be Julia Kristeva?

TIPPI HEDREN: Drop the pretense! No one believed you for a minute playing that cop infiltrating the Hasidic Jews of Brooklyn! Or how about you as the top Allied resistance agent in *Shining Through* with Michael Douglas!

MELANIE: Oh, wow! Look who's talking! America's greatest actress Tippi Hedren! Hitchcock couldn't get Grace Kelly, so he found you in some Swedish meatball joint!

TIPPI: I never made meatballs. I'm a vegan.

MELANIE: You were never an actress. Or a mother! Or a vegan.

TIPPI: I don't know how that Swedish thing got started anyhow.

MELANIE: Because you're so weird, Mother! People had to blame it on something!

ANDY GRIFFITH: Whoa, whoa—ladies, please!

MELANIE: If she hates those birds so much, why does she always travel with them? Why the seclusion? Why the bird preserve in Africa?

TIPPI HEDREN: I never worked with meatballs, nor have I been to Sweden. People say terrible things about a star just because she's difficult and cold. Andy—I mean, Mr. Karl Lagerfeld—do me a favor? Get me a heating pad from my trailer.

ANDY GRIFFITH: Will do!

[*Exit ANDY GRIFFITH.*]

TIPPI HEDREN: Okay, I have my problems. When I see the color red I grow dizzy, faint, I steal things—little things—valuable things. And I'm a bit frigid. I lied to the world about the father of my baby, but wouldn't you? Who says we have to tell the truth to the world? Where is that written? Has the world ever told the truth to us?

MELANIE: When it was my birthday all the other kids got parties in Mayberry, and all I got from Hollywood was these little dollsize coffins, with a little doll of you in it, dead, dressed like you were in *Marnie*!

TIPPI: That wasn't me, I had no time for presents! I was too busy combatting the rumors about me being from Sweden!

MELANIE: And why are you so against me drinking? What was there to do, in Mayberry, except drink pine cognac and meet Don Johnson?

[*Enter MARCELLA, with a glass of cognac.*]

MARCELLA: I'll take your side, silvergirl. Ah, your lips are dry!—which is like saying, my lips are dry. Drink—drink—feel good. Try not to turn onto problems that upset you, cause it's cool and the unguent's sweet, there's a fire in your hands and feet—

MELANIE: You're telling me!

MARCELLA: I'll sit here by your side, and after you've resigned from Tippi Hedren, you will join me at my new clinic, the Marcella Devlin clinic.

MELANIE: Fine.

TIPPI HEDREN: It's true, I have a complex relation to my birds. It's a love-hate relationship. [*To an invisible bird.*] Hi there! Do you love me? I had a girl, a girl who doesn't love me back! I see a bird, and I feel—antsy inside, as though some grand part of me had been crumpled up, then flown away!

BILLY: Mother, I've been meaning to ask you, are you a lesbian?

MELANIE: I can't sit here and make comments. I am Julia Kristeva.

[*A STUDENT stands up from the audience, waving.*]

STUDENT: Miss Kristeva?

MELANIE: Who?

STUDENT: Julia Kristeva?

MELANIE: I don't understand the question. Marcella? Where's my pine cognac?

MARCELLA: Here, dear. Miss Kristeva's off right now, she'll be investigating the power of horror at the Marcella Devlin clinic. Miss Hedren—vicious, obstinate, Miss Hedren? I have a telegram for you.

BILLY: I'll read it as her representative. [*Rips open telegram.*] Oh my God! Your performance as Laura Mulvey has won you the Academy Award! Melanie's been kicked out of Hollywood, and you'll be starring in all her future roles!

MARCELLA (*to MELANIE*): Come dear, I have your dose in the Maybeck.

TIPPI (*breathless*): Vindicated!

MARCELLA: Goodbye, Billy. Goodbye Berkeley.

MELANIE: Occasionally I always drink too much.

[*MELANIE stumbles off stage. MARCELLA is confronted by STEVE.*]

STEVE: Okay, Marcella, who's it gonna be, me, him or her?

MARCELLA: What kind of dish am I, Steve? I'm the sixty-cent special—cheap, flashy, strictly poison under the gravy.

STEVE: Why'd you lie to me?

MARCELLA: Why'd I put on these shoes? Some things you do, some things you don't.

STEVE: Just don't leave me in a minor key.

MARCELLA: That's what they all say.

STEVE: You're a bitter little lady.

MARCELLA: It's a bitter little world. I've got something on my conscience, but what woman hasn't?

[*Exit MARCELLA.*]

BILLY: Go ahead, cry on my shoulder.

[*Enter CHITA*]

CHITA: Or mine, big-faced man.

BILLY: Here she is, my Lancome girl. I'm poised to become the Matthew Marks of show business, if that's not an oxymoron,—boosting the Old Masters with one hand—[*grabs TIPPI's hand and raises it high*]—but also [*drops her hand—she sinks into a chair*] giving a boost to the new young promising stars of tomorrow, like my other properties, Chita du Sumatra and Steve Lacrosse. What a day it's been—first, I brought fun to Berkeley, then, I got to fuck my own father, and now I'm representing clients!

[*Exit BILLY.*]

STEVE: What's money, just a piece of paper crawling with germs. Without Marcella Devlin, I'm like a man set free from a Turkish prison.

TIPPI: I'm no ordinary girl, in a red dress and a French twist, I steal, I cheat, people laugh at my wooden patrician face. Yet here I am, still, without motion or a clue, rushing secret harmonies with all kinds of things I can't explain. I'd coil my fingers round your neck, push the cloth from your heart, Robin Redbreast. Ever hear the one about the two circumcisionists? "The first cut is the deepest."

CHITA: I should be happy, with my cobra jewel, but what about the love I denied? From Bard, to Sumatra, to now, I wanted a woman made of tears, for which all the jungles of my country have been stripped of rubber. I would call it to your memory now—

TIPPI: Robin Redbreast, a bird so sorrowful the quiet forester gives a low moan.

STEVE: Ferret teeth in the breast of a red bird.

CHITA: —that a phantasmal fog of love had enthralled me to her, then, but not only then, in these my words, I was born when she kissed me. I died when she left me. I lived a few weeks—while she loved me.

TIPPI: The quiet forester gives a low moan. Wake up!

ALL. Let's go see Bava's final masterpiece, *Red High Heels of Death*!

END

The anarchic and transhistoric energies of Kiki Gallery were given a wider context by curator Lawrence Rinder and artist Nayland Blake when in 1995, they opened a show at the Berkeley Art Museum, *In A Different Light*, which was widely touted as the first museum show devoted to gay and lesbian art. Many of the regulars in the poets theater were selected to show their work (among a storied, international roster). Larry asked me to write a play that could be presented in conjunction with the exhibition, and the propinquity of the film-goers paradise the Pacific Film Archive did the rest. "Cut" seemed like a natural fit. Like the show it represented, it went back a hundred years to propose and deconstruct a queer reading of Hitchcock and carried it right up to the present day, into the lives of the children of his greatest stars—children still strangely popular in 1995. And plus we got to work with the incandescent writer Mary Gaitskill. The old timers were always saying, that if you didn't see Laurette Taylor in Tennessee Williams' Glass Menagerie, then you missed out on legend. While we were acting with Mary Gaitskill from moment to moment we were continually thunderstruck, knocked out, made silent and confused—it was a roller coaster trying to keep up with her Tippi Hedren.

Sometime later I was asked to bring a typical script of the SF Poets Theater to the Poetry Project in New York, and I picked "Cut," casting it through long distance from the poets and artists I knew from precious visits, or those who had passed through San Francisco. I had an incredible cast in NYC, but what I didn't realize is that poetry politics had already reached a pitch in New York that didn't hit the Bay Area until 2014, and so when I arrived for our rehearsal I discovered to my horror that inadvertently I had arranged for a whole stage of people who in many cases hadn't spoken to each other in years. The rehearsal was terrible. When I was done, Lynne Tillman cheerfully reminded me that I didn't have to go through with it, I could just cancel the event. But for some reason I decided not to cancel, and the whole evening was a shining success. From what I understand, it was the last time Eileen Myles—playing Marcella Devlin, the discontented faculty wife—wore a dress, ever. In one scene they even wore a bustier: I felt so honored. And some of those who had come to the rehearsal as enemies mended their fences, at least for an evening.

Produced on April 2, 1995 at UC Berkeley's University Art Museum/Pacific Film
Archive in conjunction with the exhibition "In a Different Light"
(January 11--April 9, 1995)

"ALFRED HITCHCOCK"/STEVE POITRINE ....Clifford Hengst
BILLY HAMMER ....Jonathan Hammer
MARCELLA DEVLIN................................... ....Margaret Crane
CHITA DU SUMATRA................................ .... Phoebe Gloeckner
DEVLIN... .... Wayne Smith
STEPHANIE, PRINCESS OF MONACO... .... Eleni Sikelianos
TIPPI HEDREN.............................. ....Mary Gaitskill
MELANIE GRIFFITH ....Andrea Juno
ANDY GRIFFITH.......................... ....Rex Ray
ISABELLA ROSSELLINI.................................. ....Caroline Azar
JAMIE LEE CURTIS................................ .... Scott Hewicker
JAMIE LEE CURTIS................................ ....Michelle Rollman
KARL LAGERFELD...D-L Alvarez

Revived by St. Mark's Poetry Project on April 29, 1998, with the following cast:

"ALFRED HITCHCOCK"/STEVE POITRINE
cub reporter for the Berkeley Times...Tim Davis
BILLY HAMMER,
gadabout son of Marcella and Douglas Devlin...................................Kevin Killian
MARCELLA DEVLIN, his mother,
a discontented faculty wife... Eileen Myles
CHITA DU SUMATRA,
the maid of Tippi Hedren..Michelle Rollman
DOUGLAS DEVLIN,
director of the Berkeley Film Archive ....Kenward Elmslie
STEPHANIE, Princess of Monaco,
the daughter of the late Grace Kelly .... Eleni Sikelianos
TIPPI HEDREN,
abiding star of "Marnie" and "The Birds" ....Laurie Weeks
MELANIE GRIFFITH, her daughter..Lee Ann Brown
ANDY GRIFFITH, the legendary "Andy of Mayberry" ....D L Alvarez
ISABELLA ROSSELLINI,
Lancome model and daughter of Ingrid Bergman........................... Lynne Tillman
JAMIE LEE CURTIS.. Joe Westmoreland
JAMIE LEE CURTIS...Sianne Ngai
KARL LAGERFELD,
top haute couture man from Europe ....Bruce Andrews

Cut (revival), produced at Small Press Traffic (San Francisco), October 7, 2000, with Taylor Brady, Wayne Smith, Jocelyn Saidenberg, Marisa Hernandez, Rex Ray, Yedda Morrison, Margaret Crane, Karla Milosevich, Craig Goodman, Norma Cole, Rupert Adley, Tanya Hollis and Kota Ezawa

Revived by Small Press Traffic (San Francisco) on October 7, 2000, with the following cast:

"ALFRED HITCHCOCK"/STEVE POITRINE,
cub reporter for the Berkeley Times........ ....Taylor Brady
BILLY HAMMER,
gadabout son of Marcella Douglas Devlin....................................... Wayne Smith
MARCELLA DEVLIN,
his mother, a discontented faculty wife... .... Jocelyn Saidenberg
CHITA DU SUMATRA,
the maid of Tippi Hedren...................... ....Marisa Hernandez
DOUGLAS DEVLIN,
director of the Berkeley Film Archive ....Rex Ray
STEPHANIE,
Princess of Monaco, the daughter of the late Grace Kelly............Yedda Morrison
TIPPI HEDREN,
abiding star of "Marnie" and "The Birds" ....Margaret Crane
MELANIE GRIFFITH, her daughter.......... ....Karla Milosevich
ANDY GRIFFITH,
the legendary "Andy of Mayberry"......... ....Craig Goodman
ISABELLA ROSSELLINI,
Lancome model and daughter of Ingrid Bergman............................Norma Cole
JAMIE LEE CURTIS.................................. .... Rupert Adley
JAMIE LEE CURTIS.................................. ....Tanya Hollis
KARL LAGERFELD,
top haute couture man from Europe .... Kota Ezawa

Wet Paint

characters

OFFICER BIGARINI, a North Beach boy
BOB KAUFMAN, a Beat poet
SASHA CHOLNAKY, a Hungarian refugee
EVA, his sister
MICHAEL MCCLURE, poet and neighbor of Jay DeFeo's
COUNTESS CHOLNAKY, their mother
WALLACE BERMAN, artist
DOROTHY MILLER, curator for the Whitney Museum
MAGDA FILBERT, psychoanalyst
JAY DEFEO, artist
KAY DEFEO, her imaginary twin sister
JANIS JOPLIN, Texas transplant new to North Beach
HALL MARK, founder of a fledgling greeting card company
WILMA VAPE, his assistant
LEONORA WELD, stage mother
TUESDAY WELD, 14 year old Hollwood starlet
DIEGO RIVERA, painter
FRIDA KAHLO, a painter as well
HELEN ADAM, Scots poet and balladeer
BOBBY BEAUSOLEIL, not yet in the Manson family
KENNETH ANGER, visionary filmmaker
CLERK, in a hardware store, in a flashback
REBECA, an artist in a flashback who was there first

[*Scene—North Beach 1959. Music cue. Jazzy North Beach music like Take Five by Dave Brubeck Quartet, or some sort of Take Five pastiche.*]

OFFICER BIGARINI: Here I am in North Beach, 1959, wandering the streets round Grant and Green, a sworn officer of the law looking for those no good beatniks. I've been on this beat since Hiroshima and it's just getting worse and worse. Every day a new menace to law and order and today it's Bob Kaufman.

[*Enter BOB KAUFMAN.*]

OFFICER BIGARINI: Half Jewish, half black, Bob Kaufman represents everything wrong with North Beach today. When I was a boy my father hid me in his lunch pail, in the hull of the Nina, the Pinta and the Santa Maria from Genoa, but how did this kook get here, I ask you? I see his grinning beatific face and I reach for my gun. I'm Officer Bigarini, the cop the Beats call the scourge of North Beach,

KAUFMAN: Greetings, Little Big.

BIGARINI: What's this Little Big shit, stand up when I'm talking to you, Kaufman!

KAUFMAN: I am standing, Bigarini.

BIGARINI: That's Officer Bigarini to you, you worthless vagrant piece of—

KAUFMAN: And that's Saint Bob to you, blue boy, tedious excuse for a senator of Broadway. Those could have been wings on your shoulders, for you wear the look of an angel, but instead, malice has melted your mambo.

BIGARINI: Why you! Run off to your coffee shop lifestyle and co-exist.

KAUFMAN: Man, I feel sorry for you. This is San Francisco, not Selma, Alabama. Your head in the wrong year. Hitler and his youth camps burnt up in the bunker! Don't let your mouth write a check your nightstick can't swing, Little Big.

BIGARINI: I'm-a run you out of town if it's the last thing I do!

KAUFMAN: On yardbird corners of embryonic hopes, drowned in a heroin tear.
On yardbird corners of parkerflights to sound filled pockets in space.
On neuro-corners of striped brains & desperate electro-surgeons.
On alcohol corners of pointless discussion & historical hangovers.
On television corners of cornflakes & rockwells impotent America.

BIGARINI: Translation?

KAUFMAN: Go peddle your hate to the mediocre, Big. You're living in the Beat State now, and you, like every man and woman, should be on fire with love!

[*Exit KAUFMAN.*]

BIGARINI: Thing I can't figure out about Bob Kaufman, is, he knows my beat, he knows where I am every minute of the day. He knows how to avoid me, if he cared. It's like he's throwing himself in front of my face, like he wants another arrest. Bah!

[*Enter SASHA and EVA.*]

SASHA: Oh, sister, there is so much life here in San Francisco, and how good it is of our wonderful lady to give a corner of her flat to hide us.

EVA: I do not know, Sasha. North Beach is scary place for young girl.

BIGARINI: Why not go back to where you came from?

SASHA: Officer Bigarini! I have my papers.

BIGARINI: If it's not the Beatniks it's the foreigners, we're overrun. These Hungarians, only thing they're good for is their goulash.

SASHA: But Officer,—

BIGARINI: And Zsa Zsa Gabor, now there's a woman!

EVA: Let me pass.

BIGARINI: Pass for an American? No way.

SASHA: Sister, he is only, what's the word, kidding you.

BIGARINI: You live with Jay DeFeo, don't you? Lemme give you some free advice.

EVA: What's that, Bigarini?

[*Enter MICHAEL McCLURE.*]

BIGARINI: Flee! —Oh for Christ's sake, another poet! You two know Michael
McClure?

EVA: He is the upstairs neighbor of Miss Jay DeFeo.

SASHA: Michael McClure is the coolest cat in the Fillmore.

BIGARINI: Yeah? Well, he's Kansas garbage to me! McClure, you think you're
something special, don't you, with your beast language and your meat science energy
and your pants made of shoe leather.

MICHAEL McCLURE: You and your kind would make peyote illegal! But until
that dark day let's take a handful and really go to town.

[*Offers BIGARINI some peyote buttons.*]

BIGARINI: No thanks.

MICHAEL McCLURE (*offering some to the Hungarians*): Huh, Eva and Sasha? All
is cool and boundless as a rolling lamb of jazz! I see the shades slipt behind me.
Officer Bigarini!

[*BIGARINI circles McCLURE examining his pants.*]

BIGARINI: I keep walking around those pants and thinking, they're obscene
according to the statute of California. I can see every little bump and freckle on
your what's it.

MICHAEL McCLURE: I invented these pants, true—but the wild lions told me
how.

EVA: Lions! Oh my!

[*Music cue—some sort of menacing Stravinsky-like chords endlessly repeating like the lions' growls.
Or like the On the Waterfront theme song.*]

MICHAEL McCLURE: I sit at the zoo with the lions in their cage, and I speak
to them in the beast language I learn from my brain, my heart, soul, and my balls.
This is what I say to them. GRAWR! And they pad up to me—they lean against
the bars—and roar back at me.

SASHA: GRAWR!

MICHAEL McCLURE: GRAWR. Now everybody do it.

SASHA, EVA, BIGARINI: GRAWR!

MICHAEL McCLURE: GRAWR.

SASHA, EVA, BIGARINI: GRAWR!

MICHAEL McCLURE: This is how we lions talk to each other and how we eat our prey and feel the heat of the sun on our haunches.

[*He caresses his hips as though feeling the sun on them.*]

EVA, BIGARINI: GRAWR!

MICHAEL McCLURE: How's Jay? Haven't seen her in three hundred thousand light years in the tree core of sequoia.

BIGARINI: I'm giving you a warning this time, McClure, but next time I'm turning you in for indecent expositure.

MICHAEL McCLURE: Maybe you'll go your way, I'll go mine.

[*Exit OFFICER BIGARINI and MICHAEL McCLURE—in opposite directions.*]

SASHA: I know you miss Budapest, Eva, but here in California we are free. No tanks, no guns.

EVA: It is gloomy in this apartment, painted black, black, like eternal night.

SASHA: It is the black color of my love of freedom! Sings: "From the hillsides, black with foam! God bless America—"

EVA (*reluctantly*): "My home sweet home!"

SASHA: Even Officer Bigarini is somewhat friendly. He did not arrest you, Eva.

EVA: I detest him.

[*Aside.*]

And yet I find him strangely attractive. Poor refugee girl, that cop on the beat makes your heart bigger than Budapest.

[*Enter COUNTESS CHOLNAKY, their elderly mother.*]

COUNTESS: Why you wake an old widow with the screaming play of cats in alley?

SASHA: Excuse me, Mother dear, I did not hear you sleeping with my ears.

COUNTESS: Last night I pose for your favorite, the dark woman who owns this house of hell. Your precious Jay DeFeo.

SASHA: Mother, why so ungrateful? Here we come, family of needy Magyars, with no pockets, and she take us in, stick us in corner.

EVA: In corner, I sleep and dream terrible dreams. And always, the smell of wet paint.

COUNTESS: And it is dirty in here, many Christmas trees. "Edelweiss, edelweiss—"

EVA (*reluctantly*): "Bless this homeland forever!" Sasha, when we go back to revolution? I miss many friends—Bertha, Frieda, Hedy, and Muumuu.

SASHA: You, sister! You, mother! Cheer up, will ya!

EVA: I don't even remember the tanks. Tanks. No tanks.

COUNTESS: All night long, I pose, standing in corner with arms akimbo, while your Saint Jay DeFeo make mocking picture of old hag, call it "The Veronica."

SASHA: A very good likeness say I.

EVA: I think our brother loves Jay DeFeo!

COUNTESS: She's one strange lady, always her hands in lead paint, —like Stalin. I spit on Stalin. And her friends, all in black—Beatniks.

SASHA: She has heart of gold.

COUNTESS: I wear bright colors, the colors of Hungary, to spite her charity! I, the Countess Cholnaky, am proud woman!

EVA: Mother dear, I take you to Beatnik Lounge for heavy tea.

COUNTESS: Take me to big gold bridge, I jump, like Weldon Kees. You will be happy, Sasha, to see me go. Goodbye.

[*Exit EVA and COUNTESS.*]

SASHA: All day long, the jazz music, the Chet Baker, the Ella Fitzgerald, the Charlie Parker. Strange, mad assemblage and funk. Mother and sister, they don't like. Me, I like it lots. Jay DeFeo—the magical name of the rose. I greet great friend of Jay DeFeo. Hello, neighbor! Hello, Mr. Wallace Berman!

[*Enter WALLACE BERMAN. Music cue.*]

WALLACE BERMAN: Good morning.

SASHA: Holy cow!   Of all the swinging cats Frisco has to offer, Mr. Wallace Berman, you Number One.

WALLACE BERMAN (*calmly*): Let me in—and quickly, Sasha. I just saw Officer Big out on Green Street. He's the man who arrested me for obscenity at the Ferus Gallery in 1957.

SASHA: So heroic a victim!

WALLACE BERMAN: He's a vice squad goon, on the take, like a locust with teeth.

SASHA: Come in, come in!

WALLACE BERMAN: Is Jay home?

SASHA: No, Mr. Wallace, Jay DeFeo is at doctor! Brain doctor, she not sick, except in head.

WALLACE BERMAN: Psychiatry! Science of limits, free zone of trick quart chick bride. Drive the psychiatry bat to Hell!

SASHA: No, Mr. Wallace, no bat!

WALLACE BERMAN: Psychiatry, the cold cure, the anti-Semina.

SASHA: She's seeing Magda Filbert on Greenwich Street! Is that your baby,
Wallace Berman? Your baby in beat up old brown bag?

WALLACE BERMAN [*placing bag on table*]. All matter is illusion. Tosh might as
well be in a bag as not in a bag, for this is 1959, when all Americans are living in
an existential trap, caused by the specter of the A-Bomb and the separation of
God from man. Tosh might as well suck this up via the medium of brown paper.

SASHA: I give him little cherry roll [*opens bag and slips in cherry roll*] as we do to the
babies of Hungary.

WALLACE BERMAN: Can I buy your outfit, Sasha? The Hungarian things you
are wearing on your body? I will give you one silver dollar for clothes, then rip
them to shreds, hang them like parachutes, the Cold War dangling from Columbus
Avenue like the Hanged Man of the Jewish Tarot card.

SASHA: You have the fun of a goose, you amaze me. Doorbell rings.

[*Enter DOROTHY MILLER.*]

You answer door, Mr. Wallace. I strip in the closet.

[*Exit SASHA.*]

WALLACE BERMAN: Who shall I say is here to see Miss DeFeo?

DOROTHY MILLER: Tell her it's Dorothy Miller.

WALLACE BERMAN: No! Not the Dorothy Miller, from New York!

DOROTHY: None other.

WALLACE BERMAN: Everyone in North Beach knows you're here in San
Francisco putting together your famous "Sixteen Americans" exhibition for the
Whitney!

DOROTHY: True.

WALLACE BERMAN: I am Wallace Berman, perhaps you've seen my work.

DOROTHY: Yes. [*Pause.*] I have.

WALLACE BERMAN: I hate you, Miss Miller. I'm glad you're not putting me in your show. We hate New York! We keep our work private, pure and clean—like snow on the mountains.

DOROTHY: Are you the butler for Miss DeFeo?

WALLACE BERMAN: No. I am a free spirit. I work for no one, I create my idiosyncratic, Kabbalah-influenced art works, I let them speak for themselves, then throw them away. Is this your purse?

DOROTHY: Yes.

WALLACE BERMAN: I'll make a piece of it, then destroy it!

DOROTHY (*to the audience*): Get me Walter Hopps on the phone right now. He told me it would be safe to approach these North Beach radicals.

WALLACE BERMAN: Without your filo-fax you New Yorkers don't even know who you are! I'm from L.A. where the winds are flat but we know our names like our cars.

DOROTHY: I'll be back.

[*Enter KAY DeFEO, disguised as her sister.*]

KAY DeFEO: Dorothy! Come in to my garret, I am Jay DeFeo. Dorothy Miller, marvelous Manhattanoiselle!

DOROTHY: Refreshing to be treated as a dignitary.

KAY DeFEO: I am making this wonderful life-changing painting called, "The Rose." You, a seasoned New Yorker, will understand what I am doing.

WALLACE BERMAN: You told me you hate New Yorkers.

KAY DeFEO: Silence, please. [*Sotto voce to WALLACE BERMAN.*] Later I will reward you with some chick action.

WALLACE BERMAN: I'll never understand you, Jay.

KAY DeFEO: Of course you won't.

WALLACE BERMAN: Everything about you, from your name to your exquisite madcap dead Christmas trees, screams of abstraction.

KAY DeFEO: Doesn't it! Who was it said, life is nasty, brutal, and short? Brittle and short's more like it.

DOROTHY MILLER: Then what happens to "nasty"?

WALLACE BERMAN: It winds up at the Whitney.

KAY DeFEO (*with great savoir-faire*): Right this way, I'll show you "The Rose."

[*Exit DOROTHY MILLER and KAY DeFEO. Baby remains on table.*]

WALLACE BERMAN (*opening bag*): Tosh—what do you think? Did I queer my chances of getting into the Whitney? Well—I'm a Berman, not a flatterer. You be too.

[*Enter SASHA, in his underwear, his clothes folded in a neat pile. He steps in front of the chaise longue, extends his pile of clothes to the audience.*]

SASHA: My beat wardrobe is yours.

WALLACE BERMAN: O the pure of heart!

SASHA: Make a piece of it. Before I came to San Francisco, I never heard the saying, make a piece of it.

WALLACE BERMAN (*accepts gift of clothes*): Thanks, Sasha. I just had a vision, staring into the sun. One day I'm gonna be on the cover of Sergeant Pepper.

SASHA: Right next to Tony Curtis.

[*Exit WALLACE BERMAN and SASHA. BERMAN leaves paper bag on table. Enter ANALYST and JAY DeFEO.*]

ANALYST: Miss DeFeo, we must get to the root of your problems.

JAY DeFEO: I'll lie down here in my usual place on your couch, Dr. Filbert.

[*She does so, and ANALYST takes chair behind her.*]

ANALYST: You tell me that you're an artist, working inside a male-dominated art culture in San Francisco's North Beach?

JAY DeFEO: Yes, and it's so exciting. But sometimes I wonder, is it really worth all the frustration? Maybe I should have just married and moved to Daly City or the Richmond, wherever that is.

ANALYST (*coldly*): I live in Daly City.

JAY DeFEO: Oh! I didn't mean that—you know, that Daly City—your city—isn't filled with creativity and beauty. Is it?

[*Pause.*]

ANALYST: The days are fair there.

JAY DeFEO: Actually, I live in the Fillmore.

ANALYST: Now, Miss DeFeo, you manifest some difficulty when articulating your own case.

JAY DeFEO: All of my problems can be summed up in one word—Kay.

ANALYST: Ah yes, your imaginary twin sister.

JAY DeFEO: "Imaginary"—far from it! She's sneaky, that's all.

ANALYST: Kay DeFeo. How handy that a painting subject like yourself should have an imaginary twin sister who comes in at night and makes her painting larger and larger.

JAY DeFEO: And my studio is so dark now that she's made the painting so big it blocks out the window.

[*Enter KAY DeFEO.*]

KAY DeFEO: She doesn't think I'm real.

JAY DeFEO (*blinking and extending her hands as though she were blind*): I feel like Bette Davis at the end of *Dark Victory*.

KAY DeFEO: You didn't like "seeing" anyhow.

JAY DeFEO: Leave me alone!

ANALYST: Need some quiet time?

JAY DeFEO: Can't you see her?

ANALYST: No—I must have my glasses checked by my optician. My optician in Daly City.

KAY DeFEO (*to JAY*): Touché!

JAY (*to ANALYST, defeated*): Touché.

ANALYST: And you are married, I think?

JAY DeFEO: Yes—to Wally Hedrick.

ANALYST: What is it like, to be Jay DeFeo?

JAY DeFEO: Oh, sometimes it's this, sometimes that. Only rarely do I have the day to myself. I signed this stupid contract, when I was young and poor, trying to beat a shoplifting rap. Actually, Kay signed it.

KAY DeFEO: But I used her name. We're like two letters of the alphabet, "J" and "K," linked together by proximity and rue. A contract with Hall Mark cards. They wanted a simple little picture of a rose.

JAY DeFEO: Please, no details!

ANALYST: Details! Of course not, I'm not a Freudian by any means. You rented me from the Jung Institute. I was trained by Joseph Campbell.

KAY DeFEO: I bet!

JAY DeFEO: Please keep a civil tongue in your head.

KAY DeFEO: Rather than do so, I will return to the hardware store and fetch some more paint.

[*Exit KAY DeFEO.*]

ANALYST: I'm interested in your use of the rose as a sacred symbol.

JAY DeFEO (*sighing*): Well—

ANALYST: But our hour is up!

JAY DeFEO: Oh please, let me tell you about myself—

ANALYST: Walk briskly, then, I'm meeting Lenny Bruce at high noon in the Broadway Tunnel.

JAY DeFEO: And about my contract with Hall Mark—

ANALYST: Lenny Bruce will not be kept waiting!

JAY DeFEO: And my recessive subjectivity—

[*Exit ANALYST and JAY DeFEO; enter HALL MARK and WILMA. Music cue: James Bernard's theme for the Hammer Dracula movies.*]

HALL MARK: Wilma Vape?

WILMA: Yes, Hall Mark. I am here.

HALL MARK: Let us proceed to the house of the rose woman, Jay DeFeo. We shall make her follow our bargain. Have you the contract, Wilma Vape?

WILMA: In my reticule, Hall Mark, like a tragic leaf.

HALL MARK: "Reticule," what we in Germany would call a "knap-sack."

WILMA: It is the cloth bag in which a contractual document is kept, like the ark of the covenant. Call it knap-sack, if you want to sound like a square.

[*She makes the sign of the square with her fingers.*]

HALL MARK: You have been with me since the war.

WILMA: The war, the war. Always in my mind I hear the bombs, the shelling. As if, perhaps, you and I came as stowaways to San Francisco to found our fortune.

HALL MARK: I remember the porthole bringing closer to my hands the Golden Gate.

WILMA: Dear Jeanette MacDonald singing, "San Francisco."

[*Music cue. Instead of "San Francisco," again we hear the Dracula theme.*]

HALL MARK: Ah, you are a naughty one, Wilma Vape! Do you know the little sailors on our ship, and how I dandled them on my knee, each one laughing in a different Dutch argot?

WILMA: And now we own the largest card company in the world!

HALL MARK: "Hans," I said to one, the curly one with the amazing chest, "Hans, would you be my plaything in the New World?" Hans and I shared many jokes. We called the portholes our Dutch wives. [*He mimes having sex with porthole.*] That was our cunning acronym for relief—C.A.R.

WILMA: Hall Mark, let us sail on to Fillmore Street. Cold War's in bloom, and so's the need for Hall Mark cards. Soon everyone will be wearing them like state I.D.

[*Enter JAY DeFEO.*]

JAY DeFEO: Oh, look, Wallace Berman left the baby here.

HALL MARK (*to WILMA*): Let us clear our throats in meaningful manner.

[*They do so.*]

JAY (*swivels around, baby drops to floor*): Mr. Mark! Wilma Vape! I know I promised you that little picture of a rose. A year ago.

WILMA: Two years, DeFeo. Two long years you have kept Hall Mark waiting.

HALL MARK: A picture four inches by five inches, Hall Mark size.

JAY DeFEO: I'm afraid my rose has gotten out of hand.

HALL MARK: Out of hand? I'm afraid I don't—what do you say here in America?

WILMA: "Get it."

HALL MARK: "I don't get it." How could this be! You promised one cute picture of white rose for face of Hall Mark Card 2457. I and Wilma already pay you over thirty-five guilders.

WILMA: She is appealing in her misery.

JAY DeFEO: I have this sister, you see—

HALL MARK: Is she behind the Iron Curtain?

[*Enter BOB KAUFMAN.*]

BOB KAUFMAN: Silence, Jay DeFeo! Do not attempt to explain your plight to these two buccaneers of cards!

HALL MARK: Bob Kaufman? Another convicted felon.

BOB KAUFMAN: Cunning acronym for relief, dear sir. "C.A.R.D.S."

JAY DeFEO: Cards!

WILMA VAPE: From neither you—nor you—[*she points*] do we brook insolence. Hall Mark?

HALL MARK: Produce the picture at once.

JAY DeFEO: I'd need a crane.

WILMA (*to HALL MARK*): Large white bird, like the German "eglon."

JAY DeFEO: What I mean is it weighs 2,000 pounds.

WILMA: Bird known for standing on one leg, like stork.

HALL MARK: 2,000 pounds! All the sailors in my life don't weigh that much, even when laid end to end.

BOB KAUFMAN: My body once covered with beauty
Is now a museum of betrayal.
This part remembered because of that one's touch
This part remembered for that one's kiss.

HALL MARK: Vape! Seize this dark beautiful man, bring him to bedroom, sign him up to Hall Mark Cards as a poet.

WILMA VAPE: It will bring me pleasure.

BOB KAUFMAN: Today, I bring it back, and let you live forever.

WILMA VAPE: For that special someone.

JAY DeFEO: Bob—sign nothing! They'll take your soul and make greeting cards out of it!

[*Exit WILMA VAPE and BOB KAUFMAN: Enter JANIS JOPLIN.*]

JANIS: Is this big galoot bothering you, Miss DeFeo?

JAY DeFEO: No, Janis. [*In a burst of candor.*] Well, actually he is, but it's my fault, I suppose.

JANIS: I'm Janis—Janis Joplin—before I became famous. [*To HALL MARK.*] Can't you leave her be for one hour?

HALL MARK: Not even a minute. [*To AUDIENCE.*] What do you think of my US accent? I watch current TV programs for cues. I love me my favorite, *Andy of Mayberry*, and I try to mimic his stern ways of speaking. America's most powerful lawman, Sheriff Andy, tempted on the one hand by the mature curves of his old Aunt Bee and on the other by the boyish charm of young Opie. You dig?

JANIS: I swear, Jay DeFeo would have to have a hundred hands to do all the things people want from her.

JAY DeFEO: Oh, it's not that bad....

HALL MARK: Janis Joplin, a gawky girl from Port Arthur, no? In Texas, by Galveston? I know Port Arthur well, its sunny skies, its bordellos manned by cowhands.

JANIS: Port Arthur! I hated it there. I was the ugliest girl in town, they said, but here in North Beach I'm a human being with rights! Oh look, someone dropped the baby on the floor. [*Replaces baby on table.*] He'll keep, like a jar of Mama's bread and butter pickles. Miss DeFeo?

JAY DeFEO: Yes, Janis.

JANIS: Have I your permission to ham string this armadiller? We could make a skull out of his numbskull, put a candle in it, use it for Chianti. [*To HALL MARK.*] You're in North Beach now, and this lady's the hippest chick in town.

HALL MARK: Hip? Chick? She is a "hip chick," commit to memory. Rhymes with lip stick. I'll be back by night fall, and return for the painting or my name is not Walter Benjamin—I mean—Hall Mark.

[*Exit HALL MARK.*]

JAY DeFEO: "They" won't leave me alone.

JANIS: "They" never do! I'm not famous yet, but I will be, and then "they" will come after me.

JAY DeFEO: What I'd give for just one day of peace!

JANIS: I hate to tell you this, Miss DeFeo, but you have other visitors at the end of the long, dark tunnel of light you call your studio.

JAY DeFEO: I sense an innocent nature, blonde and young.

JANIS: That's the daughter.

JAY DeFEO: And a strong perfume.

JANIS: That's the mother.

[*Music cue. "Hooray for Hollywood." Enter MRS. WELD and TUESDAY WELD. Exit JANIS.*]

MRS. WELD: I was assured by Mr. Dennis Hopper that this was a decent, Christian home.

JAY DeFEO: How do you do?

MRS. WELD: An oxymoronic home.

JAY DeFEO: Are you Dorothy Miller, from the Whitney?

MRS. WELD: You've made a tragic mistake! I am Leonora Weld, and this is my daughter—[*mumbles*].

JAY DeFEO: I beg your pardon, I know the fumes are thick.

MRS. WELD (*struggling to pronounce name*): Tmbrrdwng.

JAY DeFEO (*to TUESDAY*): I can't make her out, what's your name, dear?

TUESDAY: Tuesday! Like the days of the week! I'm Tuesday Weld! Oh, Miss DeFeo, I have longed to meet you for years, and years!

MRS. WELD: Don't exaggerate. You're only fourteen.

TUESDAY: But a wise man looked into my eyes once, and told me I have the wisdom of the ancients. A wise man of Los Angeles, Dennis Hopper, now starring in *Night Tide*.

JAY DeFEO: Oh, yes. Well, your eyes are striking.

MRS. WELD: My daughter has taken a role in *The Many Loves of Dobie Gillis*, and the studio sent us here for research. Tuesday's led a sheltered life, and I intend to keep her cocooned. These black walls have to go. Black reminds me of Satan. Satan feeling frisky. Satan under the counter. Cheap.

JAY DeFEO: Tell me, Tuesday Weld, who gave you that unusual name?

MRS. WELD: That's a secret.

JAY DeFEO: Oh really?

MRS. WELD: Suffice it to say that she came with her name on a tag round her neck, like a kitten.

TUESDAY: I'm innocent, and sweet, like a cube of sugar. Let my blonde beauty radiate throughout your dark studio.

JAY DeFEO: Oh, why not! The Cholnakys have that corner over there. You can put your bags right here. Tuesday, this is where you'll learn about Beat Culture. I'm the epicenter of a new social movement that will rock this nation. And yet I keep an intense privacy around me, even as I move through life in my soon-to-be-chic painters smocks and tight cocktail gowns.

I'm particularly excited today. Important visitors arrive from the South. Oh, Mrs. Weld, think of it! The greatest artists of Mexico are coming to visit!

MRS. WELD (*visibly nervous*): Mexico!

JAY DeFEO: Yes, the land of the hot sun and shaking earth.

TUESDAY: Let's shake, rattle and roll!

JAY DeFEO: Drawn by my superb draftmanship and aura of tormented wisdom, they arrive any moment.

MRS. WELD: Artists! Which ones?

TUESDAY: Who, Miss DeFeo?

MRS. WELD: Let's all hide behind the couch. I'm afraid, I tell you—afraid of my past.

[*JAY, LEONORA, TUESDAY crouch behind couch. Enter COUNTESS CHOLNAKY and EVA.*]

COUNTESS: Ding-dong! In Budapest we no answer door for bohemian riffraff.

EVA: But here, we must. It is terrible, mother dear.

COUNTESS: I hate that painting, it is wet, always wet, and alive, like Venus Fly Trap.

EVA: I lost my American hula hoop by swinging it too close to vivid gulping painting.

COUNTESS: And I my gloves. Big painting, wet with paint, simply swallow them up! Poof, gone. Doorbell ring and ring, like finger probing my heart.

EVA: Come and lie down on American fiberglas cushion. It is like lifeboat. We dream on, maybe dreams take us back to Budapest.

[*COUNTESS lies on couch. Enter OFFICER BIGARINI.*]

EVA: Why, it's the secret police! Come in, please, do!

BIGARINI (*awkwardly*): These flowers are for you.

COUNTESS: Oh! And who are you, blue boy?

BIGARINI: Just a kid from Green Street who grew up a total hard-ass.

EVA (*takes flowers*): Yet you come to me, Little Big, with your heart on your sleeve?

BIGARINI: Mama always said, always arrest the pretty girls! One of 'em's got to put out sometime.

EVA: These flowers—they are not for our Hollywood blonde? They are for me?

BIGARINI: The boys down at the precinct are gonna think I've gone soft.

[*JAY leaps up from behind couch.*]

JAY DeFEO: I heard the doorbell—was it Dorothy Miller?

COUNTESS: Mexican people at door. I spit on you, De Feo, and your Mexican friends.

EVA: She is very strange woman, with monkeys crawling up and down her face. He is large fat man like—

COUNTESS: Like Stalin, who curdles my gut. Eva, we go. Let Mexican people come in, lounge and laugh and paint like peasants.

EVA: We go, goodbye.

COUNTESS: We go to Union Square, sit in park like pigeons of royalty.

EVA: Gumps maybe. Come with, Officer Bigarini.

OFFICER. Maybe I will, maybe I won't.

[*Exit COUNTESS, EVA, BIGARINI.*]

MRS. WELD: Mexican artists! I must go to Gump's as well. I'll follow those Hungarians, like a bridesmaid in heat.

JAY: Well, at least say "hi." This will be exposure for Tuesday.

TUESDAY: Oh, mother, please may I?

[*Enter DIEGO RIVERA. MRS. WELD hides her face.*]

RIVERA: Ola! [*To JAY.*] I am Diego Rivera, man of the people! You are lovely lady of the Rose, the mystical symbol of our love!

JAY: What an honor! Diego Rivera, returning to North Beach at last!

RIVERA: And you, American, like corned beef and kibbles.

JAY: Often I have looked at your mural at the Art Institute, studying and dreaming.

RIVERA: Now we paint together, you and me.

JAY: And Frida Kahlo? She is here, too?

RIVERA (*impatiently*): Frida is in kitchen, making tortillas for Rivera. She is little woman, little hands, she must spend long hours to wrap hands around tortilla dough. But when she finished, oh my God! A tortilla of perfection!

MRS. WELD: Goodbye, Miss DeFeo.

RIVERA: Wait! Hollywood woman, let me catch you with my hands! I know you, do I not?

MRS. WELD: You certainly do not, senor.

RIVERA: You look strangely familiar.

MRS. WELD: Release me, sir.

RIVERA: And your delicate skin, like the hide of little gray burro. I have felt this skin before, in Mexico, in my country!

MRS. WELD: Never been there. Come, Tuesday!

RIVERA (*alert to nuance*): Your daughter is called "Tuesday"?

TUESDAY: Tuesday's child is fair of face, adorable and full of grace.

RIVERA: You are regular Cantinflas! Dance for me, Miss Tuesday, while I gaze with longing and regret at the tiny body of your mother, and locate her within the deep catalogue raisonné of my memory bank!

JAY: Come and see my big picture, Mr. Rivera. Tuesday will dance for you later.

RIVERA: She is cute ballerina on top of music box, but her mother is so much more!

JAY: Enough about them! What about me?

RIVERA: Kierkegaard tells us, "The very mark of my genius is that Governance broadens and radicalizes whatever concerns me personally." [*To MRS. WELD.*] That mean you, striking phantom. Frida! Fridita! Come and see strange American woman!

[*Enter FRIDA KAHLO. Music cue: "La Malaguena."*]

FRIDA: Rivera, no shouting! [*Sees JAY, and clasps her hands.*] Muy caramba, how lovely, like a blood clot!

DIEGO: Not her, this tall woman here, ten stories' worth of tall. Did you love her, or did I, when we were young and full of bananas?

FRIDA (*gaze swivels to LEONORA, but then back to JAY*): I see her, but my eyes, my dark coal eyes, swing—like a pendulum, or a boomerang, to return to lovely dark haired, paint-stained, San Francisco woman.

JAY: I am Jay DeFeo.

FRIDA: I stab myself, with desire.

TUESDAY: Oh, darn, my little watch says, two hands on the hour, I have an appointment with the young Lawrence Ferlinghetti. He has promised to show me his paintings!

MRS. WELD: They're said to be quite unsettling.

[*Exit MRS. WELD and TUESDAY.*]

JAY: Frida, I'm flattered. But you don't understand what we're trying to do here in San Francisco. This isn't about sex or even about life. We're delving deep inside ourselves to try to find the true divination of the Holy Spirit who gave us birth.

FRIDA: Reproach me then—I beg of you.

DIEGO (*aside*): That tall woman—I know her, but where or when?

JAY: We're in the Cold War and I'm surprised they even let you two into the country.

FRIDA: Sneaked in!

DIEGO (*in agreement*): We sneak. [*Aside.*] Leonora Weld! Who is she? Now Leonora Carrington I know. Won her from Max Ernst in poker game. Oh that crazy night at Berggruen's. But this magnificent tiger woman—I don't remember remembering her!

FRIDA: Devour me, Jay DeFeo, or I put my head in paper bag and blow up like balloon. [*Picks up paper bag.*] Oh—a baby! Muchacho mio?

JAY: That's the Berman baby.

FRIDA: He is my kewpie doll, I take him to remember how a woman artist of San Francisco made me into her slave bracelet.

DIEGO (*sternly*): Put down, Frida!

[*Reluctantly FRIDA replaces baby on couch.*]

JAY: We're under pressure to conform, to be these Mom and Dad cutter cookies. Cookie cutters. But not me, me, Jay DeFeo. I don't know where I found the courage to defy the zeitgeist, but here I flicker, like a shadow in my cave, drinking my seven and sevens and making a stand.

RIVERA: You say, "no" to patriarchy.

JAY: "No," to New York values of art.

RIVERA: "No," to frivolous exploitation.

JAY: And "no" to the Whitney. —Though Kay has other ideas.

[*Enter DOROTHY MILLER.*]

DOROTHY MILLER: I've come back one more time to beg you to let me include you in my epochal "Sixteen Americans" show in 1960.

DIEGO RIVERA: Dorothy Miller! I love a curator.

JAY DeFEO: I'll send my work—and Wally will too—but I don't want to go to New York.

DOROTHY: This show will make household names of Robert Rauschenberg, Jasper Johns, many more.

JAY DeFEO: You are very kind, but Jasper and I have made a pact. I don't go to New York, and he doesn't come to San Francisco!

DIEGO RIVERA: Turf war, Jay DeFeo?

DOROTHY MILLER: May I take the Rose with me, then?

JAY DeFEO: Take anything but that!

FRIDA: Hello Miss Miller. Like a bride I come to you, blushing, roses in my cheeks, and a postage stamp pasted to my forehead. Hail, Dorothy Miller, come talk with me about new show, I propose magical "Sixteen Mexicans" show.

[*Exit DOROTHY and FRIDA KAHLO.*]

JAY: Frida's great. I love her enthusiasm!

DIEGO: Usually she just lie in bed, look depressed, like piñata without candy.

JAY: Señor Rivera, I have a professional question. Did you ever sign a contract with Hall Mark Cards, planning to make just a little picture of a rose?

RIVERA: Of sunflower, yes! Hall Mark Card 473!

JAY: And say you had an invisible twin who kept coming to your room at night and making it larger—larger and larger—

RIVERA: Like the old Spanish legend of the duende!

JAY: And now I'm afraid—what happens when I give up my painting?

RIVERA: My sunflower picture, tiny as my fingernail, grew to huge proportions. Hall Mark and Wilma come, and Bigarini slam my fingers in drawer, like Paul Newman in *The Hustler*.

JAY (*recoiling*): My hands—broken by goons?

RIVERA: You learn to live without them! Look at me, wriggle my joints!

JAY (*sinking to a chair*): It's just that—sometimes gloom overcomes me.

RIVERA: Me, too! They call me—the sad sad sack. Me and Frida, we lie in bed and brood over fate of little people under U S foreign policy.

JAY: So I told my analyst—

[*Enter ANALYST.*]

JAY: Why are my dreams so big?

ANALYST: Instead ask yourself, why has your gender been squashed, a day late and a dollar short?

JAY: I wanted one tiny perfect thing, is that too much to ask?

ANALYST: Only in America.

JAY: Here you get many, many, dozens of large imperfect things. God, I went to a US school and I felt I was passing the cemetery.

ANALYST: As you neared completion of "The Rose," did it sadden you?

JAY DeFEO: What a leading question! [*To RIVERA.*] And while I was in there discussing my problems, Kay was here, in my studio, enlarging my picture like some Carol Doda Tom Wolfe silicone explosion.

RIVERA: Kay? Que Kay?

JAY DeFEO: She's my twin sister. All right, maybe she's not my twin. Maybe she's not even my sister.

RIVERA (*to ANALYST, as he pushes JAY off the couch*): I am Diego Rivera. I like professional women very very much. I paint you as the spirit of Daly City at carnival time, I make love to you like wild Fiji of Mazatlan.

ANALYST (*lightly*): I'm expensive.

RIVERA: I sell a painting to you, we will discuss money and love at—Cafe Trieste.

ANALYST. Tell me, Mr. Rivera, why murals? Why so big a canvas?

RIVERA: My family is big—it includes the whole world, including Johnnie Ray and Walt Disney.

ANALYST: When you lived in the hacienda, were your parents having sexual intercourse in your bed?

RIVERA: In my bed? On my, how do you say, stomacho. Very messy, they ruin pjs of Mexican boy. I take you to cafe, you buy champagne for Rivera. My little toothpick, I shall insert you in gold, molar gold! [*He indicates an exit.*] This way?

ANALYST: Must be, there's no other way.

[*Exit ANALYST and DIEGO RIVERA.*]

JAY DeFEO: All good things must come to an end, I suppose. For close to six years now, I've breathed in the fumes of lead paint. Dear me, how unusual when one's psychiatrist takes a romantic interest in one's Mexican idol. I need some poetry! Poetry in my life.

I'll call Jack Spicer. No wait, he doesn't have a phone. No wait, he's said to hate women. Is it Kay he dislikes? I thought he loved me—or was he just being kind? Or am I losing—

[*Enter KAY.*]

Kay, do not torment me now.

KAY: I come with good news, sister dear.

JAY DeFEO: Are the police here to break my fingers in the drawer?

KAY: No—not yet! Here's what—

[*Enter HELEN ADAM. Music cue: Scottish music like bagpipes.*]

HELEN: Knock-knock! May I come in, like a little bird?

JAY DeFEO (*delighted*): Helen Adam! Of course, come in.

HELEN: I was passing on the street, and heard you from the window. You said you wanted poetry. Or were you just being kind? Hello, Jay. Hello, Kay.

JAY DeFEO: Oh Helen, I've been so—Wait—did you say, "Hello" to Kay? So you can see her?

HELEN: I'm Scottish you know, and we gifted ones see things! Even the invisible.

KAY: I'm as real as you are, Jay, maybe realer.

JAY DeFEO: Helen Adam, beloved Scottish poet, now the beloved poet of the North Beach bohemians, poets and artists. No one knows why you recite your old school ballads in that sing-songy voice, but you know what, we just love you to death.

HELEN: Yes, dear, and I have second sight, which came to me with the waters I drank in Loch Lomond.

KAY: And what does your second sight tell you?

HELEN: I can't see you, Kay, but I know you mean no good for our lovely Jay. Look at her, she is the curious blue jay of the highlands, and you are like the fog over the brae.

JAY DeFEO: Sing us a song, Helen.

HELEN: One of my bloodthirsty ballads that have made me famous?

KAY: Oh, why not. You're a freak, lady!

HELEN: My poem is called, I strangled my love with a scarf.
"When I was a young girl all giddy and gay,
I met a young laddie from Fotheringay."

KAY: Great rhyming! "Gay" and "Fotheringay."

HELEN: "But when he came near me I started to cough,
Hey hey,
So I strangled my love with a scarf."

[*JAY applauds, and after a bit, so does KAY.*]

HELEN: Verse Two. "The.... living fleece of my long black hair
He combed with a flair that was debonair.
But his voice was a squeak, like a rat on the wharf,"

JAY and KAY: Hey, hey!

HELEN: "So I strangled my love with a scarf."

KAY: Hey, hey, Jay! Now you're learning something.

JAY: Thank you, Helen—there's just one thing—I'm wondering about—is there
something you're trying to tell me, with your mystical Scottish cane and your pierc-
ing black eyes?

HELEN: Listen to the poem that's in all of us! It's violent and harsh, like life!

KAY: You tell em, Helen Adam!

HELEN: "In medieval Scotland, life can be cruel,
And your man will control you, if you give him the tool.
So when he comes near you, and you want to barf—"

KAY and JAY and HELEN: "Hey, hey,
Then strangle the fool with your scarf."

HELEN: And now I have to go, the spirits call—Anubis! Diana! What a lovely
visit, Jay, and no tea for once.

KAY Goodbye, Helen.

HELEN (*looking in another direction*): Fare thee well, Kay.

[*Exit HELEN ADAM.*]

JAY DeFEO: Maybe she's right! I wanted one perfect rose, but you came in, night after night, as I lay sleeping, and added extra cells and layers. It's fat in the middle, like pregnancy, and in it are lost many household items like curlers, gloves, and tears.

KAY: Yes, and you will be famous!

JAY: But I never wanted fame, only the respect of people at the "6" Gallery.
KAY: That's what you think.

[*Enter HALL MARK: Music cue: Dracula theme again.*]

HALL MARK: I must adjust my bifocals. I'm seeing double.

JAY: Hello, Mr. Hall Mark.

HALL MARK: Mr. Mark. "Hall" is my first name. Isn't it a common name here in California?

JAY: It usually refers to a kind of passageway between two rooms.

KAY: It's common as pig tracks. Hello, Hall!

HALL MARK: On the border between France and Spain, I lost most of my right ear, and grew this hair to cover it. I was all alone; the Fascist troops behind me. So you must speak up.

KAY: Your painting will be ready tomorrow morning.

JAY: I'm sorry, I'm not done with it yet.

KAY: It's 2,000 pounds, weighs more than you do.

JAY: A little rose, small as a Hall Mark card.

HALL MARK: You're confusing me, Miss DeFeo. I suspect, on purpose. I am the European man, I come from an old culture with new ideas about art, in an age of mechanical reproduction. You and your kind are doomed, as my greeting cards and allied developments burnt the heart out of your individual project.

[*HALL MARK and JAY stand very close to one another.*]

JAY DeFEO: You can't threaten me. What's the worst that could happen to a woman? It happened already—and to me.

HALL MARK: I stood in the cottage of the voluble Basque villagers, gun in hand. Should I shoot myself, or no? I thought back to all I learned in the Frankfurt School, the clever lessons of use and adversity. I, Walter Benjamin.

KAY: Why did you change your mind?

HALL MARK: With the barrel in my mouth, my gaze fell onto the little cards Spanish peasants send each other to cheer each other up when crops fail or bulls gore their sons in city arenas. Little cards, four inches by five inches. And as I gazed, gun in mouth, the bright colored cards made me happy.

JAY DeFEO: So then, you figured—

HALL MARK: You might as well live! Live, live, live! Life is a banquet, and most sons of bitches are starving to death!

KAY: What a disgusting story.

JAY DeFEO: A lovely parable.

HALL MARK: Now it is midnight. I will be back when the sun rises, to take possession of my painting. Like your studio, the future of bourgeois individualism is dark indeed.

[*Exit HALL MARK.*]

KAY: My new plan is to make a film, starring you. Tomorrow when the crane comes, I want you sitting there looking wistfully at "The Rose" as the wall comes down.

JAY DeFEO: Oh, no, Kay, I couldn't! I'm so camera-shy!

KAY: And I know the perfect man to direct this movie!

JAY DeFEO: Who?

KAY: Kenneth Anger, of course! He's here in San Francisco, over on Polk Street, shooting "Scorpio Rising." I'll go fetch him, shall I?

[Enter JANIS JOPLIN.]

JAY: No—Kay—no, please!

[Exit KAY DeFEO, JAY running after her.]

JANIS: I thought I saw two of them—whoa, Janis girl, better lay off the Southern Comfort! I lay on my back on the floor, staring at "The Rose," for twenty-four hours, till when I shut my eyes I saw this black rose spinning like a pinwheel. It was trippy, man! My throat loosened up like gravel was being shoved down my larynx, or was that Joe Namath? When I woke, I could sing, or gargle, and I traded in my cowgirl suit for the full Haight Fillmore drag. I became a woman of style, at the same time that I lost my wits. Who's this?

[Enter BOBBY BEAUSOLEIL.]

BOBBY: I'm Bobby. Kenneth Anger sent me over to add the street trash element to his magnum opus on "The Rose."

JANIS: You're Bobby McGee?

BOBBY: Bobby Beausoleil.

JANIS (*sizing him up*): "Busted flat in Baton Rouge—waitin' for a train—"

BOBBY: From the Manson family. I'm this long, lean, lanky piece of street candy poured into vinyl like liquid prime rib.

JANIS: Welcome, young stranger! I was feelin' 'bout as faded as my jeans. See this fringe? It was just hanging there like Spanish moss till you moved your hips in my rearview mirror.

BOBBY: You're pretty for a girl. In jail we didn't see many women, only each other.

JANIS: Poor boy, and now you're saddled with Kenneth Anger? I heard he was rough on his leading men.

[Enter SASHA (dressed again).]

SASHA: Janis, Janis, help me. America's #1 poet is at the door!

JANIS (*to BOBBY*): That's Michael McClure. He and I are writing a song together, "Mercedes Benz." He's as cute as you are, only dark, where you are fair.

SASHA: Michael McClure! A friend of Hungary, a friend to America!

JANIS (*to BOBBY*): Quick now—what's the one thing you want out of life?

BOBBY (*instantly*): Parole.

SASHA: The friend of lions! He has written a special poem in Beast Language in honor of Miss DeFeo.

[*Enter MICHAEL McCLURE and WALLACE BERMAN, Berman with guitar.*]

WALLACE BERMAN (*looks in bag*): How's my boy? The world treating you all right?

MICHAEL McCLURE: Dark brown, color of whale intestine!
Funky clitoral petals of rose, unfold in thrusting waves of
FEEE REEE ROW
A-BOOM FUGO FEE REEE RU

WALLACE BERMAN: Thy kisses are like lily centopads, thy thighs like Caryl Chessman preying on couples in lovers lane.

MICHAEL McCLURE: Rose painting! Like a thumbtack through my mind! The punctum of the absurd, endowed with an irrevocable punctum!

WALLACE BERMAN: Thy rich tresses like spotlights glittering along the waters of Babylon, thy cheeks like red marshmallows, soaked in blood of lovers.

MICHAEL McCLURE: At the moment of ultimate madness of zombie hesitation I, poet of ecstatic wisdom, mix butter and black paint, make a new song under the earth, under Artaud, mad cub of night outfoxed!

WALLACE BERMAN: Let thy petals fall on top of my primitive Xerox machine so I may make a sign unto Zion.

MICHAEL McCLURE: Peyote dramas of bright lights electrify my brain fence, top secret gossip surrounds the world like hands I see in the future. Row of wild beasts join trunks and tails, Barnum and Bailey animal crackers, high, high as kites.

WALLACE BERMAN: Lo, I have seen her in Estanian, where the Lord of the dark places hath rendered her native. Are you there yet?

MICHAEL McCLURE: I go, into the future, for all things are meat, with creatures springing from it in chic lavender, duende black, blue and red bacteria!

[*Exit MICHAEL McCLURE.*]

SASHA: Three cheers for Mr. Cool and Mr. Berman, hurrah.

WALLACE BERMAN: So the baby's been no trouble?

BOBBY: Gee, Janis, I'd like to be your boyfriend, but I have another girl I've tattooed to my chest, feel. [*Takes her hand, puts it on his chest.*]

JANIS (*reading chest*): Tuesday Weld!

BOBBY: I met her in a vice den down in Chinatown. I showed her the jailhouse rock, she showed me how they do it in Hollywood.

JANIS: You're out on the street, looking good, but baby, deep down in your heart, you know that ain't right.

SASHA: Someday I dream of becoming American artist and being iconoclastic. You have fun here.

JANIS: Oh! Big fun! It's Port Arthur all over again. Sasha, come with me and help me dry the painting. I've got to gangbang some quarterbacks, give me back my self-esteem.

SASHA: Okay.

JANIS: Oh, here she is again, Miss Popularity.

[*Enter TUESDAY WELD. JANIS spits at her on her way out. Exit JANIS and SASHA. TUESDAY is now quite altered in look, like Olivia Newton-John at the end of "Grease."*]

TUESDAY: Goodbye. Mr. Berman, I love your sound.

WALLACE BERMAN: You're a cute chick, but I'm a married man with a baby. [*Brings forward bundle.*] This is him. It's a boy.

TUESDAY: Teach me to play the guitar.

BOBBY: Tuesday! We cut our thighs together, rubbed blood on my chest.

TUESDAY: I had enough commitment in Hollywood, Bobby, thanks to 20th Century Fox.

BOBBY: Say, Mister, I'm Bobby Beausoleil, dig? I've got talent! Let's jam.

[*Enter LEONORA WELD.*]

LEONORA: Let me feel that inscription. It's a living scar. Young man, have you been making lewd advances to my daughter?

TUESDAY: Mother! I was innocent, but Bobby says his hobby is "corrupting Tuesday."

BOBBY (*to BERMAN*): I'm the white Chet Baker, Mister! Give me a break, I can't stay Kenneth Anger's love slave forever.

BERMAN: First, we are going to learn the Yigdal, the ancient Jewish piyyut. Kabballah tradition says that in early times, wind instruments were considered particularly sacred. Thus, says Rabbi Vohar, the word "Hanukkah" is derived from "harmonica."

BOBBY: Cool!

LEONORA: Now scat, boy!

BOBBY: Tuesday, you're just mad because I spelled your name wrong.

TUESDAY: What's so hard about "Tuesday"? It has a "u" in it. And a "T." You just skipped right ahead to the "E."

BOBBY: That weren't no "E," sorry doll.

[*Exit WALLACE BERMAN and BOBBY BEAUSOLEIL.*]

TUESDAY: Mr. Berman, you forgot your baby!

LEONORA (*advances towards the audience, miserably*): So did I. (*To TUESDAY.*) What have you to say for yourself? Make-up! Cosmetics! High heels! Intercourse!

TUESDAY: Mother, you're embarrassing me and embarrassing yourself.

LEONORA (*unrolls newspaper*): You're in Herb Caen's column. "Teenage Tuesday Weld cavorting at Trader Vic's." Vile!

TUESDAY: Mother, it's time for a heart to heart.

LEONORA: You're acting like a slut.

TUESDAY: The apple doesn't fall far from the tree.

LEONORA: What are you implying, young lady?

TUESDAY: I was having a little chat with Russ Tamblyn, he spilled some beans— jumping beans, Mama.

LEONORA: Okay. I give up.

TUESDAY: Mexican jumping beans!

LEONORA: I said, "okay"! You want to hear the whole story?

TUESDAY: Of course I do.

LEONORA: I was in Tijuana with Max Ernst, Peggy Guggenheim, Arthur Cravan—the whole Surrealist bunch. Lovely little lunch. A small orchestra—just three trumpets and a castanet. Okay, I had some rum and Coke. I was feeling good, Tuesday. Is that a crime?

TUESDAY: And?

LEONORA: And a little man asked me to dance. I thought he was a waiter. And Peggy said, Leonora, give him a tip. We danced the cucaracha. And—[*lost in thought*] and it was Tuesday, I recall! "Martes," in Spanish. Next thing I knew, nine months later. I was lying in a ward in Juarez, and tied to the leg of my bed was a basket. You were in the basket, dear. Taped to your nose, I saw a tag, like a price tag, with one mysterious word. "Martes." So I named you that. Well, Tuesday.

TUESDAY: Oh Mother, why didn't you tell me this sooner?

LEONORA: Because I wanted to watch you grow up.

TUESDAY: There are some things no mother can do for her daughter, and one is to live her whole life for her.

LEONORA: They say only a woman who forgets childbirth will have another baby.

TUESDAY: Blow out the candles, Leonora Weld. I don't like what's in so I must be out. [*Picks up bundle.*] Rockabye, baby, in the tree top . . .

LEONORA (*joining her in song*): "When the wind blows, the cradle will rock." What a cute baby, what's his name?

TUESDAY: Tosh. T-O-S-H. Like Shot spelled backwards over Bobby Beausoleil's juvenile chest.

LEONORA: "Tosh"! What an odd name! Wonder how they came up with that?

TUESDAY (*acidly*): Gee Mother, let's think. Shirley Berman woke up in a Juarez clinic and there was a little price tag on the baby's nose.

LEONORA: How can you mock my woe, my amnesia? Put down that baby and empathize!

TUESDAY (*puts baby on table*): What did this little Mexican waiter look like, Mother?

LEONORA (*haunted*): I thought he was Mexican . . .

[*Enter HALL MARK and JAY DeFEO.*]

HALL MARK: I demand my painting, now!

LEONORA: But he could have been from the Frankfurt School.

JAY DeFEO: Mr. Mark, this is Leonora Weld. And her daughter, Tuesday, an ingenue.

LEONORA (*turns her back*): I mustn't face the great Hall Mark without my makeup.

TUESDAY: Were you ever in Mexico, Mr. Mark? Do you know the cucaracha?

LEONORA: What's the best place for makeup in San Francisco?

TUESDAY: Foxy Lady, on Mission. Come on, Mother, I'll take you there. By the way, Mr. Mark, where's your assistant, Wilma Vape?

HALL MARK: She is negotiating with Wayne Thiebaud for some pictures of cake for Hall Mark Cards. She will be here shortly to supervise removal of "Rose."

TUESDAY: This way, Mother. Forward march!

[*Exit LEONORA and TUESDAY.*]

HALL MARK: Is very charming girl of the lower classes. But the other woman, the mother, mm, she stir some pine-sweet memory in ancient oaken heart.

JAY DeFEO: So, you hold me to ancient contract. [*Aside.*] Why am I talking like him? Out of some kind of protective coloration?

[*Enter ANALYST.*]

ANALYST: You ape the manners and morals of men, seeking in their absent centers the original rupture.

JAY DeFEO: Should I be lying down?

HALL MARK: I hold you to the Magna Carda, the right of card holders over all their serfs. Hand over your oils. This senseless over-painting must cease, and cease today.

ANALYST: Men always fret when they see a woman doing something twice. Why not abandon feminist art and paint Walter Keane's big-eyed waifs for him? He needs help.

JAY DeFEO: I'm torn!

ANALYST: Nothing new, due to your gender.

[*Enter FRIDA KAHLO.*]

FRIDA: I wish to have talk with you, Miss Filbert.

ANALYST: Uh-oh. [*Confiding in JAY.*] I had a little transference with her husband at the Top of the Mark.

FRIDA: Filbert, in your country the name of a nut..

ANALYST: And of a pleasant street, here in the Marina. [*To JAY.*] He left love bites on my neck that gleam like plantains. [*To FRIDA.*] Shall we walk up and down my pleasant street like two old friends?

FRIDA (*consulting monkeys*): Let me ask my monkeys. What do you say, my monkeys? This is Frida, and this is Diego. Frida says, she used to be "Friday," only a little Mexican man snipped the "y" off her nose. [*Sadly.*] Now she is Frida. [*Turns to other shoulder.*] And Diego, what do you say?

ANALYST (*patiently, still nervous*): Hi, Diego! What do you say?

FRIDA: Diego says, [*uses monkey voice*] "I slept with a psychiatrist named Magda Filbert!" Ho, ho, ho, my little monkey—very funny!

ANALYST: Cheeky thing!

FRIDA: In Mexico, I killed Trotsky for less,—Tina Modotti too.

ANALYST: Well, let's walk… towards the police station.

FRIDA: We go. And Frida says, "But I fell in love with woman, Jay DeFeo, woman of fire and mango and wine." We go, Magda Filbert.

HALL MARK: I will consult sales slip of 1953.

[*Exit FRIDA and ANALYST.*]

JAY DeFEO: That old thing. I made a Faustian bargain with you, Walter Benjamin.

HALL MARK: Yes. For $12.00, and I own "The Rose." [*Sharply.*] How would you know my name?

[*Enter KENNETH ANGER.*]

KENNETH ANGER: Ah—the children of the Night! You must be Jay DeFeo. I am the last of the performers on this bill.

HALL MARK: How do you do, Bill? I am—Hall Mark.

KENNETH ANGER: You have mistaken me for Bill. Though I know you fell asleep in my arms, aboard the Queen Mary. I am the inimitable Kenneth Anger.

HALL MARK: Ah! The genius who will film the events of tomorrow. When I take possession of my painting.

JAY (*aside*): When I lose my reason for living.

KENNETH ANGER: But you, my darling, are too old to play Jay DeFeo. [*Studies her face with hand.*] I will have Bobby playing you, walking down the stairs with light in his cupped hands, and you can be some old bag woman who looks on with regret.

HALL MARK (*rubbing his hands*): So—tomorrow morning, we meet here at dawn. I shall bring my crane, you your camera, and you your tears. In thunder, lightning or in Rainer, as I said on shipboard to a little, merry, elf sailor.

When he knelt on the floor I filled his mouth with cotton as one would an aspirin bottle, in my country. —America. [*Picks up baby.*]   I'll take out the trash on my way out.

[*Exit HALL MARK with baby.*]

ANGER: Well, as Scarlett says, tomorrow is another day! [*To JAY DeFEO.*] My dear, is there anyone in North Beach who looks like you, only less—well, less paint-scraped? I mean—there's a whole Caravaggio on your face—no, a Rembrandt or Holbein or whoever did all those elderly Dutch women touching utensils and looking dowdy.

JAY: Well—

ANGER: Is it Vermeer?

JAY: I have a twin sister, who doesn't sow, only reaps.

ANGER: And they say there are no miracles

JAY: But I've tried snapping her with a camera, and she just disappears from the frame!

ANGER: Like my famous photo of Marlon Brando! What that man can put away!

JAY: Disappears! Like a vampire . . . or a figment of—why, maybe she's not real at all.

ANGER: Well, real or imaginary, she's got to look better than you. We'll try a nice Kodachrome exposure, shall we, and hope for the best. What's her name?

JAY: Kay.

ANGER: Now, Jay, I want you—actually "Kay"—to be staring sadly out of this wall—the fourth wall [*points towards audience*]—which we will remove tomorrow at dawn. It will be you, here, Fillmore Street, there. I have a lovely swimsuit for you to wear, made of nylon, nylon from the parachutes of our brave boys of Iwo Jima, then spun by human jaws and ejaculated on by pet Marines.

Where's that Bobby Beausoleil? In French, his name means, Beautiful Sun, but just don't call him late for supper.

JAY: I wanted to do the thing Wally Berman always says, to be the creator, the kim-kam of the Kabbalah who, in the ultimate act of self-abnegation, removes herself from the site of work in order to—

ANGER: To let the work find its own space to unfold. Yes, dear, of course you did. Me too, I'm just less braggy about it.

JAY: And now it's leaving me.

ANGER: Right! But my film will make you famous, so what's a little empty nest?

[*Enter COUNTESS CHOLNAKY, with bag.*]

COUNTESS: We have a saying in Budapest . . . let San Francisco fall into the sea, the angels will laugh. I found this bag on the stairs. Bag is human!

ANGER: And who's this cheerful dowager?

JAY: Another boarder.

ANGER: I love her complexion, like a bag of cocaine broke in my pocket.

COUNTESS: You—dark woman. I give notice with this month's rent.

[*Enter EVA.*]

EVA: Mama, this woman, Jay, may be tool of Stalin, but she has let us live here free.

ANGER: How generous.

EVA: If you can call it living. Like manger!

ANGER (*to EVA*): I will put you in my film—you, my ingenue, will have sexual intercourse with a great Shetland Pony, who represents Bobby Beausoleil.

COUNTESS: And now, I leave, I marry again.

ANGER: These Hungarians! Look at Zsa Zsa, married twelve times. [*To EVA.*] A Shetland pony, brown, clop-clop, many hooves, with enormous erection and boyish grin, like Bobby.

EVA: Mama! Who you marry?

COUNTESS: I go to him now. Diego Rivera, of Mexico.

JAY DeFEO: What on earth are you thinking? He's married already.

ANGER: The virgin waits on the altar of the Rose. Slowly, on four long legs, with great neighs of pleasure, the Shetland pony approaches, bowlegged, pinned with colorful ribbons. You feed him sugar, darling, stroke his genitalia.

JAY DeFEO: Are you sure there hasn't been some mistake?

EVA: Mama, this American man's a-spooks me.

COUNTESS: We have been man and wife for many months. He may be a Stalinist, but I forgive a man his faults when he loves the Countess so deeply. Together we return to Hungary, restore feudal system.

JAY DeFEO: How on earth do you plan to dispose of Frida Kahlo?

COUNTESS: Eva, you know man on cable car?

EVA: Yes, mama. Very nice Hungarian man, Josef.

COUNTESS: Very sympathetic to cause.

ANGER: I know him. I helped him call out all the stops from Powell Street to the wharf.

COUNTESS: Frida is on cable car now. I arrange small accident with driver.

[*Enter FRIDA KAHLO, pierced by spoke from cable car,*]

COUNTESS: My plan succeeds, she useless now as woman.

EVA: Good only as spectacle.

JAY DeFEO: My God, Frida, what happened?

FRIDA: I was riding up and down your famous hills. The driver gave me funny look—the evil eye, then he slam the brakes and I fly, through your famous air, like mockingbird.

JAY DeFEO: That pole or whatever must be killing you.

FRIDA: Yes, and only you can soothe me. Take me, Jay, to your black studio where the pine trees of Jesus litter the floor and paint.

COUNTESS: Rivera divorce her now quicker than the good paprika.

EVA (*sneezing*): Ah-choo!

ANGER: God bless you. I mean—Satan bless you.

JAY: I know I have some band-aids and mercurochrome, unless Kay added them to the painting.

FRIDA (*to JAY*): I, Frida, rent with pain, look at your angelic face and find rest there.

ANGER: Madame Kahlo, with that pole through your middle you are now an interesting example of California funk junk assemblage. Half human being, half iron rod, half goddess. Will you play Anais Nin in my new film, "Wet Paint?"

KAHLO. If Jay wants me to do so, Kenneth Anger.

JAY: We must see to your wound at once.

KAHLO. Ah, I was hoping you would, mm, say that.

[*Exit JAY DeFEO and KAHLO.*]

ANGER: You two are evil, and that's the nicest thing I can say about anyone, male or female.

EVA: We make wedding gown now, for Mama. Cream lace and cherries, like proper bride of Hungary.

COUNTESS: Man of anger, you shall throw rose petals in my wake.

[*Exit COUNTESS and EVA.*]

ANGER: I've lit the fireworks. Jay DeFeo—walking a perilous tightope between obscurity and fame in the late 1950s. The brilliant romantic artist, taunted by sister Kay DeFeo. Kay, who sneaks in night after night to dash more paint on Jay's finished production. Jay, woman, rebel, artist, haunted by a shoplifting arrest in her past, and puzzled by how dark her apartment seems to be getting . . .

[*Enter DIEGO RIVERA.*]

RIVERA: Are they gone?

ANGER: You are not marrying that Countess, I hope.

RIVERA: Nor her daughter, Eva, either. I have made love to both, but a man has got to do what a man must do, for Stalin.

ANGER: Substitute "Satan" for "Stalin," and there, in a nutshell, is the reason I made "Kustom Kar Kommandos."

RIVERA: Feel, the sweat on my brow, flowing like wet bull sperm.

ANGER: *Olé!* Señor Rivera, have you seen my brand, Bobby Beausoleil? I bought him from Bigarini at juvenile hall for two bottles of Dr. Pepper and a rookie Roger Maris.

RIVERA: They are throwing rice in my direction. What was it Burt Bacharach said, ten years from now? "I've got the wedding bell blues."

ANGER: There's a large statue of the Great God Beelzebub in my studio on Polk Street. Hide in it. I'll wait here and throw them off the track.

RIVERA: You are a good man under layers of lurid homosexual vice.

ANGER: I'm in no mood for compliments, I think.

[*Enter TUESDAY WELD.*]

TUESDAY: Mother's told me everything.

RIVERA: Then she is lying *mentirosa*!

TUESDAY: If you are my father, at least you can advise me.

RIVERA: I never laid a finger on that woman, Leonora. If she says she was at the Restaurant, I was out sick that day.

TUESDAY: So you were never a waiter.

ANGER: Father and daughter, escape your lies, run to Beelzebub. Starlet and Stalinist, only if you enter the body of the Dark Master shall ye escape your own damnation.

RIVERA: We take your advice, leave now, come back later for filming.

TUESDAY: Where are we going—Daddy?

RIVERA: We coat our bodies in grease, then force them through the anal cavity of a great bronze she-bull.

TUESDAY (*after a pause*): Tora, tora, tora, I suppose. [*To ANGER.*] Let my mother know I'm off hungering for new experiences.

RIVERA: Andale! Andale!

[*Exit RIVERA and TUESDAY. Enter WILMA VAPE.*]

ANGER: Tell me, Wilma Vape, how did you get involved in this man Hall Mark's circus?

WILMA: Who told you I knew that man?

ANGER: I heard it through the Vapevine.

WILMA: It's a long story. I was one of many brave men and women who helped prominent theorists escape Europe and bring them to America.

ANGER: You risked your neck for Hall Mark?

WILMA: I had my reasons. Sexual ones. So we reach San Francisco. Here nothing is sacred—except, as I find to my disgust, Richard Diebenkorn. I help Hall Mark found great business built on ideas. Powerful ideas.

ANGER: I was hoping to interest you in a business proposition. "Kenneth Anger Cards." I'll paint small pictures of Satan, we could have a whole franchise—once you've made your escape, Vape.

WILMA: You share an interest with Hall Mark. An interest in sailors.

ANGER: Tattoos, fireworks, leather pants, yes, the open sea. The breeze in my face!

WILMA: I'll think about it.

[*Enter WALLACE BERMAN.*]

BERMAN: Hi, fellas. Gee, did I put the baby down somewhere? I think I lost him. He's in a bundle, looks like a Duchamp kind of Meret Oppenheim thing.

ANGER (*eagerly*): A human baby?

BERMAN: Don't get your hopes up, he's been circumcised already.

WILMA (*shortly*): No. No baby. Scram.

BERMAN: We haven't met—I'm Wallace Berman.

ANGER: You, Wallace Berman, the great artist of the 20th century. I love your movies.

BERMAN: I've only made one.

ANGER: I'm thinking of Bruce Conner. You or Bruce Conner intersect from frame to frame, TV news, still photos, white noise, found footage. I worship you, like a graven idol. I kiss your sandals.

[Enter KAY DeFEO.]

KAY: Hello everyone.

BERMAN: Jay—

KAY: I think he might have gotten sucked into the painting. I heard some wailing coming from the painting—I remember it vaguely, as one might recall a previous life, a la the Search for Bridey Murphy. Was I an Irish colleen, beating the sod? Or was I applying thick firm brushstrokes over the baby?

WILMA: In that case, baby is now part of the contract between this woman and Hall Mark Cards.

BERMAN: It's just like the story of Abraham and Isaac. Father in heaven, did I deliver my first born son to the altar of Beat Culture?

[Pause while ALL consider this.]

WILMA: Could be.

KAY: What a pity, eh?

BERMAN: But, but, but, this isn't cool!

WILMA: I hear baby cry now. Come, Wally Berman, let us remove bag from painting, and baby from bag, like Eskimo pie.

BERMAN: And so it was written.

[Exit WILMA and BERMAN.]

KAY: If I'm only part of Jay, why do I feel so alive, so independent? I step towards my only window and look into the dark. Thousands of stars spin round me, slowly circling planet Earth like Sputnik. Like butterflies. I close my eyes tight as I can and my heart comes pounding up in my throat. "I'm alive," I say.

ANGER: I never feel that way—except when I'm sacrificing a goat, or watching Norma Shearer in *The Women.*

KAY: Then she comes in and takes over. Walks through my skin like rain through a window, and I shut down, no one can see me.

ANGER: So let's try this Elizabeth Taylor, *Suddenly Last Summer* kind of burst of recovered memory.

KAY (*amused*): I remember going into the hardware store . . . and a young man—

ANGER: A handsome young man, like a Greek god—or a faun—

[*Enter a paint store CLERK.*]

CLERK: Need any paint today?

ANGER: He will have to do!

KAY: My name is Jay DeFeo.

CLERK: Why, yes, Miss DeFeo. You've been coming in daily for years. Two buckets of lead paint?

KAY: Yes. (*Aside.*) Thick white paint with metal running through it, like the calcium of my bones.

CLERK: Can I just finish waiting on Miss Bollinger? She has an actual career!

[*Enter PAINT SHOP CUSTOMER.*]

PAINT SHOP CUSTOMER: Yes, and I was first on line.

KAY: Were you?

PAINT SHOP CUSTOMER: I heard the bells over the door ring when you came in behind me.

CLERK: I too heard bells, heard the screen door slam, and there you stood, all weird like.

ANGER: Good, Ryan. Like she's utterly strange, like Maya Deren. No! Mamie
Eisenhower. Rebeca?

PAINT SHOP CUSTOMER: Yes, weird. You go to Berkeley, right? I've seen you
in there [*improvising*] without makeup.

CLERK: Will that be cash?

ANGER: And you say—

KAY: I am stealing these two cans of paint.

ANGER: That's putting it a little baldly.

PAINT SHOP CUSTOMER: A female thief!

KAY: Remember my name, paint clerk boy?

CLERK: Yes, but you can't do that!

KAY: I can and will. I have no money, I'm an art student at Berkeley. I need this
paint for my masterpiece.

ANGER: "Give to me what I need."

KAY: "Give to me what I need."

[*Enter JAY with the brown paper bag in her arms.*]

JAY: No, Kay, don't do this to me.

KAY: You are not strong enough to stop me or say no.

JAY: I saw the paint.

KAY: Two heavy cans that made my arms ache to lift my brush.

JAY: I saw the paint, felt it enter the veins of my heart. But—

KAY: He said—

JAY: Shoplifting is a serious crime.

CLERK: A serious crime.

JAY: I can't do that. I'm a good girl, I am.

PAINT SHOP CUSTOMER: She will be a felon. Her art career blighted. Who would hire that woman to teach? She's got a record.

JAY: I saw the paint. Sealed in drums like pig poison. My hands reached out—my long white arms—

KAY (*takes baby*): I reached out and told the clerk,—

CLERK: I'm afraid I can't just let you take the paint, Miss DeFeo.

JAY: Two heavy cans, that felt wrong in my hands.

ANGER: Like the scrotum of the devil!

CLERK: Here in America, when you want something, you have to pay for it.

PAINT SHOP CUSTOMER: And I was first. One day I'll invent surveillance cameras that would prove it.

CLERK: That's economics 101!

JAY (*to CLERK*): "Fuck you." [*To audience.*] And I left the shop with my paint. The clerk knew my name, my address.

KAY: At home I sat and panted, sweating, like a dog.

JAY: Breathing in the open tins of paint, the life line.

CLERK: Hello, Operator, get me the police.

KAY: My painting had to be fed, like a dog.

ANGER: Bobby! Bobby Beausoleil! Get out here and play some throbbing chords, like the theremin of *Forbidden Planet*.

[*Enter BOBBY, who goes to the piano and plays some chilling chords.*]

JAY: I felt her in my body like running blood, a fever, high and hot, blood like fire. My pulses were pounding.

KAY: The pounding at the door, who is it?

[*Enter OFFICER BIGARINI.*]

BIGARINI: "It's the police, open up, lady."

KAY: Open the paint. Dip in the brush. Apply lead paint to brush.

BIGARINI: Artists come in, they ruin a town.

JAY: I get tired.

KAY: Above you, as far as you can see, in either direction, all the way up , then all the way down, stands the rose.

BIGARINI: She was a hot chick, but she shoulda stuck to painting her nails.

JAY: Read me my rights.

BIGARINI: That's a laugh. There's only one right here, the badge of Bigarini.

JAY: I'm so tired.

KAY: Yet the rose must be fed.

[*Enter MICHAEL McCLURE.*]

BIGARINI: GRAWR! GRAWR!

MICHAEL McCLURE: GRAWR!

[*Enter BOB KAUFMAN.*]

BIGARINI, McCLURE: GRAWR! GRAWR!

KAUFMAN (*opens his mouth to growl, but no sound comes out*).

McCLURE: Bob Kaufman has taken a vow of silence, in protest of a social system that allows black oppression, enforced shoe wearing in restaurants, corrupt policemen like Bigarini here—

BIGARINI: Hey! I'm right here, sir! Am I invisible to you Beat people?

McCLURE: GRAWR! GRAWR!

[*Enter SASHA.*]

SASHA: Miss Jay, Miss Jay, the crane is here. Big day on Fillmore Street!

JAY (*raising her arms to the audience, as though sleepwalking*): They led me away in handcuffs. My picture in the paper.

ANGER: Under arrest. Look haggard, Jay!

McCLURE: Look at Bob, he's crying for all the injustice in the world.

[*BOB KAUFMAN cries, his back wracked with sobs no one can hear.*]

KAY: I never felt more alive.

ANGER: Bobby, more soul in those chords. Sex power, Bobby. Look at him crying, what is the aural equivalent of that grief?

JAY: I never felt more restrained.

[*Exit KAY.*]

ANGER (*to BOBBY*): Pathos, shock, steel! Think of the cattle prod, that took your cherry in juvie. Tuesday! Wallace Berman, Diego Rivera, get out here and tune up. Jay—give it everything you've got, and more.

JAY: I did. I am. I was.

SASHA, McCLURE, BIGARINI: GRAWR!

BOB KAUFMAN: [*Again KAUFMAN growls but no sound comes out.*]

[*Enter TUESDAY, BERMAN, RIVERA.*]

SASHA: The walls have collapsed. They're lifting the painting right out of the room I live in. Will I ever see it again?

[*Enter ANALYST.*]

ANALYST: It could be worse, Miss DeFeo. They could be sealing up your painting behind a wall for thirty years.

WALLACE BERMAN: Or selling it to the Whitney.

ANGER: Every cloud has a silver lining.

[*Enter HALL MARK, WILMA, LEONORA.*]

HALL MARK (*pointing*): It's like a rose in the sky.

WILMA (*pointing*): Or the dead skull of a white cow.

HALL MARK: "Crane … above road's dusty surface."

WILMA: "C.A.R.D.S."

LEONORA: Like the mother who's found her daughter only to lose her to men, mink and Manhattans.

ANGER: And now—Janis Joplin, with a very special tribute to "The Rose."

[*On the wall behind them a giant projection of Jay DeFeo's painting "The Rose," appears. Enter JANIS JOPLIN.*]

JOPLIN (*singing that old Bette Midler song. "The Rose" a la Joplin.*):

Some say love, it is a river
that drowns the tender reed.
Some say love, it is a razor
that leaves your soul to bleed.

Some say love, it is a hunger,
an endless aching need.
I say love, it is a flower,
and you its only seed.

JOINED by ALL: It's the heart afraid of breaking
that never learns to dance.
It's the dream afraid of waking
that never takes the chance.

It's the one who won't be taken,
who cannot seem to give,
and the soul afraid of dying
that never learns to live.

JOPLIN: When the night has been too lonely
and the road has been too long,

JOPLIN, JAY, and KAY: And you think that love is only
for the lucky and the strong,

ALL. Just remember in the winter
far beneath the winter snows
lies the seed that with the sun's love
in the spring becomes the rose.

[*As JANIS sings, a slide appears as big as possible on the stage backdrop or back wall, a slide
of the completed Jay DeFeo painting, "The Rose."*]

END

"Wet Paint" was once my most controversial play. Poet Bill Berkson at the San Francisco Art Institute commissioned a work from San Francisco Poets Theater to celebrate the restoration of Jay DeFeo's The Rose, which notoriously had been sealed up behind plaster walls in SFAI's anterooms, a huge artwork prone to decay but too expensive and unwieldy to think about right now until the Whitney Museum, preparing its huge "Beat Culture and the New America" show, bought it, excavated it, and spent years restoring it. The "Beat Culture" exhibition played in New York, and now was coming to San Francisco's De Young Museum. Berkson asked for a play that would be a sort of pageant of the poets and painters working together in San Francisco in the 1950s, laid in North Beach which is where the Art Institute was, and I remember it was going to be a benefit for Poets in Need, the charity group headed by Lyn Hejinian and Leslie Scalapino among others, to supply emergency $$$ for writers in immediate trouble.

SFAI's publicity for the "Wet Paint" performance including a saucy postcard which caused most of the trouble—my fault, I guess. Ad copy described the play as an irreverent look at the Beat artists of the 1950s, especially Jay DeFeo, but also including Kenneth Anger, Bruce Conner, Wallace Berman, Joan Brown, Michael McClure and plenty more. The tag line read, "They invented a new kind of **ART**.... (turn over card) .... and a new kind of **SEX** to go with it." The De Feo Foundation didn't like it: its director told me that she was only letting the play go on because Berkson had assured her I was a true artist in some unthinkable way, but she couldn't subject herself to this travesty—it would be too hurtful. Bruce Conner's attorneys served me a cease and desist order. I'm there in my boxers having answered the doorbell at some ungodly hours, looking at the legal document in my hand, and ruing the day I'd crossed the famous iconoclast. I had no recourse, and no money to defend my stupid play, I did what he asked and got rid of "Bruce Conner" as a character—that's why he doesn't appear in the play at all. At the actual performance the audience seemed to enjoy themselves, especially the grand finale in which Janis Joplin and the whole cast sing "The Rose" while a huge transparency of De Feo's painting covered the entire stage area from ceiling to footlights. Michael McClure was there, and he sought out the young woman, Kathi Georges, who had played him in the piece, while Tosh Berman assured me that his dad would have loved it. So I felt somewhat better, but still hated by the establishment, which isn't I realize today, a totally bad feeling to have when you're an artist.... Years later, The Whitney and SFMOMA cosponsored a Jay De Feo retrospective, and to my surprise, Leah Levy of the De Feo Trust asked me if I would supervise a revival of "Wet Paint" at the Phyllis Wattis Theater at the museum. She just had to say five words and I started to cry: "I was wrong about you." What a lesson! I have tried ever since to ape her magnificent style and her compassion. It's true, "Wet Paint" was the same play really, only now it was understood as a gigantic declaration of a love big enough to forgive and celebrate flaws.

Produced at San Francisco Museum of Modern Art, in conjunction with the Jay de Feo retropsective in 2012 (revised version).

SASHA CHOLNAKY ....Tucker Bennett
EVA, his sister..D. Scot Miller
COUNTESS CHOLNAKY, their mother.. Steve Orth
WALLACE BERMAN.. Wayne Smith
DOROTHY MILLER..Kate Delos
ANALYST...Karla Milosevich
JAY DE FEO .... Phoebe Gloeckner
KAY DE FEO.. Norma Cole
JANIS..D-L Alvarez
HALL MARK ....Jonathan Hammer
WILMA VAPE...Leslie Scalapino
MRS. WELD .... Alicia Wing
TUESDAY WELD .... Scott Hewicker
DIEGO RIVERA...Cliff Hengst
FRIDA KAHLO ....Margaret Crane
BOBBY BEAUSOLEIL...David Buuck
MICHAEL MCCLURE .... Kathi Georges
KENNETH ANGER..Rex Ray
CLERK..Ethel Chase
PAINT SHOP CUSTOMER,
an artist in a flashback who was there first ....Rebeca Bollinger

Originally produced by San Francisco Art Institute, October 10, 1996, with the following cast

SASHA CHOLNAKY...Craig Goodman
EVA, his sister..Cait in Mitchell-Dayton
COUNTESS CHOLNAKY, their mother......................................Michelle Rollman
WALLACE BERMAN...Wayne Smith
DOROTHY MILLER...Kate Delos
ANALYST..Karla Milosevich
JAY DE FEO..Phoebe Gloeckner
KAY DE FEO...Norma Cole
JANIS...D-L Alvarez
HALL MARK..Jonathan Hammer
WILMA VAPE.. ..Leslie Scalapino
MRS. WELD...Alicia Wing
TUESDAY WELD.. ....Scott Hewicker
DIEGO RIVERA.. ....Cliff Hengst
FRIDA KAHLO.. ...Margaret Crane
BOBBY BEAUSOLEIL...David Buuck
MICHAEL MCCLURE...Kathi Georges
KENNETH ANGER..Rex Ray
CLERK.. ....Ethel Chase

The Big Keep

characters

FRIEDA HUGHES
KEVIN KILLIAN
JORIE GRAHAM
ST JOHN OF THE CROSS
ALISON
JIM
MIKE
STEVE DICKISON
LAUREN BACALL
LARS VON TRIER
ETHEL CHASE
MUSICIAN
DOGME 95
URSULA ANDRESS

[*The scene is an expensively furnished office lined with books and photos of famous poets. Enter FRIEDA HUGHES and KEVIN KILLIAN.*]

FRIEDA: Hi Kevin. Oh God, another day of work.

KEVIN: Aren't we bright and cheerful?

FRIEDA: I stayed out too late last night.

KEVIN: I know how you feel. I've worked here at the Poetry Center for twenty years—and it's never been so busy. It's our fiftieth anniversary and I'm feeling like I'm fifty years old.

FRIEDA (*confessing*): I went to see Eve Ensler—at the Commonwealth Club.

KEVIN: You didn't!

FRIEDA: I know—I should have taken you. But she is brilliant. What a mind!

KEVIN: It's nine a.m.—I'm going to unlock the doors. Ready?

FRIEDA: Ready as I'll ever be, I guess.

[*KEVIN unlocks door and JORIE GRAHAM rushes in.*]

JORIE GRAHAM: How long did you plan to keep me waiting?

KEVIN: Couldn't say.

JORIE GRAHAM: You do realize I am Jorie Graham?

KEVIN: That name rings a bell.

JORIE GRAHAM: "Rings a bell"? You people drive me crazy. [*She plays with her hair.*]

FRIEDA (*stepping forward*): Oh, Miss Graham, hi. So sorry. Steve Dickison, our director, has been terribly busy. He's all apologies.

KEVIN: Frieda, do you feel a draft? [*To JORIE.*] Oh no, that's you, swatting your hair around. People told me, "Kevin, wait till you meet Jorie Graham, she's the white Diana Ross," but until now I didn't realize what they meant.

JORIE GRAHAM: I've been here almost two hours.

KEVIN: Just like me, except I've been here twenty years. And freaks clog this office from nine to five. Ever since the Poetry Center got that one hundred million-dollar donation from Ethel Chase, all of a sudden we're popular.

[*Enter students ALISON, MIKE and JIM.*]

ALISON: Excuse me, can somebody help? I need to get the Sylvia Plath tapes.

KEVIN: You must be a student.

MIKE: I've been here since Tuesday waiting for Ezra Pound on tape.

KEVIN: We're on a number system here—like a bakery.

JORIE GRAHAM: Did my importance escape you? Official TV spokesmodel for the Poetry Center, the Naropa Archives, and the Poetry Project at St. Mark's Church, I, Jorie Graham, have a direct dial-up connection to St. John of the Cross.

FRIEDA: What number are we up to?

KEVIN: 29.

JIM: I'm 29!

KEVIN: Hmm, 29, just perfect. Not too old, and not too young. You've been around the block a few times, just like a car right out of the dealers.

JIM: I want to show Steve my presentation.

KEVIN: Come a little bit closer—I love that new car smell.

JIM: For the new poetry money.

VOICE: Jorie Graham . . .

ALISON: Somebody's calling you, Ms. Graham.

JORIE (*to ceiling*): Is that you, St. John of the Cross?

VOICE: It is indeed. I give you visions for your poetry. *The New Yorker* then buys it. Everyone's happy.

FRIEDA (*waving at ceiling*): Hi, St. John of the Cross. It's me, Frieda.

VOICE: Hello, Frieda.

JORIE (*to St. JOHN of the CROSS*): What's happening here, all of a sudden I have to sit in these chairs with all these loser students?

KEVIN (*to JIM*): Just go through that door there, and sit down, and wait in another chair.

[*Exit JIM.*]

VOICE: To be filled with God, your soul must empty itself of self.

JORIE (*impatiently*): Yes, but I'm meeting Mei-Mei Bersenbrugge at Agnes B. at 3.

VOICE: The spiritual capital sins, the passive purgation, Jorie.

JORIE (*hardly listening*): Agnes B. herself will be showing us around.

VOICE: And you are being fired here at the Poetry Center.

JORIE (*this catches her attention*): What?

VOICE: Oh, not because of your human failings, it's because Steve Dickison, the director of the Poetry Center, has—

JORIE: Fired!

VOICE: —Has replaced you with someone even more statuesque and legendary. A woman who really knows how to shop. Someone photogenic, with a growl in her voice that makes the Carmelites snap to attention.

KEVIN: Are you talking to someone?

JORIE: Yes, to—oh why bother explaining it to you, Kevin Killian. Where is Dickison anyway?

KEVIN: Don't ask me.

JORIE: Then—where is Ethel Chase? I hate to go over his head, but—[*laughs*]— actually what else are heads for?

ALISON: Excuse me, Frieda, someone told me you were Frieda Hughes.

FRIEDA (*waving*): Hello students, yes, the daughter of Sylvia Plath and what's his name. I'm an intern here. I used to live in London where I worked as an intern to Stella McCartney but I realized here, in San Francisco, the Poetry Center's where the action is.

ALISON: What was your mother like?

FRIEDA: I don't remember, I was just a baby when what's his name killed her.

KEVIN: Frieda's a poet herself.

FRIEDA: And so is Kevin I believe.

KEVIN: We're all one big happy family. [*Aside.*]—With an ugly secret.

FRIEDA: Families are like that.

JORIE GRAHAM: Not my family.

FRIEDA: You know, Alison, you remind me of my favorite writer.

ALISON: I do? How flattering.

FRIEDA: Many must have commented on your amazing resemblance to Eve Ensler. The author of *The Vagina Monologues*?

KEVIN: As for you, Jorie Graham, you will have to cool your [*he looks at JORIE's shoes*] heels right here in my office. Admire the art work. Now that we have one hundred million dollars from Ethel Chase, Mr. Dickison has been able to furnish up. That's a De Kooning over there and that's a picture of his favorite star, Lauren Bacall.

VOICE: I love her too.

MIKE: How come we can't get any tapes? What's going on?

KEVIN: Incidentally, we've also hired St. John of the Cross, so [*swivels to JORIE*] he will not be your exclusive link to the divine any more.

JORIE GRAHAM: What do you mean?

VOICE: What do you think he means? I'm doing the broadcasts now, Jorie.

[*KEVIN turns up radio and the VOICE talks on the radio.*]

VOICE: "Among these tapes, you'll find original recordings by William Carlos Williams, Langston Hughes, Marianne Moore, Robert Lowell, Muriel Rukeyser, Louis Zukofsky; the Black Mountain poets, the poets of the San Francisco Renaissance, and the Beats."

JORIE: I used to say that!

VOICE: Well, Jorie, now I say it. And I get paid too! Think I'll go down to Agnes B. with Mei-Mei Bersenbrugge, give her a thrill. Bye.

FRIEDA: Bye!

VOICE: Bye, Frieda.

[*Enter STEVE DICKISON.*]

STEVE: What's this unholy ruckus?

ALISON: Please, Mr. Dickison! The Sylvia Plath!

MIKE: How about Ezra Pound? I've been waiting since Monday.

KEVIN: Tuesday.

MIKE: Whatever.

STEVE: Now, now, everyone, you can't speak all at once. [*Aside.*] —Or at all. [*To STUDENTS.*] One at a time—like the Maximus poems.

ALISON: I demand those tapes of Sylvia!

JORIE: What about my appointment?

MIKE: Do you have the Cantos or do you have the "Can-not-tos?"

JORIE, MIKE, ALISON, FRIEDA (*in unison, in scary mechanical voice*): How will this anarchy end?

KEVIN: What?

JORIE, MIKE, ALISON, FRIEDA: How will this anarchy end?

STEVE: Jorie, Jorie, Jorie, you're kicking up one heck of a fuss. My high tech cameras are everywhere—even in your hair.

JORIE: I hear I've been let go?

STEVE: Think of it as retired.

FRIEDA: Or refried. Like old, Mexican beans.

STEVE: Boys and girls, many of you have asked, what has the Poetry Center done with that 100 million dollar Chase grant. Well, it's a case of out with the old and in with the new—who happens also to be the old. Ladies and gentlemen, meet our new celebrity spokesman—I mean woman—and oh boy, do I ever mean "woman." Let's hear a big San Francisco welcome for Miss Lauren Bacall!

[*Enter LAUREN BACALL.*]

LAUREN: How are you all?

[*She swaggers around about the stage as befits her star status.*]

MIKE: Oh my God, it's Lauren Bacall.

FRIEDA: She looks a bit like Eve Ensler . . .

ALISON: Thought you were dead.

LAUREN: After ten months of filming in Denmark for Lars Von Trier I thought I was too. [*Laughs in a sophisticated way.*] But instead, I'm very much here alive, come to San Francisco to do my bit for the Poetry Center—and those delicious checks from the Ethel Chase fund. [*To someone offstage.*] The suitcases, please. The black one, the red one, and the blonde one. [*Lightly.*] Thank you!

KEVIN: Miss Bacall, have you met Miss Graham?

JORIE: How do you do?

LAUREN: Martha Graham? Sure, Martha and I are old friends.

JORIE: "Martha"?

LAUREN (*jovially*): We were legends together—back in the day, when she could still dance. Remember that "Clytemnestra," Martha? I nearly spilled my drink. —And that would have been tragic.

JORIE: Martha Graham was my grandmother. That was not I.

LAUREN: Oh yeah, she did have this relative invented Graham crackers. That you by any chance? If so, let me shake your hand. You helped keep Bogie alive. He loved the little brown squarey things—I think. He'd sit there, acting tough, but when the gang had gone home he'd say, "Mommy, get me one of those Graham crackers."

JORIE (*with controlled fury*): No, I did not invent—

VOICE: Lauren Bacall? She's enchanting.

STEVE: Hear that, ladies and gentlemen, even St. John of the Cross loves Lauren Bacall.

ALISON: But when I can hear my tapes?

MIKE: Yeah what's with the tapes?

FRIEDA: Quiet please!

LAUREN BACALL (*to STEVE*): You didn't say there'd be civilians here. What kind of press conference is this?

STEVE: You're a day early.

JORIE: You're replacing me with her? I wash my hair with champagne. I give prizes to my unrewarding students. Even when I'm gardening, I'm angelic. And yes, I spend money. But there are two things I don't do. I don't forgive and I don't forget and you, Lauren Bacall, and you, Steve Dickison, will regret this step till the day you die! I'm going to Ethel Chase and telling her some good old-fashioned Iowa truth.

[*Exit JORIE GRAHAM.*]

FRIEDA: Oh good, she's gone.

LAUREN BACALL: I just spent the last ten months in Iceland! I'm playing Nicole Kidman's twin sister in *Dogville*, by Lars Von Trier.

KEVIN: You're her twin sister?

LAUREN BACALL: Well, her older twin sister. Everyone said, "Lauren, it's a great chance for you." Lars von Trier is the Dogma guy, you know. From Iceland.

KEVIN: Wasn't it Denmark?

LAUREN BACALL: Now where are my lines? Denmark—Iceland—it was cold. It was like looking into the bottom of Frank Sinatra's so-called heart.

Oh yes, here we go. "Naropa's archive includes leading poets from the Beat Movement, such as Gregory Corso, Diane di Prima, Lawrence Ferlinghetti, Allen Ginsberg and Gary Snyder; New York School poets John Ashbery, Bill Berkson, Ted Berrigan, Kenward Elmslie, Barbara Guest, Kenneth Koch, Bernadette Mayer and Anne Waldman."

Wait a second. What's with this "New York School poets?" I went to school in New York and we didn't have any school poets.

We had Longfellow, Tennyson and what's her name who wrote, "Only God can make a tree."

KEVIN: Joyce Kilmer.

LAUREN BACALL: Her! So who's my director? And for God's sake get rid of these civilians.

STEVE: Okay, everyone, you heard the lady. Out!

KEVIN: But, Mr. Dickison, some of these young people have been waiting for days to access the tapes.

LAUREN BACALL: I'll handle this. [*To STUDENTS.*] Now, you all heard the man, just give us one hour and you can come back and listen to all the tapes you want.

ALISON and MIKE (*agree enthusiastically*).

STEVE: No. Tell them they're unavailable.

LAUREN: They're unavailable.

[*Exit STUDENTS, grumbling.*]

LAUREN: Someday I'll find out what that means, "unavailable." But for now, I really don't care. After you've lived through World War II, the McCarthy Commitee and playing the mother of Barbra Streisand, you really don't care. Let me look at those school poets again (*she studies teleprompter*): "Gregory Corso." Never heard of him. "Diane di Prima." In my day she'd-a had to change her name. I wasn't born Lauren Bacall. They made me an anapest.

VOICE: Go ahead, Miss Bacall, you're doing fine.

LAUREN: "Kenward Elmslie," now there's a mouthful. Why, I know him. I used to go by his place, he invented Ritz Crackers. [*To FRIEDA.*] You—girl with the glasses. Run down to Tommy's Joint, get me a box of Ritz Crackers.

FRIEDA: Right away, Miss Bacall.

LAUREN BACALL: It's a red box.

[*Exit FRIEDA, nodding.*]

KEVIN: Mr. Dickison, Lars Von Trier is here for his appointment.

STEVE: Send him right up.

KEVIN (*on the phone*): Come right up, Mr. Von Trier.

LAUREN BACALL: Not Lars Von Trier from Iceland!

STEVE: Yes, I've hired him to be the director of your commercials.

LAUREN BACALL: But he—but we—

STEVE: Why? Is there a problem?

LAUREN BACALL (*annoyed*): You know how to whistle, don't you, Steve? You just put your lips together and blow me.

[*Enter LARS VON TRIER.*]

LARS: Lauren Bacall. Lady of the fat heart.

LAUREN: Well, well, well. Of all the Poetry Centers in all the towns in all the world, you walk into mine.

LARS: I had to see you again. One film together was not enough.

LAUREN BACALL: I'm not the woman for you, Lars Von Trier. Why don't you go back and see if Nicole Kidman is free.

LARS: I don't care about Nicole Kidman, she's tall woman, very cold.

LAUREN BACALL: You gave her star billing in "Dogville."

LARS: She is dog. You are very different, you are. You catch this Danish man unawares, he thought, "Lauren Bacall, freak oddity," but then when he met you, he flip.

LAUREN BACALL: So you came to San Francisco. I won't play the sap for you, Lars Von Trier.

LARS: Remember those long nights on the sound stage, the fairy lights at the Tivoli Garden.

LAUREN BACALL: Go home now, kid. We don't want no stinkin' Dogme 95 on these TV spots. People want glamor. They want poetry and they want glamor. [*To STEVE.*] Say, could someone get me a Dr. Pepper?

STEVE: Kevin?

KEVIN: I'll have a Tab.

STEVE: No, I mean, could you hurry downstairs and bring back a big Dr. Pepper for our newest superstar?

LAUREN BACALL: It's a clear bottle; the soda itself is brown.

LARS: And I'll have aquavit.

KEVIN: Now I know have Gray Davis felt, when they announced the recall. Twenty years devotion to poetry, and what does it gain me? "Fetch."

[*Exit KEVIN.*]

LAUREN BACALL: My audience wants me in makeup, furs, jewelry. None of your "Dogville" potato sack costumes like I never left the Bronx. Reciting your inane dialogue and playing working class. Yeah, yeah, we'll always have Paris.

LARS: In Denmark we have a saying, "A woman says no to Dogme, she says yes to love."

LAUREN BACALL: Oh yeah? And over here we have a saying, "Never date a man with more names than you have." Lars. Von. Trier. Tell me about it! Let's face it, I dated John Dos Passos, Sean "Puffy" Combs, James Van Der Beek. J. Edgar Hoover was no picnic either. All of them little men without the strength to tame a tigress.

LARS: I change my name for you, Lauren Bacall. Call me "VT" as a poet might.

LAUREN: We've got work to do. Got your camera?

LARS: Ja, ja . . .

[*Enter ETHEL CHASE.*]

STEVE: This is the one and only Ethel Chase!

ETHEL: The modest philanthropist who gave you one hundred million dollars to spread poetry throughout the land.

STEVE: And look what we've bought with your money! Poetry's popular all over again, it's becoming an art form.

LARS VON TRIER (*to ETHEL CHASE*): You will work in a factory, and big machines will crush you like tomatoes. And everybody sing. "Money, money, money—money."

LAUREN BACALL: Ah, leave her alone, she's a good kid.

ETHEL CHASE:　Why are all those young people lying out in the corridors in protest?　They have signs that say, "No tapes."

STEVE:　I think it's "No tapas," they're protesting gentrification.　[*He makes frantic signs to LAUREN BACALL to help back him up.　She obliges even though she is confused.*]

LAUREN BACALL:　"No tapas!"　"No tapas!"　They tried to put up a tapas place in the Dakota, I just gave them the Look.

LARS VON TRIER:　Then the waves crack open and sharks come and swallow you, your mouth stuffed with tapas.

ETHEL (*afraid of him*):　I'll just sit over here and watch the rehearsal.　Thank you.

LARS VON TRIER (*to BACALL*):　I need you the way a camera needs film.

LAUREN BACALL:　Let's not talk about love, let's get rolling.　Okay—the school poets.　"Anne Waldman, Bernadette Mayer" . . . hmmm, I knew Louis B. Mayer when I worked for MGM.　Wonder if this one chases you around the desk like her Dad did.　"John Ashbery, Kenneth Koch . . . " [*Snickers.*] Ethel Merman and I used to call him Kenneth Cock, for very good reasons.　Oh, you don't live a lifetime at the Dakota without seeing the seedy side of love.

LARS:　You torture me with your tales of the other men in your life.

LAUREN BACALL:　You tortured me by putting me in that burlap sack!　Meanwhile Nicole Kidman looked pretty.　Okay, we were both supposed to be poor.　But there's pretty poor, and there's potato sack poor.　[*To ETHEL CHASE.*] You've got style, Ethel Chase.　I'll give you that.

ETHEL CHASE:　Thank you again.

LAUREN BACALL (*to LARS VON TRIER*):　Do Icelandic women fall for your spiel?

LARS:　I am from Denmark.

LAUREN BACALL:　Bjork warned me about you—in the basement of my building, the Dakota, at the washer dryer.

LARS:　Bjork?

LAUREN BACALL:　She could hardly get a word in edgewise.　The dryers were making such a racket. Tears ran down her round cheeks. All I could hear was, "Lars Von Trier, Lars Von Trier." I thought it was a new, Danish detergent. I should have listened to Bjork more closely but hey, whatever happened to mentorship?

LARS: Then—you reject me?

VOICE: Lauren Bacall—don't be so hasty.

LAUREN (*glancing at ceiling*): Who is that?

VOICE: I am St. John of the Cross with a message from beyond.

LAUREN: A ghost, eh?

VOICE: Think of me as a friend from Spain. From Spain of a long time ago. A friend with great admiration for your stellar work in *Written on the Wind* and *How to Marry a Millionaire.* One who saw you twelve times on Broadway in *Applause!*

LAUREN: Yeah—well, what do you want?

VOICE: Look at this man who comes before you pleading his love.

LARS VON TRIER: I'm sorry I put you in rags. The man in me said, dress her in silver. The artist, indeed Dogme itself, said, make her wear old potato sack and suffer.

LAUREN (*to St. JOHN of the CROSS*): He's nothin'. You forget, I've had Adlai Stevenson and Harold Pinter.

VOICE: Let not he be the excuse for turning away your last chance for love.

LAUREN BACALL: Not to mention Bogie.

LARS: Then I go now—heartless woman, back to the cold receipt of Scandinavian snow vista. I too have pride.

VOICE: Stop him.

[*Exit LARS VON TRIER.*]

LAUREN (*to audience*): Am I cutting myself to thin slices like those bridge and tunnel girls who cut themselves for fun? Am I shutting my heart to a great, vacuous love from Denmark and becoming a stodge?

VOICE: Yes to both questions.

[*Enter KEVIN and FRIEDA.*]

KEVIN: Here's the Dr. Pepper!

FRIEDA: Did we come at a bad time?

STEVE: Shall we continue our rehearsal?

LAUREN: I'll be right back. Hey! Danish! Wait up. [*To ceiling.*] And you—
Spanish. —Gracias. [*To audience.*] I'm hard to get, Lars von Trier. All you got to
do is ask.

[*Exit LAUREN BACALL.*]

ETHEL CHASE: I like these commercials. I think you've done right by poetry.
Now let's see the pilot program I commissioned.

STEVE (*puzzled*): Pilot program?

ETHEL CHASE: You don't remember?

FRIEDA (*to STEVE*): Mr. Dickison—

STEVE: Oh yes! The Federal Government of Laura Bush, impressed by the Poetry
Center's commitment to all weird poets from all over the world, and by our 100
million dollar grant from the lovely, effervescent Ethel Chase, gave us funds for a
new kind of pilot program. Frieda?

FRIEDA: They came to us and asked us to re-design the new American currency.

STEVE: Everyone was tired of seeing the same old faces on their
money—Washington, Jefferson, Andrew Jackson.

KEVIN: "Let's put the faces of poets on our dollar bills," said Steve Dickison.

[*Enter JIM.*]

JIM: That's where I entered the picture. [*Giggles.*] Kind of bizarre in a way, I just
kind of walked in here to try and borrow a tape, and before I knew what I was

doing, they had whisked me into another room, stripped me naked, and asked me to draw a picture of Hart Crane's face.

KEVIN: At that moment, all young Jim knew of Hart Crane was that he invented the Life Saver.

JIM: And then they sprung it on me, see, I'm a designer too, and I was going to get the chance to make a real difference in the way people see money. So here are my prototypes.

KEVIN: Let's start with the hundred dollar bill.

FRIEDA: It used to be Benjamin Franklin.

KEVIN: Now it's Walter Benjamin!

[*As JIM displays it, STEVE, KEVIN and FRIEDA applaud.*]

STEVE: Fifty dollar bill, does anyone remember?

It was Ulysses Grant.

Now it's *Ulysses*, by James Joyce.

FRIEDA: No more Andrew Jackson on the 20. It's Jackson Mac Low, and when you turn it over, it's Janet Jackson.

KEVIN: That was my idea. I'm a stone Janet fan.

ETHEL: Bravo! I'm well satisfied. Steve, I don't mind telling you I came today a bit suspicious of the way you're using my money. But I'm a happy woman now. I'll be back in half an hour to review the condition of all the tapes. Now, I have an appointment at Agnes B.—but I'll be back.

[*Exit ETHEL CHASE.*]

FRIEDA: We've bought a little time.

JIM: I didn't even get a chance to show my quarter, with George Oppen on it instead of George Washington.

STEVE: Jim, do you have a car?

JIM: Sure, Mr. Dickison.

STEVE: Take me to the Agnes B. shop on Union Square. I have one more trick up my sleeve.

KEVIN: And we're supposed to hold down the fort?

[*Exit JIM and STEVE.*]

FRIEDA: Oh, Kevin, what are we going to do? That crowd is fierce out there.

KEVIN: I know.

FRIEDA: They're asking for tapes by Clayton Eshleman.

KEVIN: No—better—Bruce Andrews.

[*Enter LAUREN BACALL.*]

LAUREN BACALL: Bruce Andrews? I thought of marrying him, once. But eventually I realized we didn't speak the same—L=A=N=G=U=A=G-E.

FRIEDA: You're alone! Didn't you catch up with Lars von Trier?

LAUREN: No—but I'll find him. Don't worry about that. See that blue light over there—that's the light of lovers.

FRIEDA: How saccharine.

LAUREN: Now that it's just the three of us, you can fess up.

KEVIN: What do you mean?

LAUREN: There's some funny business with Ethel Chase's money, isn't there. Admit it. Tell Mama.

FRIEDA: Well—

LAUREN: In fact you don't have a penny left of Ethel Chase's millions.

FRIEDA: Not a blooming shilling.

LAUREN: You're so British, I admire that in a person. Harold Pinter whispers those sweet nothings in my ear, my knees kind of buckle.

KEVIN: So, you're our last chance, Miss Bacall!

LAUREN: You spent $100,000,000.00? On what?

FRIEDA: Expenses.

LAUREN: Expenses?

KEVIN: Oh, Frieda, just tell her the truth.

FRIEDA: All right. I saw *The Vagina Monologues* and had a few questions for Eve Ensler. So I asked her.

KEVIN: I wanted to ask Larry Harvey if success is killing his original idea for Burning Man. So I did.

LAUREN: You mean—?

KEVIN: Yes. We spent all our money at the Commonwealth Club.

FRIEDA (*defiantly*): And it was worth it. I wondered why Johnnie Cochran said he was "90 per cent sure OJ was innocent." So I asked him.

KEVIN: You see, Ms. Bacall, in the modern world, access is everything. We here at the Poetry Center know that better than anybody.

LAUREN: I see.

FRIEDA: But access costs money! And so when Ethel Chase gave us a hundred million dollars for poetry, we just took a little.

KEVIN: Oh, that Eve Ensler! Her "Vagina Monologues" are priceless.

FRIEDA: I was going to tape it.

KEVIN: Did you?

FRIEDA: I guess I was too starstruck.

KEVIN: Oh well.

LAUREN: But there must have still been tons of money left. Listen to me, carrying on about money, you'll think I'm awful.

FRIEDA: We've been afraid you'll think we're awful.

LAUREN: Oh, Frieda, far from it. Nobody knows better than I that when you want something, you have to go get it, by hell or high water.

FRIEDA: Eve Ensler's like the Ruth Draper of a new generation.

LAUREN: Oh absolutely.

FRIEDA: So, we asked Larry Harvey what we should do with our money and he advised us to construct a forty-foot sculpture of twigs and bark, of our favorite poet—and then to burn it in the desert. That took some doing.

KEVIN: Larry is wonderful. As it turned out, success did kill his original idea for Burning Man, and he's okay with that.

LAUREN: But there still must've been a bit more money, left over? And my God, what will your boss say when he finds out you two have been embezzling?

[*Enter STEVE DICKISON.*]

STEVE: If Daniel Ellsberg leaked the Pentagon Papers today, would he be tried for treason? I asked him.

LAUREN: No, no, not you too!

STEVE: Daniel Ellsberg has the sexiest eyes.

LAUREN: Oh, my God.

FRIEDA: It was the first thing I noticed about him, at the Commonwealth Club. Next to Eve Ensler, Daniel Ellsberg is the sexiest tomboy beanpole on the planet.

KEVIN: He said he used to know you, Ms. Bacall.

LAUREN: Did he? I can't remember. Oh yes, we were engaged. That's right. I met him at Truman Capote's "Black and White Ball" at the Plaza. There was Kay Graham to my left and Daniel Ellsberg to my right, so I introduced them. You know it was really I who leaked the Pentagon Papers. [*Fiercely.*] And I'd do it again all over again—if I knew what they were!

STEVE: Did you? We should get you a gig at the Commonwealth Club.

LAUREN: You, dear man, are in hot water up to your—[*she surveys him.*] -- Oh, never mind. How can I help? And, by the way, will I be paid?

STEVE: Your check is good. It's the others I'm worried about. And also, the tapes.

LAUREN: Why—what's wrong with the tapes?

KEVIN: Well, when funds were running a little low, and the Commonwealth Club called and said they were bringing—oh, who was it, Frieda?

FRIEDA: It was Monica Lewinsky.

KEVIN: And none of us had a penny in our pockets, I looked around and saw all these tapes on the shelves just gathering dust, and four letters appeared across my field of vision. Ebay.

FRIEDA: And we sold them.

LAUREN: You have none left?

STEVE: What could we do? If it wasn't Eve Ensler, it was Matthew Barney.

KEVIN: I saw the Cremaster Cycle, and I wanted to ask Matthew Barney what it feels like to cover your whole body with Vaseline and slither like Spiderman across the ceiling of the Vatican.

FRIEDA: So we asked him!

STEVE: We had a small account on Ebay and one day we offered a copy of the W H Auden tape and were we ever shocked, someone bought it!

KEVIN: Two people bid on it. That's two more people than ever came in here and listened to it for free.

STEVE: So we knew we were onto something big.

LAUREN: Did I ever tell you that Ursula Andress asked me to have her baby for her? I said, "No, thanks, sweetheart, I've been through childbirth, and I'd rather do a picture with Sinatra than go through that meshugineh again."

FRIEDA: What went for the most?

KEVIN: I think the Dylan Thomas tapes. Things got bad when we started to notice we had competition. Other sellers were undercutting us viciously. We'd have our Adrienne Rich tapes up for, say, twenty dollars, and all of a sudden someone else was offering Adrienne Rich for ten cents.

FRIEDA: With free postage.

STEVE: We soon figured out it was the staff at St. Marks' and at Naropa.

LAUREN: So—they're in the red too?

KEVIN: Guess so. It's tough to live in New York.

FRIEDA: As for the people at Naropa, it turned out they were sending all their money to the Dalai Lama to make Boulder more sacred. He'd send them back little cuttings of mountain plants, and little vials filled with his urine, and for that it would be ten thousand bucks a pop.

STEVE: Sacred! As though an hour with Johnnie Cochran doesn't have its own spiritual ineffability.

LAUREN: I understand.

STEVE: And with Anne Waldman always in Prague, her razor sharp financial mind hasn't been at the controls.

LAUREN: Her I don't care for. Vulgar little thing. Those scarves, that clanking jewelry, those silver bracelets, all stolen from me. That hair across her eyes a la Lauren Bacall?

KEVIN: Well, sure, but—

LAUREN: But I must shake myself out of Waldman negativity. [*She shakes.*] How can I help?

STEVE: It's easy. We sold our last John Cage tapes—

FRIEDA: Nothing but dead silence anyhow—

STEVE: To bring you here, the world's greatest actress, and you can impersonate all the different poets and thus pull the chestnuts out of the fire.

LAUREN: Well, I'm flattered, naturally, but—

FRIEDA: Oh do say you'll help us, Miss Bacall!

KEVIN: It's our last chance! Think of it as preservation. We don't want to go to Attica, or even to one of those cushy so-called country club prisons for white collar crime.

STEVE: And you'll be helping to keep the world safe for poetry.

LAUREN: The big keep, eh? Y'know, Bogie always said, Baby, when you go ahead and do something, don't do it halfway. [*Snaps her fingers.*] I'll do it. But I'm rusty, I need my lines.

STEVE: Okay, so you speak into the mike—

KEVIN: Let's start out with something easy. Dylan Thomas.

STEVE: He was Welsh.

LAUREN BACALL (*acidly*): That's helpful.

[*Enter STEVEN TAYLOR.*]

KEVIN: And here's a musician to put you in the mood. That old Welsh mood. Coal mines, heavy fog.

LAUREN BACALL: All right. Whatever. [*Clears her throat then begins.*]

You, my father, there on the sad height,
Curse, bless, me now with your fierce years, I pray.
Do not go gentle into that good night.
Rage, rage against the dying of the light.

ALL. Three cheers!

STEVE: That's great, Lauren, and now let's keep moving on shall we? [*To STEVEN
TAYLOR.*] Let's have a little New Jersey music to go with this next one, Springsteen,
Bon Jovi, Patti Smith?

LAUREN BACALL: "This is just to say—

I have eaten
the plums
that were in
the icebox

and which
you were probably
saving
for breakfast—Bogie—

Forgive me—

KEVIN: That was just beautiful.

FRIEDA: Almost as good as the original, which I used as a coaster at a party
for Czeslaw Milosz.

STEVE: Let's save the compliments for one big bunch, shall we? We're really
under the gun.

LAUREN BACALL: Under pressure, eh?

[*STEVEN, can you play that repetitive bassline from Queen's "Under Pressure"?*] How about
Sylvia Plath?

Bastard
Masturbating a glitter,
He wants to be loved.

I do not stir.
The frost makes a flower,
The dew makes a star—

KEVIN: You are a star!

LAUREN BACALL: The dead bell.
The dead bell.

Somebody's done for.

FRIEDA: Exactly like my mother. [*Moving downstage towards AUDIENCE, speaking confidentially.*] We worked for hours that afternoon, racing against the clock. For we knew our careers were in the balance.

STEVE: More! More!

LAUREN BACALL (*exhausted*): I can't! I can't!

FRIEDA: Finally, Lauren Bacall faced the biggest challenge of all.

KEVIN: And now we need Anne Waldman.

LAUREN BACALL: Oh, not that hack.

STEVE: She's always in demand.

FRIEDA (*to BACALL*): She's the vortex, we're just the dead leaves that scatter in her wake.

KEVIN: Here's the script, it's called "Rogue State."

LAUREN BACALL: Well, I'll give it a whirl. [*In a flat, colorless voice.*] I'm in a rogue state, honey.

FRIEDA: Oh, no, more drama, Miss Bacall!

KEVIN: Give it oomph.

FRIEDA: Make those operatic trills that frighten little children!

LAUREN BACALL (*in an affected voice*): "I'm in a rogue state, honey,
Getting unpredictable and strange." --How's that?

STEVE: It just lacks something.

VOICE OF ST. JOHN OF THE CROSS. "I'm in a rogue state, honey,
Getting unpredictable and strange."

LAUREN BACALL: Who's that?

VOICE: You never let Bogie down—make sure you don't let poetry down.

LAUREN BACALL (*with renewed confidence*): That's right, I never did! Thanks! [*To STEVEN TAYLOR*]. Hit it, Maestro.

[*STEVEN TAYLOR plays "Rogue State" music. STUDENTS are drawn in by this bizarre music—ALISON, MIKE, JIM—all of whom will clap and scream wildly when she finishes.*]

LAUREN BACALL (*a la Waldman, scaring small children, etc*): I'm in a rogue state,
honey, getting unpredictable and strange . . .
Just a rogue state itching to
Test my harridan ballistic range.

National Missile Defense System
Got nothing on me
I can pierce through the genome project
With a cyborg's vitality . . .

I'm in a rogue state, Mr. President
Don't tell me what to do
Your rules aren't my rules
Cause I'm the Lady of Misrule . . .

[*Enter JORIE GRAHAM.*]

JORIE GRAHAM (*when clapping has died down, she continues to clap bitterly and slowly*):
The scope of your evil astounds me.

LAUREN: Look who's back, like a bad penny.

JORIE: I told you. I don't forgive and I don't forget. And when I see someone
push me into the grave I climb out like Carrie's mother.

LAUREN: Sitting pretty, Jorie Graham?

JORIE: I don't care about pretty, and I haven't been sitting. While you were in here trying to cover up the crime of the century, I was out shopping. At Agnes B. on Union Square.

KEVIN: Big news.

JORIE: And look what I bought.

FRIEDA: So—a ring?

JORIE: Look what came with it.

[*Enter LARS VON TRIER and DOGME, a four year old child.*]

LARS (*embarrassed*): She said she was having my baby.

JORIE: And here's the baby. —We call her, "Dogme 95."

FRIEDA: Oh, my God, how rude.

KEVIN: Are you two married now?

JORIE: You replaced me on TV, I replace you with VT.

[*All look blank, mumbling.*]

JORIE (*impatiently*): Von Trier. VT. TV? It's the kind of word-type pun only a poet knows how to execute.

LARS VON TRIER: Lauren Bacall, listen to me! This was not my idea, I swear!

LAUREN BACALL: Don't worry, Danish, I know all about it. [*She points to DOGME.*] That's not Jorie Graham's baby. That's the baby I had for Ursula Andress.

JORIE: Who told?

LAUREN BACALL: Jorie Graham, you've tried once too often to pull the wool over my eyes. [*To FRIEDA and KEVIN.*] You don't live at the Dakota your whole life without slipping on a snaily trail of deceptive rivals.

LARS: You mean—I'm free?

LAUREN BACALL: Lars von Trier, you big hunk of Danish film genius, does a girl have to throw herself at you to get you to marry her? I will if you need me to.

LARS VON TRIER: What'd you do that for?

LAUREN BACALL: Been wondering whether I'd like it.

LARS VON TRIER: What's the decision?

BACALL: I don't know yet.

LARS VON TRIER (*to DOGME*): Come here, baby. Give Daddy a kiss.

[*DOGME and LARS VON TRIER hug.*]

BACALL (*ironically.*) It's even better when you help.

FRIEDA: Shame on you, Jorie Graham!

STEVE: Loser.

JORIE: I suppose I've made a fool of myself once again, but what's a poet to do without her spiritual link to the divine? Ever since St. John of the Cross left me, I've lost my bearings.

LAUREN BACALL: Listen, Missie. I've been around the block a couple of times. A woman doesn't pull this kind of trick unless she's got something on her mind.

JORIE: On my mind?

LAUREN BACALL: Ever hear of—overdetermination?

JORIE: I believe I've heard Helen Vendler mention it on occasion.

VOICE OF ST. JOHN OF THE CROSS. Jorie—Jorie—

JORIE (*brightening*): Yes, St. John of the Cross!

VOICE: Say what's on your mind. About those tapes. About poetry. About extinction.

JORIE: Well, I—

VOICE: And let it be your own voice, don't echo mine, the broken down voice of a Spanish mystic who couldn't even order a taco at El Toro.

JORIE: You're so sweet. Actually I do want to say—

VOICE: But wait! I hear the footsteps of an important legend.

[*Enter URSULA ANDRESS in a beatific state.*]

KEVIN: Isn't that Ursula Andress?

FRIEDA: My favorite from the James Bond movies.

DOGME: Mama!

STEVE: And the new celebrity spokesperson for the Poetry Center.

LAUREN BACALL: You mean, I'm out?

STEVE: Hate to break it to you, Miss Bacall.

LAUREN BACALL (*to JORIE*): Now I know how you feel.

JORIE: Sauce for the gander, Lauren Bacall?

STEVE: But you had a great afternoon!

LAUREN BACALL: And there are some things bigger than our mere jobs and egos, I suppose.

JORIE: Yes, that's true.

STEVE (*annoyed*): Enough with the philosophy, you two. Shut up and listen to a real star for a change. Miss Andress?

URSULA ANDRESS: I made the difficult trek from Switzerland to bring this important message to the world. With me, I brought my baby, and I brought my dial-up connection to the divine. Tell us, St. John of the Cross, Spanish man.

VOICE: You'll all cheer up when I tell you what happened down at Agnes B. on Grant Avenue. Agnes B herself came out of the back room and when I explained to her the seriousness of the situation, she spoke right up. "I'll fund the Poetry Center," she said.

LAUREN BACALL: Good for her!

VOICE: "And Naropa, and St. Mark's." Incidentally it has been Agnes B. herself who's been buying up all the old tapes on Ebay, and I've brought them all back with her apologies.

FRIEDA: That's a relief.

VOICE: And she says she'll stop slaughtering cows to make her fine ladies' handbags.

JORIE: Let the voices sing! —That's my message.

[*STEVEN, can you improvise some martial, atonal chords during these speeches. Stir things up.*]

FRIEDA: Preserve the heritage of all poets everywhere.

LAUREN BACALL: Make the world safe for poetry.

URSULA ANDRESS: Give money to the Archives Project of Naropa, the Poetry Center at SF State, and St. Mark's Poetry Project.

ALL (*taking one step towards audience*): Let the voices sing,
Give money to preservation.
Open your checkbooks,
Fight time's strange power.

[*STEVEN, during next speech music will change to "As Time Goes By."*]

LAUREN BACALL (*at center stage*): What a day I've had. First flying into San Francisco in October, blue city, white sea, dozens of Starbucks to light my way. Then I meet poetry and it hits me like a sock in the kisser. Then love backs up like a cement truck and drowns me in Danish pastry. Then I get involved in this preservation thing and you know me, I don't do nothin' halfway. I'm a full-time woman with a 24/7 crusade. Back at the Dakota, Yoko Ono will greet me on my return and give me a white pillowcase filled with John Lennon's old pubic hair . . . [*Lost in thought, then abruptly.*] My God, know what I just remembered?

I was married—for eleven years—to Jason Robards Junior. Funny the way time slips away and some things you just blank out on.

[*MUSIC returns to martial spirit as before.*]

ALL: Let the voices ring,
Give your money to preservation.
Open your checkbooks,
Fight time's strange power.

END

The Big Keep was another unusual commission. Poet Anne Waldman, who had seen a number of poets theater plays at Naropa, where I was sometimes used to teaching a class for their Summer Writing Program, devised an entertainment consisting of a play that would argue for the value of preserving poetry readings and performances digitally. It would be a play written with a part in it for her, since she planned to tour it around to raise money for Naropa's efforts to digitize decades of readings and lectures which now sat rotting on tape. It was to be a play with an underlying panic about technology, and what better place to premiere it than San Francisco?

Today it holds up pretty well but there's one subplot (one might call it—or "running joke") that has been lost to time, and that's the bit where all of the characters have joined the Commonwealth Club to hear popular speakers like Eve Ensler and Larry Harvey. I don't know why but the airwaves and billboards were jam-packed with an unusual ad campaign trying to make the dreary old Commonwealth Club seem as hip and relevant as a must-hear podcast. They must have spent a fortune on these commercials, which all of us could parrot word for word. The punch line was always the same. The speaker wanted very much to get certain information from a famous person. "So I asked her!" he announced triumphally. The promise of instant and complete access (at a price) had always been the promise of Silicon Valley and it seemed to fit in with the characters of our play, who wanted immortality or, at any rate, to hear the living words for the immortal. Anne Waldman's guitarist Steven Taylor came on to play pretty much himself, able to indicate in a few notes and chords dozens of different moods—they played off of each other like Penn and Jillette or Nureyev and Fonteyn.

FRIEDA HUGHES ....Cecilia Dougherty
KEVIN KILLIAN...Rex Ray
JORIE GRAHAM...Jocelyn Saidenberg
ST. JOHN OF THE CROSS.. Wayne Smith
ALISON...Tanya Hollis
JIM.. Will Yackulic
MIKE.. Zakary Szymanski
STEVE DICKISON... Himself
LAUREN BACALL..Anne Waldman
LARS VON TRIER .... Kota Ezawa
ETHEL CHASE.. Mary Kite
MUSICIAN ....Steven Taylor
DOGME 95 .... Zora Ezawa
URSULA ANDRESS..Karla Milosevich

The Lenticular

characters

KABIN KARKI
an art writer

GRETA COURT
a registered nurse

ALLISON
her sister, an adept of the lenticular

MIDGE
a caterer

"DR TIM"
a prominent GP

[Play opens in Rosedale, an affluent suburb north of Toronto. In the salon of the Court sisters, guests gather for dinner.]

[Enter KABIN and GRETA.]

KABIN: But Greta dear, where are the goldfish I adore? I couldn't help notice the empty bowl out in the foyer.

GRETA: It's complicated.

KABIN: Their wee, mincing tails—so flirtatious. Tell me, is Allison home? I tell you, I'm dying to hear the latest about—oh, what is it that interests her so? Those little picture things that change.

GRETA: The lenticular, Kabin. That's her King Charles' head.

KABIN: Why do I so frequently think of lentil soup when you mention that word? *[Snaps fingers at an unseen audience.]* Greek experts, come, trace their common derivation.

GRETA: I shouldn't know this, but somehow I do, through osmosis I guess—my sad fate—lenticular images in fact do derive their name from the same root as the quotidian lentil.

KABIN: You nurses must know all sorts of things.

GRETA: I suppose we do.

KABIN: Between lentil beans, and those gerbils, and flashlights—

GRETA: When they learn I'm a nurse, men will always hone in on one ordinary extraction procedure. But in my case, Kabin, I'm concerned about my sister. She's obsessed. She's turned our entire dining room into a large lenticular artcube, that stretches from hutch to sideboard and gives the unsettling illusion that one has already eaten. You can't even make out the food on your plate, it seems to bilocate each time your fork makes a jab for it.

KABIN: I wonder if the extraction procedure to which you allude is the same one I'm thinking of.

GRETA (*wearily*): It is. The question is, what to do with Allison? You were engaged to her once, Kabin—give me some advice. I don't really love her the way a sister should.

KABIN: Ah me! She and I set a date,. and she broke it off. Why? Hard to say. But I still love her, speaking as an aesthetician. She's quite extraordinary looking, and she sure can rock a caftan.

GRETA: This time she's gone too far.

KABIN: Dear, you can always get new goldfish!

GRETA: She's called Tim! My boss! Doctor Tim! I couldn't be more embarrassed. And your mission, Kabin? Somehow distract Dr. Tim when dinner starts, don't let Allison browbeat him with her LQ test.

KABIN: Have I met Tim?

GRETA: I don't know, but I love him the way meat loves salt, as much as, or more than, my sister loves her lenticules.

KABIN: Oh, OK. What's cooking? It smells divine, and neither of you were ever known for your cuisine.

GRETA: Our salons are now catered, out of household things.

KABIN: And what's an "LQ test?"

GRETA: Here's the chef now.

[*Enter MIDGE, a caterer.*]

MIDGE: Miss Greta, we're going to start laying down the food in a minute. Hope you're hungry! Oh! Who's this?

KABIN: I'm Kabin Karki, from Nepal. Don't bother re-pronouncing my name, just remember it's like the little log cabin, and under its mat you'll find my car key.

MIDGE: I'm Midge. Of Midge's Digestibles. May I give you my card?

KABIN: But I would rather you let me give my heart—to sir, with love.

MIDGE (*puzzled*): Oh Miss Court, that mural in your dinette! It frightens me. I walk in from one door, I see a field of African veldt. Coming from the pantry, it's like a flowery apron on an amateur cook—you know, all violets, no real rigor.

KABIN (*to GRETA*): When we used to "date," Allison was all about grilling the wait staff. "Is this produce raw?" It was mortifying and I see she hasn't changed.

MIDGE (*producing a tray with hors d'oeuvres*): While we wait for the final guest, won't you try some nibbles? This is (*scrunches face to remember*) goldfish almondine, raised locally. Indeed within eight feet of the eat site.

GRETA: I'll have to check my own heart rate, after I scream.

MIDGE: "Tino Sehgal, 2011."

KABIN (*fretfully*): —Yes, think of Allison's work as performance art of a sort. You stood on line for eight hours at the Met, to watch Alexander McQueen fit Marina Abramovic. This you get every day, no waiting.

GRETA: No goldfish for me, thanks, Midge. Gee, it's like a Gershwin tune.

MIDGE: Miss Allison has ordered the Abbott Henderson Thayer special. Camouflage birds. From above, they're blue to match the sky, from below, nature gives them white underbellies, so their enemies think they're snow and burrow.

GRETA: I said no thank you.

MIDGE: Think of penguins!

KABIN: Midge, dear, let's meet again at the eat site.

[*Enter ALLISON COURT, binoculars in hand.*]

ALLISON: And who's this—is this the famous Doctor Tim I hear so much about?

[*Exit MIDGE.*]

KABIN: Allison, don't be so disconnected! You were my fiancée; you know I'm no doctor. You've known me since RISD where we worked with Dale Chihuly.

ALLISON: Rings a bell.

GRETA: Please, Allison, relax. Let this be one occasion where you don't whip out your LQ test at the drop of a napkin ring.

KABIN (*soothingly*): That's OK, Greta. Allison dear, try it on me! I love taking tests, it puts me firmly on the side of the federal.

GRETA: Oh dear!

ALLISON (*pleased to get a chance to let her LQ test sparkle*) My famous Lenticular Quotient test, the LQ test, is really cool. First step, Doctor, peer through these lenses and tell me what you see on my dining room wall.

KABIN (*obeying her*): A peacock's tail?

ALLISON: It's actually only more lenses, infinitely small, though I'm trying to enlarge them by one method or another.

GRETA: She thought she might found a new size of lenticule on the golden backs of my little fish.

ALLISON: We call this a lenticular print. It may look like a peacock feather to you, Dr. Tim, but it's really only superb printing by my factory elves.

GRETA: "Now run over to the other side and see what appears."

ALLISON: Now run over to the other side—[*to GRETA, sourly.*] Stealing my thunder, sister mine?

GRETA: I'm sorry!

ALLISON: Re-apply these binoculars to your eyes, Doctor, uh—Mr. whatever. And turn them to focus into the room on the far side of the threshold. What appears?

KABIN: Hastily, I see what looks like a gravestone in an autumn cemetery.

GRETA: Poor little innocent fish, sacrificed to lenticular science.

KABIN: A grayeyard in old Nepal, IMHO.

ALLISON (*assuming the attitude of a museum tour guide*): What the public came to love about the lenticular was its way of emblematizing the loss of the past to the present, or the present to the future.

KABIN: It makes time pass by quickly—a boon to the bored! One step and you're in the grid of life, proud as a peacock, but blink and, well, you're dead.

MIDGE (*from kitchen*): Not literally!

ALLISON: The Lenticular is death, but only the sort of death Massumi, echoing Michel Foucault, calls incorporeal materialism. And step back to where you were, or shut your left eye, and the grave disappears, and you're back to life (*or the next thing to it*)—you're back in the past. The past recaptured, the future negated. Proust would have loved it, and in his honor Midge is passing around some delectable goldfish almondine.

MIDGE (*calling from the kitchen*). Half a mo!

GRETA: Is it really about the passage from death to life?

ALLISON: And back again.

KABIN: Cher had a sizeable hit with that Massumian insight. "If I Could Turn Back Time," remember Allison? It was going to be our first dance as newlyweds. Cher stood atop an enormous battleship and made the world listen to itself! The tortoise nearly mated the hare.

ALLISON (*slowly*): I think I remember…. Doctor Tim.

[*Enter DR. TIM, a wealthy resident at Lovecraft General and GRETA's boss.*]

DR. TIM: I'm Dr. Tim! Are there two of us?

KABIN: I'm Kabin. And this is Allison, Greta's little sister. [*Lowering his voice.*] She looks sweet and innocent, doesn't she doctor, but believe me, she's Satan with that strap-on, as I'm sure you've heard.

DR. TIM: How do you do, Ms. Court? Now you have an interest in things lenticular, or so I hear from your charming sister.

GRETA: Hello, Doctor!

DR. TIM (*ignoring her*): Administer your LQ test, Allison, or should I say, Dolores, our Lady of Pain? A Swinburne touch to the lenticular, or so I have always thought since its adoption by medical science in the 1950s.

> Could you hurt me, sweet lips, though I hurt you?
> Men touch them, and change in a trice
> The lilies and languors of virtue
> For the raptures and roses of vice.

ALLISON (*eagerly*): Finally, one who understands! As a little girl I was drawn to the flame of the candle, rather than its wick. Daddy gave me a set of tiny cards, no bigger than your mandible, Doctor, each revealing a scene from nature. In one a green tree on a hill. Tuck up the card and the leaves turned red, tuck it up another notch and the tree is shining white with cold.

GRETA (*in a low voice*): That was my card, sister mine! Yours was the lighthouse.

ALLISON: In a second card a lighthouse stood wet and dark on a mossy cliff, but when I spun the card around my head, beams of light burst out ot its lens, under its dome, circling the dark bloody sea below.

GRETA (*low voice*): That was my heart, not the sea.

DR. TIM (*grabbing binoculars from KABIN*): My nose tells me dinner's ready in the next room. Shall I see what's cooking?

ALLISON: I've convoked this dinner to show off my newest work of art. That mural which performs life and death is lovely, but it's very 2008. My elves have been slaving day and night, weaving a carpet made of lenticules. You'll feel like you're walking on a cloud—and you will be!—and the next step you will be greeted by the hounds of Hell.

DR. TIM (*impressed*): By Jove! (*Sotto voce, to KABIN*): Satan with a strap-on, for sure!

KABIN: Allison, where's Greta?

ALLISON (*flippantly*): Have you checked the—nurses' station? That old-fashioned white she wears, the no-color of a movie screen. No wonder all you men prefer me, for I come in colors, everywhere. Do you know this poem, which I sort of adapted to my own style sense?

> Whenas in silks my lensic self goes,
> Then, then, methinks, how sweetly flows
> That liquefaction of my clothes.

Next, when I cast mine eyes and see
That brave vibration each way free;
O how that glittering taketh me!

DR. TIM: Do I hear raised voices from the pantry?

KABIN: Somehow Greta exited without being seen!

ALLISON: And you doubted the power of the purposive lenticular!

[From offstage we hear the raised voices in the pantry. Fearfully MIDGE screams out, "I'm sorry I killed your fish!" GRETA rumbles. "They were my heart, they were not fish. They were the lenses of my youth as a girl." A shriek.]

KABIN: Maybe "doubted" is the wrong word. I never "doubted" per se. But when we were an item, Allison, you used often to exaggerate your influence in world affairs.

DR. TIM: Mistress Allison, do you ever see clients alone? I have a bit of an extraction problem your arts might assuage.

KABIN: Remember when you said you met J.D. Salinger in—where was it, dear, somewhere doomy, like New Hampshire? And you talked him into putting those brassy stripes on the corners of his books?

ALLISON. "Brassy!" I think not. They do the trick, don't they? For Jerry, the lenticular bounces us back and forth from the illuminations that sometimes rattle our lives, turning us into quiz kids, and then back into the doldrums of the mundane, where we realize wisdom is but a fleeting thing. We're really as phony as the squares we despise.

KABIN: "Jerry"?

ALLISON: That is the name his intimates used to bark out erotic orders to him with, while tightly encased in black vinyl, as he lay moaning on the damp floor of his homely, Buddhist, dungeon basement. "Jerry, you piece of shit," began many perorations.

DR. TIM *(impressed)*: My word, Miss Court, you're a firework! Come on, show me what you're worth!

[*Enter GRETA, in a daze, her hands bloody, her maquillage whitened, drawn. Her formerly crisp nurse's uniform is stained and crumpled. She carries a large mirror.*]

GRETA: There was the real world, Allison, and then the world you took from me.

ALLISON: Hold up the mirror, do, angle it so we can see into my newly carpeted dining room.

KABIN: Doctor Tim, do something, poor dear's at the edge of shock!

GRETA: I'll be fine. Let's hold the mirror up to dialectic, shall we?

[*GRETA raises large mirror so that AUDIENCE can see the interior of the dining room. One enormous wall is woven with lenticules which seem to twinkle as the mirror trembles. On the new carpet, we see the dead body of poor MIDGE.*]

KABIN: How ghastly! Isn't she that catering girl so keen to pass on her card?

ALLISON: Perhaps!

[*Pause.*]

[*DR. TIM walks offstage to MIDGE's body, realizes that he's dead. We see him do so in the mirror. TIM realizes the horror of the situation and begins to scream.*]

ALLISON: Blow out the candles, Greta!

KABIN: My eyes are playing tricks on me! Is that Midge, or is it a whole system of values dead on the rug?

GRETA: It is not one person who ruined our lives, but a whole nexus of market demands.

DR. TIM (*from offstage*): By Jove, I think it's capitalism!

END

"The Lenticular" is the second of two plays I wrote as closet dramas, never imagining that they would be put on stage. The first was "The Pre-Poetic," written in spring 1998 as my contribution to *Shark #1*, a short-lived journal edited by poet Lytle Shaw and artist Emilie Clark. Eighteen of us wrote on the theme of the "pre-poetic," and I remember not even knowing what it was. Eventually the little play took its place among the poems in my collection *Tweaky Village*, while director Ajit Chauhan filmed it for an episode of his projected public access TV program Poets Theater Public TV. The Canadian-born, NYC-based artist Gareth Long asked me to write something creative for a show of his, *Never Odd or Even*, opening in November 2011 at Southern Alberta Art Gallery, Long had done lots of work with lenticularity, so I thought of what would happe`n if you went off the deep end and tried to live your life through the tightly coiled lens of the lenticule. "The Lenticular" seemed even more impossible to stage, so I didn't even try, but when the poet JenMarie Macdonald asked me for some short plays for her Philadelphia poets theater ensemble. I sent her both "The Pre-Poetic" and "The Lenticular" and to my surprise, she reported that Philly audiences loved the double bill.

"The Lenticular" was written as a catalogue essay for Gareth Long's mid-career retrospective exhibition *Never Odd Or Ever* (Southern Alberta Art Gallery, November 11, 2011—August 1, 2012).

The play was first produced by Vox Populi in Philadelphia on Saturday, March 20, 2015, directed by JenMarie Macdonald, with the following cast:

KABIN KARKI, an art writer .... Phil Mittereder
GRETA COURT, a registered nurse .... Jenn McCreary
ALLISON, her sister, an adept of the lenticular... .... Alexa Smith
MIDGE, a caterer.. Mel Bentley
"DR. TIM," a prominent G.P... Jason Mitchell

Box of Rain

characters

MARY MULHAIR
director of the Rumaker Gallery

RACHEL RUMAKER
her boss

RYAN TREE COLLINS

JASON JOHANSON
apparently his boyfriend, actually his son

JORDAN GADGET
police inspector investigating a theft

SIRI
computerized voice of a smart phone

HEIDI BROAN
reporter for the *Nob Hill Gazette*

PABLO PICASSO
the modernist painter

RODNEY
the inventor of the fax

THOMAS KINKADE
the painter of light

DORA MAAR
French painter and photographer

THIEF
a child of nine or ten maybe

[A contemporary gallery in San Francisco, with a fax machine prominent in the center of the office. MARY is seated, RACHEL standing looking over some papers in a folder. Enter RYAN and JASON, slightly drunk.]

RYAN: Guess what, you guys, Jason and me are starting an office pool! It was going to be about the 49ers, but then we figured—

JASON: It's summer, and that would be stretching it.

MARY (*absently*): That's nice, boys, count me in. I need a lift.

RACHEL: Mary, did my fax come yet?

RYAN: Rachel, Mary hasn't even heard what the pool is about—

JASON: What it embodies—

RYAN: And still she's willing to put money in.

JASON: That's what I call a good sport.

RACHEL: Oh for God's sake, leave Mary alone! The poor dear's been through enough what with the tragic loss of her husband.

MARY: No, I'm OK. But thank you, Rachel.

RACHEL (*to RYAN*): Your fly's open.

[He turns his back and adjusts. RACHEL rises to examine the fax machine]

MARY: Now what's this pool about?

RYAN: We did nothing but talk about it all night long at Absinthe!

MARY: Sorry I couldn't go help you celebrate.

JASON: I know, Mary—the death of Rodney is still such a painful memory.

MARY: Monday we were watching *Game of Thrones* re-runs, and by Tuesday—oh! It's just too awful to think about, even in this lovely gallery, in the heart of San Francisco.

JASON: There, there, Mary Mulhair, why you came back to work so soon I'll never know.

MARY: Because Rachel needs me.

RYAN: She needs to stop mooning over her star client, the painter of light, Thomas Kinkade. He was at Absinthe with Nancy Sinatra.

[*RACHEL returns.*]

RACHEL: Boys, forgive my snapping at you. We need you here at the gallery, you're our two, highly ornamental, gallery pets. I put you up front to give the place a bit of life.

MARY: Gay life.

JASON: In turn we think the world of you, Miss Rachel.

RACHEL: I'm afraid our days and nights at Absinthe are numbered. We're just about down to our very last Picasso.

MARY: And once Rachel was the dealer that Picasso always visited on his rare vacations to San Francisco.

JASON: Absinthe was absolutely packed last night, with actual celebrities, not just our San Francisco celebrities.

RYAN: In scare quotes.

RACHEL: Someone tell me, what is wrong with our damn fax machine? It keeps spitting out non-confirmations!

JASON: Even Danielle Steel gave up on our pokey old city of love. But you wouldn't know it from Absinthe last night, in one booth sat Jennifer Aniston and Fred Frith!

RYAN: You know what's tragic, there's not one person in all of San Francisco who knows who both of them are. We all know one or the other, but—

JASON: But we're compartmentalized, I agree. That is tragic.

RACHEL: What's tragic is that poor Mary here has lost her husband in a truly awful manner and all you two can do is talk about your death pool!

MARY (*slowly*): Death pool.

RYAN: That's characterizing it in a reductive way, Rachel.

JASON: That's like saying the World Cup is a yacht race.

RYAN: That's like saying Lou Harrison was only a San Francisco celebrity.

RACHEL: Cute as you are, I wash my hands of the two of you.

RYAN (*reading the monitor*): Here's a fax! Oh my God, Thomas Kinkade died!

JASON: The painter of light?

RACHEL (*sharply*): Tom?

RYAN: It's from his wife, she doesn't give many details.

MARY: That's two then—Rodney, my husband, and now Tom. Thomas Kinkade, who personally painted me and Rodney in the chapel that was our bedroom.

RYAN: Don't people always say that when one celebrity dies, there'll be three in a row?

JASON (*hysterically*): And Picasso!

RYAN: Jason, he's been dead since, I don't know, before I was born. I think.

RACHEL (*sits down again, dramatically*): Tom—dead?

MARY: Ah, Picasso! The dear old Catalan fool. I remember him coming into this gallery on his last trip, it was the 70s, he was in his 90s, but still he had that his eye for the ladies. I was just a silly gallery girl, but even I knew that he was the master.

RACHEL: Being Picasso's exclusive dealer in the Bay Area kept us afloat for years.

RYAN: But thank God you bought in on Thomas Kinkade early.

RACHEL (*to herself*): Oh my God, that I did!

MARY: I remember Thomas Kinkade when he was just a struggling grocery clerk at Safeway, bagging the lobster and greens I would make for Rodney when first we were wed. Kinkade gave me his card, can you imagine, a grocery boy with his own business card helping me with my bags, handing me his card, all covered with snow, and gold, and lighted windows of Christmas.

JASON: And now he's dead too.

MARY: Now this old business card is worth nearly as much as my Picasso.

RYAN: Rachel, I have something awful to tell you.

RACHEL: I don't know if I can take more bad news.

RYAN: We had that beautiful Picasso on an easel in the front room? By my desk?

RACHEL: What do you mean, "had"?

RYAN: The painting showed a strong woman's face, like Susan Sontag, or you know, what's her name from *The Lion, the Witch and the Wardrobe*? Swilda something.

JASON: Swilda Tinton.

RYAN: She's so mean in that.

JASON: She's strong. They're both strong. Like you, Rachel.

RYAN: And now's the time to show that strength.

MARY: Jason, could you do me a favor? You have such tiny fingers and you're always texting. Could you see if you could unjam our Fax machine? I tried this morning and it gave me a nasty shock, it did.

JASON: Yes, Mary. First let me get my WD40 or whatever it's called.

[Exit JASON.]

MARY: Like a goose walking over my grave. Do you remember, Rachel? That was Pablo's saying. One of his many Catalan sayings that had us in stitches, in the 50s, 60s, and 70s.

RACHEL: So Ryan, what do you mean, "had"? Past tense? Pablo's wonderful picture of Dora Maar, that I was planning to sell to keep our tottering gallery from going under?

RYAN: You know the first thing I noticed when I came in here, fresh from the Art Institute, looking for a job? That very picture, sitting on an easel as though Pablo Picasso himself had just signed it. And now?

[*Enter JASON with a can of WD40.*]

JASON: Dad, you're always embarrassing me.

[*Enter INSPECTOR.*]

MARY: I know you from somewhere!

INSPECTOR: From the Police Academy, perhaps, where I taught for many years? Were you a cadet?

MARY: That's not it, but welcome, sir. I'd get up but I'm still so upset about my husband, Rodney, and his sudden—well—I can't even say it.

RYAN (*whispers*): Suicide.

RACHEL: Ryan Tree Collins! You're not telling people that Rod killed himself, are you? Leave the poor man be.

RYAN: Of course not, I'm just asking this distinguished man if he's here to buy some art?

MARY: Rodney Faxenheimer would no more take his own life than he would—I don't know—than he would cheat on me with another woman.

[*Exit MARY.*]

INSPECTOR: We've had a call at the precinct that an important painting has been stolen.

RACHEL: My Dora Maar that Pablo gave me last time we—

JASON: Last time you what, Rachel?

RACHEL (*improvising*): Had a drink together at Tosca.

JASON: OK, this is what happened. We were both watching the painting from our desks, me and Ry both— Guarding it with our lives the way we usually do.

RYAN: It was about two p.m and I was a little sleepy after the long lunch celebrating our office death pool—

JASON: But all four of our eyes were absolutely fixed on the painting as it sat there, a liquid shock of paint, on its customary easel.

INSPECTOR: Now who are you two?

JASON: Oh! I thought you knew, I'm Jason Johansen, a young artist.

INSPECTOR: Oh?

JASON. Yes, and this is my dad, Ryan Tree Collins.

RYAN: Hi!

INSPECTOR: He's your "dad" in some complicated gay sense?

RACHEL: They are actually father and son in the biological sense.

JASON: I know it's weird kind of.

RYAN: May I finish please? So then chloroform filled the room, and the last thing I remember, a little boy walked off with the painting.

INSPECTOR: Run down the street, Ryan, see if you can identify the boy in a lineup.

[*Exit RYAN.*]

INSPECTOR: Down at the station house we're still reeling at the news about Thomas Kinkade.

RACHEL: My Dora Maar!

JASON: Here one minute, gone the next.

INSPECTOR: Meanwhile a piece of old technology like this old Fax machine just sits here dominating the entire gallery space, much as the stone heads of who knows what stand severe and menacing at Easter Island. [*INSPECTOR GADGET moves towards the fax machine.*] Does this thing have a camera in it? Maybe one that could see into the exterior lobby and tell us who stole the painting.

RACHEL: Did you meet Mary Mulhair, my director? Her husband only recently died.

INSPECTOR: The beautiful woman in black? Yes, I saw her.

RACHEL: Her husband, Rodney Faxenheimer, was the inventor of the fax machine, and this was the actual prototype, the very first one.

JASON: I don't understand Fax machines. Why did anybody bother to have them when you could just e-mail it or send it over your Blackberry.

INSPECTOR: You're too young, boy, to remember, but back in the day the Fax machine hit us like Picasso hit the art world with his blue period and broken guitars and women with three noses.

[*RACHEL and INSPECTOR are drawn towards each other as if by magic, and their conversation should reflect that.*]

RACHEL: Or when Thomas Kinkade hit the art world with his painting in light! It revolutionized the way we viewed our lives. After Picasso, what was the point of classical mimesis—of learning to draw?

INSPECTOR: Though he could do that too.

RACHEL: After Kinkade, and his diamond dust paintings of Christmas trees and pet shop windows glowing with candles and fire, you didn't really need electricity any more. One painting could light up a whole village.

INSPECTOR: Fireflies ceased to mate and reproduce.

JASON: Well, me and Ry—[*he is interrupted by the others*].

INSPECTOR: There was no categorical imperative, no need for the firefly to continue as a species.

JASON: I mean my dad—

RACHEL: Nor any need for flashlights. So when Rodney invented the Faxenheimer—later shortened to Fax—

INSPECTOR: Simple "fax," pure poetry.

RACHEL: All of a sudden it was, why did we ever mail letters, hire messengers, send documents overland? You didn't even have to do anything, just press a button.

INSPECTOR: You just had to believe, like Tinker Bell, that at the other end, the party you were trying to reach was reading your words.

RACHEL: Or viewing your image.

[*RACHEL and INSPECTOR freeze.*]

JASON (*to audience*): It's like I'm not even here. They're on a wavelength of their own. Must be a generational thing, when people had these Faxenheimer what's-its and to them it was a big deal.

[*He rises and moves around them, dialing a number, as SIRI enters silently, without speaking.*]

JASON: Hello? Fax people? We have a lifetime warranty on one of your machines, and we need service?

The serial number? Where is that supposed to be?
Repeat that please? Was it, "SIRI, Jason needs serial number of fax machine"?

SIRI: It is on the back.

JASON (*on phone*): It is number [*extremely slowly*] 000... 000... 1.

Or is it 4?

SIRI: It is definitely a 1. Rodney Faxenheimer was a complex man, but even the tormented begin with a binary code of good and evil.

JASON: Have the machine replaced, and send us a new one. If you still make them any more.

SIRI: They're not made any more.

JASON: That figures.

SIRI: Jason Johansen.

JASON: Yes, SIRI?

[*To audience.*] Weird, because she usually doesn't speak without being spoken to.

SIRI: If I were you, I would not ask to have Fax machine repaired. Let the dead be!

JASON: It's just that my father keeps me on apron strings! He won't even let me have a drivers license because he says, my mother died in a car wreck.

SIRI: "He says"? Have you verified the death of your mother with the car wreck people?

JASON: What are you saying? That she didn't die in a car wreck? Oh surely not. If she's alive I would hope she'd have been watching over me and for my graduation from SFAI she'd have given me a Lexus.

SIRI: I would not be so sure, or as they trained us to say, I would not be so SIRI.

JASON: Wait—don't go—tell me more—!

SIRI (*beckoning at RACHEL and INSPECTOR*): Stir from thy sleep, Inspector Gadget and Rachel Rumaker, out of the fog of love that time and loss have brought thee, a consolation prize for losing everything.

JASON: What about my mother?

[*Exit SIRI.*]

RACHEL: My goodness, where was I?

INSPECTOR: I've awakened from a deep refreshing sleep, by Jove.

RACHEL: I think you were there in my dream, Inspector Gadget.

INSPECTOR: And you in mine, Miss Rumaker, looking splendid in something by, oh what is the name of those two strange twin girls in LA.

RACHEL: Inspector, before I say anything more—

INSPECTOR: (*answering himself*). Rodarte!

RACHEL: I must ask you. Have you solved the puzzle of who stole my Dora Maar Picasso?

INSPECTOR: All reports, and video footage, indicate the crime was committed by a little boy. Perhaps nine. Or eight.

RACHEL (*looking at JASON*): A boy working under the direction of an adult?

JASON: I think I better go now.

[*Exit JASON.*]

INSPECTOR: Under the direction of an adult? Except in the imaginary kingdom of William Burroughs' Wild Boys, that is, sadly, the burden of all boys.

RACHEL: For girls it's worse! You wouldn't believe how difficult it was for me to become Picasso's San Francisco dealer. I was too pretty, haters said. Too elegant. Too smart and too sexy.

INSPECTOR: Well, the joke's on them. [*Picks up piece of cardboard.*] What's this—a photograph of the missing painting?

RACHEL: I took it with my iPhone just yesterday—funny! Almost as if I knew, or the iPhone knew—what would happen today. Kinkade always said, "Rachel, you're psychic, like the leprechauns of Ireland."

INSPECTOR: Funny—this face reminds me of my first wife.

RACHEL: Oh?

INSPECTOR: She was a terror.

RACHEL: Many wonderful men put up with harpies for first wives. You wouldn't be the first to suffer from the "Rebecca Syndrome."

INSPECTOR (*misunderstanding*): Oh no, her name was not Rebecca, her name was Dora. Not a harpy exactly, just a woman with a big appetite for life.

RACHEL: Hate that.

INSPECTOR: This looks just like her.

RACHEL: It's Picasso's portrait of Dora Maar.

INSPECTOR: Could be my wife to the life, and her name was Dora too. Coincidence?

RACHEL (*worried*): In what sense?

[*Enter HEIDI BROAN.*]

HEIDI BROAN: Inspector Gadget, have you at least identified the little boy at the center of this daring daylight heist?

RACHEL: Do you have children yourself, Inspector?

INSPECTOR: Only one.

HEIDI BROAN: I'm Heidi Broan from the *Nob Hill Gazette*. Tell me, Officer Gadget—

INSPECTOR: Inspector Gadget, from the Matthew Broderick flop.

HEIDI BROAN: Inspector, we have the testimony of not one, but two, drugged, gay men that they saw a little boy make off with the Picasso.

INSPECTOR: Ryan and Jason remain our primary suspects. Not no little boy, see?

HEIDI BROAN: You are homeschooling a young boy fitting the description given you by Ryan and Jason?

RACHEL: Nothing wrong with homeschooling! Thomas Kinkade, the painter of light, was homeschooled in a grocery store near here. And he turned out just fine!
[*Aside.*] Just fine—when he was in my arms. But when he walked out into the world he let dreams and daiquiris seduce him.

[*Enter MARY.*]

MARY: Hi Rachel! I had a call from the fax people. Turns out the fax machine isn't broken at all. They've made an extensive, systemwide check of their network and they say there's an open line from here to Colma.

HEIDI: Colma? Brrrr! There's nothing out there but graves!

MARY: So we're getting faxes from Colma only, but that's a start, isn't it?

RACHEL: No, some people live there. Tom's family hailed from Colma. There's a chapel deep in Colma Valley for travelling strangers in distress. They nestled among the ghosts of the pines in the shadow of a precipice.

INSPECTOR: Is that your fax now? I can almost hear its groan.

MARY: Is that the fax you've been waiting for, Rachel?

HEIDI: *Nob Hill Gazette* readers know that you, Rachel Rumaker, have had a long romantic career. You have bedded, if not wedded, some of the great artistic names of the previous century. Including Picasso and Thomas Kinkade. Now you've moved on to policemen?

RACHEL: I'm drawn to him, Heidi, though I don't know why!

INSPECTOR: For me the connection was instant, like a switch.

MARY: It's from Pablo!

RACHEL: Oh for goodness sakes, Mary, how can that be?

[*Enter PICASSO: On the left side of the stage, where from now on only the dead will gather, while the living remain on the right hand side of the stage.*]

PICASSO: The miracle of the fax!

RACHEL: He's been dead since 1973.

HEIDI: And he was plenty old then, and look at this, it's the handwriting of a young man.

MARY: He always had young handwriting.

INSPECTOR (*grabbing fax*): Dear Rachel,

PICASSO (*in unison with INSPECTOR*): Thanks to the miracle of the fax,

INSPECTOR and PICASSO: I am speaking to you from the land of the dead. Here is a little picture of a guitar to prove it is I, I Pablo Picasso.

RACHEL: That was "our instrument"—the guitar,

INSPECTOR and PICASSO: As you will remember, that was our instrument, Rachel Rumaker.

MARY: Fax him back! Maybe it works both ways.

RACHEL: I don't know what to say.

MARY: He's in the land of the dead, isn't he? Ask him if he's seen Rodney!

RACHEL: I hate to be a downer, Mary, but that seems like such a waste of a fax.

INSPECTOR and PICASSO: Many souls wander this desolate valley, in the shadow of the precipice.

[*Enter SIRI.*]

SIRI: Fax transmission slows and halts.

INSPECTOR and PICASSO (*slowly*): Goodbye, Rachel.

MARY (*bitterly*): Thanks, Rachel!

RACHEL: OK, get me a pen, I'll write whatever you ask.

HEIDI: Ask them if they've seen, you know, famous people like Michael Jackson and whoever. JFK.

SIRI: Many ask for Marilyn! And Hitler, of all people.

RACHEL (*reading what she's written*): Pablo, hi. Say, have you run into a guy called Rodney Faxenheimer—rather recently?

SIRI: Very nice.

MARY (*insistently*): He's cute.

RACHEL: Oh, Mary.

MARY: He was cute!

RACHEL (*re-writing*): A cute man called Rodney Faxenheimer. He may have a bullet hole in his chest.

INSPECTOR: In hell that's common. Thug life destroys.

SIRI: What color were his eyes?

MARY: I don't know, he was always wearing shades.

INSPECTOR: Was he tall?

MARY: Well, I had to look up.

SIRI and RACHEL: Yeah? Well I hear he was bad.

MARY: Mmmmm, he's good-bad, but he's not evil!

RACHEL: I should ask Pablo about Tom, too.

INSPECTOR: Tom who?

RACHEL: —Nobody.

SIRI: Yes, we see!

HEIDI: Let's bring in the TV cameras for this one. B.R.B.Y.—be right back, y'all.

[*Exit HEIDI BROAN.*]

PICASSO (*reading fax*): "Hi Pablo. Say, have you met a cute guy called Rodney recently?" Bah! "Bullet hole." Oh yes, *si, si,* he's the man we call Bullet Hole. Hey! Bullet Hole!

[*Enter RODNEY.*]

PICASSO: What'd they put on that bullet hole, *hermano,* that looked fierce when you came in! When was that, yesterday?

RODNEY: Tuesday, I think. Right after *Game of Thrones.*

PICASSO: Exchanging rounds with the Fascists?
SIRI: That's private, Picasso.

PICASSO: Everything's private in the land of the dead.

[*He presses the fax button.*]

[*On the other side MARY reads from his fax.*]

MARY: "Rodney is here, Rachel. Cute Rodney. Were you his lover, Rachel? He came here blown away by huge *Guernica*-size hole in belly."

Oh, how awful!

PICASSO: Big fucking hole, man.

RODNEY: I still feel a little nauseous. Is that normal?

SIRI: Yes, Rodney, it is normal. Want some Pepto?

RACHEL: I was never his lover.

MARY: I know.

RACHEL: I like guys, but Rodney I never felt that, you know, that yen for. He only had eyes for you, Mary.

MARY: Then why did he do it?

RACHEL: Maybe—oh, who knows.

RODNEY: SIRI, fetch me some paper. No, better yet, write down what I say.

SIRI: Yes, Rodney?

RODNEY: Tell her that I did it because I was upset, upset that no one was using my innovation, the fax machine. I was on the discard table like an old—what were those little dolls called?

PICASSO: The Beanie Babies?

SIRI: Message sent.

INSPECTOR (*nervously*): I think there's been too much faxing here and not enough detective work. [*He points to his butt.*] See this? That's the seat of my pants and that's how I cracked the Patty Hearst kidnapping and many other crimes in the cool gray city of love.

RACHEL: I'll go with you, but isn't this sort of—wow?

INSPECTOR: Depends on how often you've heard from the dead.

RACHEL: Now how about your wife, Dora? Is she still with us?

INSPECTOR: You mean—?

SIRI: Human catching on!

RODNEY: We're human too, SIRI: we don't stop being human just because we die—of old age, Pablo Picasso—or of suicide, the pain that's too great to keep living with.

PICASSO: In Paris, during the Spanish Civil War, did I, Picasso, keep from painting? When paintbrushes ran out, I used my, how do you say, my dick!

SIRI: All disperse.

RODNEY: You disgust me, Picasso.

PICASSO: Pendejo.

RODNEY: Your disgusting dick.

SIRI: I say, disperse!

[*All leave the stage, under hypnosis and walking like sleepwalkers with their arms outstretched. Enter RYAN and JASON on the right hand side.*]

RYAN: Where can we go, to be alone?

JASON: Why? At home you don't even speak to me.

RYAN: We have to talk about Rodney!

JASON: That funny little man?

RYAN: I liked his big bulky sweaters.

JASON: That matched his eyes.

RYAN: His dirty fingernails,

JASON: Oh boy what a prize.

RYAN: He was kinda cute.

JASON: Tight tapered pants.

RYAN: High button shoes.

JASON: He was always looking, like he had the blues.

RYAN: And that means [*pause*], sad.

JASON: I can never—

RYAN: Never—

JASON. Never—go home any more.

RYAN: No, you can never—never—never—go home any more.....

RYAN: We can't tell Mary Mulhair. She'll flip.

JASON: It's not like anything ever happened, Dad.

RYAN: Where did I go wrong? I tried to bring you up as any gay dad might, once he learned his son was gay. I tried to preserve a youthful look; I worked only at entry-level positions hoping that someday you would join me, Jason—And I'm glad you did. And dating the same guys worked, didn't it?

JASON: Up to a point, but one of us should have kept his paws off the late Rodney Faxenheimer.

RYAN: I resent your implication that it should have been I.

JASON: Well, you're older and wiser. Supposedly.

RYAN: I wish your mother was alive to wash your mouth out with soap.

JASON: Whatever.

RYAN: But she died in that plane crash.

JASON: Plane crash!

RYAN: Car crash I mean.

JASON: Look, Dad, we've had fun in the past but maybe, if we brought a man to suicide, that's the proverbial little voice that says, "Jason and Ryan, break up."

RYAN: You can't break up a father and a son! That's what blood is all about.

JASON: And that means [*pause*]—sad.

[*Enter MARY.*]

MARY: Hello Jason and Ryan! My God, I've been through the treadmill what with Rod's suicide, et cetera. Thank goodness I have you two and your bright, sunny, vivacious personalities when I come to work every day.

RYAN: Mary, have you considered maybe a break?

JASON: Ry and I have friends in Guatemala—who would love to have you as a sort of permanent houseguest.

MARY: You boys are so sweet, but I can't leave the fax machine.

JASON and RYAN (*in unison*): The fax machine?

JASON: That old thing?

MARY: Haven't you heard?

RYAN: Heard what? We've been busy assisting clients, dealing with paparazzi,—

RYAN and JASON: "I'm your biggest fan/ I'll follow you until you love me,/ Papa, paparazzi."

MARY: They fixed the fax machine and we've been hearing from the dead and I'm hoping Rodney will fax me.

JASON: But that's crazy!

MARY: Maybe so, but I just feel so—well—I guess I'm looking for closure. Though it was nice that when he died, he was at your apartment, so he was surrounded by friends.

JASON: We were watching TV and heard a shot from the bedroom.

RYAN: We ran in and found poor Rod exactly halfway between my bed and Jay's.

MARY: As though he couldn't decide! He was always that way—indecisive, like he couldn't make up his mind. Anyhow boys, I am so grateful to you for making him your "straight friend." He often said that my introducing him to you two had changed his life utterly.

JASON (*to RYAN*): We destroyed his suicide note! Now he'll send as many as he needs to till she gets the message.

RYAN: Then unplug the thing, Jason! You young people are geared for high tech, I'm not.

[*Enter INSPECTOR.*]

INSPECTOR: Now which one's Ryan, and which one's Jason?

[*They identify themselves briefly.*]

INSPECTOR: So half knocked out by chloroform, you saw a little boy drag away the Picasso painting right off the easel.

JASON: He was a tiny runt, no bigger than Kylie Minogue.

RYAN: He was like a child's version of Kylie. Like Kylie as seen by a child.

JASON: An imaginative child.

RYAN: He had to reach up to the easel to grab the bottom of the painting, and pull it down on himself, like a cat unplugging a fax machine.

JASON: Dazed as we were, that detail struck us both. And his clothes. Rather quaint, like he's been reading Dickens or maybe trying out for *Billy Elliot*.

INSPECTOR: Tell me more about the death of—

RYAN: Of who? Haven't we had enough questions? It's like the video for "Paparazzi"!

RYAN and JASON: "Baby, you'll be famous/ Chase you down until you love me,/ Papa, Papa-razzi."

INSPECTOR: The death, of course, of Thomas Kinkade, the painter of light!

MARY: Why? Have there been developments?

INSPECTOR (*pulls out fax*): We've had a communiqué from the haunted fax machine, purportedly from the painter of light himself!

MARY: Oh really, what does he say? You know he and Rachel were very close.

INSPECTOR (*alarmed and jealous due to his new passion for Rachel*): Oh really? How close?

[*While MARY looks away, JASON and RYAN fill in the inspector by making the pantomime gesture for fucking, darting an index finger into the circle made by the thumb and index finger of the other hand.*]

MARY: Oh, Thomas Kinkade, what a wonderful artist, they'll be nobody like you for ever and a day!

[*Enter THOMAS KINKADE, on other side of the fax machine.*]

THOMAS KINKADE: I hear voices!

MARY: He was blind, you know.

INSPECTOR: A blind painter?

RYAN: There are many such, Inspector. And wow, there are some hot blind guys in general, wouldn't you say, Jase?

THOMAS KINKADE: Mary, if you can hear me, send me a fax—in Braille of course.

JASON: Kinkade could see when he started out—

MARY: When he was a grocery boy at Safeway, he could see like an eagle.

RYAN: They promoted him to the guy who sits in the booth and watches for shoplifters.

JASON: What Foucault called the panopticon.

RYAN: He could catch a thief stuffing a pot roast down his pants like nobody's business.

THOMAS KINKADE: I was the painter of light, and even in the dark I could remember little things no one had noticed or remembered, the tear on a face; the blood beating beneath the wrist. The crunch of a light bulb, the taste of whiskey.

INSPECTOR: At home my wife had his brilliant recreation of her French childhood in Argentina, replete with thousands of tiny star-like Christmas lights on the pampas.

MARY: Your wife? Inspector Gadget, I thought you were a single man.

JASON: Don't you have a little boy?

RYAN: About the size of a child Kylie Minogue, dressed in a play suit?

INSPECTOR: Look, I'm the one asking the questions here.

JASON: I guess we can tell when we're not wanted, eh Dad?

RYAN: We may be gay but we're not totally insensitive!

JASON: You'll miss us when we're gone.

MARY: That's what Rod used to say, how I'd miss him once he left.

RYAN: Aw, we didn't mean it like that, Mary, we're just feeling snubbed.

JASON: We're going down to the corner for a couple of coconut flips and we'll feel warm and toasty all over again—

RYAN: Not just suspects!

[Exit RYAN and JASON.]

THOMAS KINKADE: Someone write a fax for me! Ask the authorities, has there been an autopsy yet—on my body!

INSPECTOR: I don't know, Mary Mulhair, want to join them?

MARY: Why don't we go to a straight bar and have some regular drinks?

[Exit INSPECTOR and MARY.]

THOMAS KINKADE: One minute I was walking in the Stanford Shopping Center eating a hot dog cooked in beer, next minute I woke up here, with weird music like Kraftwerk playing, and a voice in my ear saying,

[Enter DORA MAAR.]

DORA MAAR: Hello, darling, welcome to hell.

THOMAS KINKADE: You again!

DORA MAAR: Might as well learn my name! It's Dora Maar.

THOMAS KINKADE: That's a racetrack near my house.

DORA MAAR: Dora is easy enough…..

THOMAS KINKADE: Near one of my many houses. I'm at the pool lounging and sipping a Mai Tai, and I sniff and there's the unpleasant odor of horse.

DORA: And Maar, it rolls off your tongue, they named a planet after me, Mars, the red planet.

THOMAS KINKADE: Could this really be hell?

DORA MAAR: I shrug. I don't know, darling, it could be heaven depending on if, when you were alive, you came from Palo Alto.

THOMAS KINKADE: It feels like heaven in a way. Then why can't I see again?

DORA MAAR: No little bright specks in your iris? It happened to De Kooning when he crossed over, and he wasn't even blind.

THOMAS KINKADE: De Kooning told me that I was the best painter of my generation.

DORA MAAR: Then maybe he was blind.

THOMAS KINKADE: I bought the town he lived in and he gave me a brush. I sold the little hairs of the brush, and recouped what I spent on the town.

[*Enter SIRI.*]

DORA MAAR: Ah, Madame SIRI, with your little voice like the eye of a needle, you understand me?

SIRI: A fax has come from the outside world.

THOMAS KINKADE: For me? I'm opening a retail store in Poughkeepsie tonight at 6:30, with my DNA.

SIRI: I'm sorry, Mr. Kinkade, this fax has come for Mademoiselle Maar.

DORA: Dora Maar! From the red planet?

SIRI: Oh, no, I'm looking for the Dora Maar who was Picasso's mistress on planet Earth I guess you'd call it.

DORA: Ah, forget my little irony, SIRI. I'm sorry. That fax is for me! But what is a fax?

[*Enter RODNEY*]

RODNEY: This is so typical. "What is a fax?" So easily they forget! The fax was once the most important tool in business! Without my machine, we would never have been able to engineer neoliberalism. NAFTA bill would still be sitting on Clinton's desk, unsigned. Now people are throwing away my machines! Literally bound for the junk heap.

SIRI: Miss Maar of earth, your question to SIRI was, "What is a fax?"

DORA MAAR: And then this big strong manimal came in despair, tearing out his hair, and I was enchanted—like a little girl in Argentina on a balcony.

THOMAS KINKADE: He's a loser!

RODNEY: Loser!

THOMAS KINKADE: He wears the invisible marks of the suicide, that even a blind man can see.

SIRI: A "fax" is any message or image transmitted electronically from what is known as a fax modem, and transported over distant places. For example, I could "fax" you from Scientology headquarters near Fort Lauderdale, Florida.

DORA MAAR: Read to me my fax. Is it from Picasso? He made me the weeping woman over and over again in many statues and paintings.

THOMAS KINKADE: Lady, you're out of luck. I'm blind, see? Though wait! I do see little dabs of light, like butter, melting, across the curtain of black.

DORA MAAR (*grabbing fax from SIRI*): No—it is not from Picasso at all—it is from (*her voice chokes*)—My former husband, my earth husband.

RODNEY: You see—fax works!

THOMAS KINKADE: If it's so great, how did you wind up in that bedroom, on the floor, halfway between the bed of one man and the bed of another?

DORA MAAR: What do you do after Picasso disappears? For me there was God, and there was my career! In time I came to eclipse the old Catalan goat, nowadays all connoisseurs know, Picasso nothing, Dora a star. But anyway I went to San Francisco, and married a cop.

[*Silence.*]

DORA MAAR: You heard me! A cop! And here he is, "Dora—if I can reach you in the kingdom of the dead, I need to see you. Can you meet me at the Rumaker Gallery, by the empty easel?" Easier said than done, policeman!

RODNEY: Go to Colma! That's where the membrane is thinnest. Concentrate, and you can hear the footsteps of the living right above our heads.

DORA (*waving fax*): That's all he says! Not even a word about—about our little boy?

ALL: You had a son?

DORA: I did not say that, I am in denial, what little boy?

SIRI: Let us each write a fax detailing our most secret desires and send it on to the land of the living.

KINKADE: I'd like to send a fax to *Artforum* or whoever pointing out that whatever Olafur Eliasson has or had, they were all tricks stolen from the man they call—the painter of light!

SIRI: Don't speak! Write it down, and yes, Thomas Kinkade, you can use Braille.

RODNEY: I hate to be a Johnny one note, but—fax works, it's simple as that.

DORA MAAR (*mutters in French*).

SIRI: You had a son?

[*ALL characters disperse. On the right side of the stage RACHEL and HEIDI enter.*]

RACHEL: Back when I met Picasso, the Grateful Dead came into the gallery looking for a skull and roses. Pablo took to the boys right away and produced skull after skull, rose after rose for them. But Heidi, you know all this, right?

HEIDI: Rachel Rumaker, you have lived a lifetime of adventure and still you look approximately 32 years old. I know you patronize many fine *Nob Hill Gazette* advertisers, looking for beauty.

RACHEL: Heidi, we both know beauty comes from within. Lean in, lean in to my magical fax machine. If you listen hard you can hear whispers.

HEIDI: Okay—I'll give it a shot. It's sort of kooky. I can't wait for the movie where Miranda July or Zooey Deschanel play me.

RACHEL: What do you hear?

HEIDI: Why—it's by the Grateful Dead, isn't it?

RACHEL: Yes, the song they wrote for Pablo after he cut off Jerry's middle finger with a spackle drill. "Look out of any window, any morning, any evening, any day…."

HEIDI: Are there ants in the machine? It's like a chorus of little ants singing.

RACHEL: They're not ants, they're the tiny voices of the dead, missing me in their different ways, I expect.

HEIDI: "But it's just a box of rain/ Or a ribbon for your hair/ Such a long long time to be gone/ And a short time to be there."

RACHEL: So if I lose my gallery to creditors, it's not the end of the world! How much, if you don't mind me asking, do you make at the Gazette?

HEIDI: It's a volunteer newspaper actually. So I don't know. We do get paid, but we're not allowed to look at the check.

RACHEL: Do you know what it's like to love a married man who is slowly growing blind? I joked that if in the future I ever got a wrinkle, he wouldn't even know.

HEIDI: I think every woman knows that feeling.

RACHEL: Kinkade said he didn't need to see in order to paint, he would just plunge the brush into the paint and Christ would take care of the rest.

HEIDI: He had such sparkling eyes for an old man.

RACHEL: Heidi! He was no older than a really great Rauschenberg combine. And those sparkling eyes? He just painted them on himself, the sparkle was actual diamond dust. Eyes, painted on a pair of dark glasses.

HEIDI: Eyes that twinkled when he walked toward you in a crowded fern bar.
[*Pause.*]

RACHEL: Et tu, Brute?

HEIDI: Don't Brute me, I was his fiancée, and who were you, just a parasite! Was Picasso married too, when you had your way with him during the summer of love?

[*Enter RYAN.*]

RYAN: Rachel! Reporter! What am I to do, that Inspector won't believe my story about the chloroform and the little boy!

HEIDI: He asked me if you had a little boy, and I said, "Only Jason Johansen."

RACHEL: I never expected loyalty from a reporter, but can't you see, Jason's been scared half to death."

[*Enter MARY.*]

MARY: A fax for Jason!

RACHEL: An ordinary one, or a—special one?

RYAN: I'm gulping. Like [*he demonstrates*]. Now I'll read it aloud. "Dear Ryan, don't worry, the truth will come out and you will be cleared."

RACHEL: Who wrote that?

RYAN: It's like they're watching us!

HEIDI: And then Inspector Gadget asked me about who was Jason's mother.

RACHEL: Can we talk about this in my office, Heidi Broan?

[*Exit RACHEL and HEIDI.*]

MARY: What are you telling them about Jason's mom?

RYAN: Mary! You know I would never tell, even if they poured hot coals in to my rectum.

MARY: It was so long ago—we were both so young and foolish. And both involved with other people—I was newly married to Rodney Faxenheimer—

RYAN: And I, involved deeply with the late Harvey Milk.

MARY (*lifting a fist to the skies*): Rodney, God help me, you drove me into this man's arms with your neglect of a woman's needs! I know you were inventing heavily, and betting your shirt that the fax machine would become universally used and beloved—which it did, Rodney, it did!

RYAN: During your pregnancy—did he never suspect?

MARY: God help us, he had his brain inside that imaginary machine—He never saw that deep within me, I was growing your child, Ryan Tree Collins. And he didn't even notice that I had given birth. I was annoyed, I guess you might say.

RYAN: So awkward, Mary dear.

MARY: I waved him in Rodney's face, making the baby wave as if to say, "Hi Dad," but he never blinked an eye. So one day I just decided to give the baby to you, for you to raise him.

RYAN: Oh my God, that's right!

MARY: That's why I thought it was so nice when, in recent months, Rodney seemed to take an interest in you two, and spent all his time with his two gay friends.

RYAN: I couldn't tell him that Jason was your son. It would have violated the terms of the pact you and I made, back in the 80s.

MARY: Instead you just—

RYAN: Well, I had to make up some reason why I'd be interested in him!

MARY: You sort of led him on a little bit?

RYAN: Well, he was great at parties, for I could introduce him as my friend who invented the fax machine. People just couldn't believe it! One queen was like, and was it you who painted those poker playing dogs?

MARY: He had the patent to prove it.

RYAN: One of the very first patents ever issued in the US—

MARY (*giggling*). And he could prove it. He had it tattooed on a very private place.

RYAN: Well, on his cock. Not so private. He would pull it out at a moment's provocation, and after awhile he would do it even without asking. Patent 115. I'll never forget that number, it was in my face so often.

MARY: Oh, those hot tub parties! He would tell me all about them.

RYAN (*aside*): Dear Rodney, why did you say we had a hot tub? Now I can never have Mary over my place again. [*To MARY.*] Hold on, Mary dear, I'm just sending a fax. No, not that kind of fax! Just to the press.

MARY: Anyway, anything that could get Rod together with little Jason, I was all for. [*Giggling.*] Did he show Jason his tattoo, too?

[*Embarrassed pause.*]

RYAN: You loved him, didn't you?

MARY: I never understood him.

RYAN: Oh my God, it's like that song from *Chess*! [*To SIRI.*] Help me with this one, SIRI!

[*Enter SIRI.*]

SIRI: Yes, Ryan Tree Collins. The big, ABBA-inspired duet from *Chess*.

RYAN and SIRI:

Looking back,
I could have played it differently,
Won a few more moments,
Who can tell,
But it took time to understand the man,
Now at least I know
I know him well.

MARY: That was very nice, Siri. Come, let us all go to confession, and remember our sins in our different ways.

[*Exit RYAN, SIRI and MARY. Enter PICASSO and DORA MAAR.*]

PICASSO: So we meet again, Dora Maar. You're lovely as ever. Still a spitfire?

DORA MAAR: Yawn! I've seen this movie, when I lived on earth and it was called *Pretty in Pink*.

PICASSO: We have frozen to our Platonic ages—as we look the best. Do you have a studio?

DORA MAAR: If you can call it that. You?

PICASSO: The whole kingdom is my atelier, the kingdom of the dead, like my famous picture, *Guernica*.

DORA MAAR (*evenly*): I was there when you made your *Guernica*, Pablo Picasso. Out of my bones, my tears, Picasso, you made your *Guernica* and then it was Dora who?

PICASSO: I had to laugh, someone faxed me an article from the other place, and in it the writer said, that I would be remembered if at all as an important man in the life of the artist Dora Maar.

DORA MAAR: I'll laugh with you. Ha, ha, ha.

PICASSO: So who stole my picture of you, in San Francisco, at the Rumaker Gallery? Your feminist minions? Yes, even Picasso has his Valerie Solanas girls.

DORA MAAR: The girls who hate you. Yet this was a boy. Or so they say.

PICASSO: Always with the "or so they say," you suggestive tease. For once say it the way you feel it. Tell the truth in blue and rose, like your periods, like my periods.

DORA MAAR: The truth? OK.

PICASSO: Was it not a boy?

DORA MAAR: This is gonna sound like I'm playing you for a fool, Picasso, but the truth is, I don't know who that little boy was. If only we weren't so far away, under the earth, and the curtain over our heads, of grass and dirt, weren't so thick. Why don't they just bury us under glass?

PICASSO: Remember when I painted sheets of glass, and the *pendejo* under the glass filmed me with his movie camera?

DORA MAAR: So we could see better.

[*Enter SIRI.*]

SIRI: It was a little boy—not yours, Dora Maar?

DORA MAAR: I have no issuance.

PICASSO: Sing us a Spanish song, Siri, bring back to me the days when I was a child of nine or ten, running drugs in Catalonia with no ass in my short trousers.

SIRI: Spanish songs are numerous, Pablo Picasso. Developed in—

PICASSO: Just pick one, and sing it!

DORA MAAR: Above the grass, maybe the sun is shining, birds are singing, no rain is falling from a heavy sky.

SIRI: All right, Picasso. "Tropical the island breeze/ All of nature wild and free/ This is where I long to be/ La isla bonita./ And when the samba played/ The sun would set so high/ Ring through my ears and sting my eyes/ Your Spanish lullaby."

[*Enter THOMAS KINKADE.*]

KINKADE: Hi everyone, what's up? Looks like a party!

PICASSO: Where are the dark spectacles, Kinkade?

KINKADE: Don't need them no more! My eyesight is back, better than before. I can see every drop of sin in your eyes, Picasso. And as for you, Dora Maar, there are holes in your soul deeper than the potholes on Sand Hill Road in Palo Alto, where I went to high school.

DORA MAAR: So you have been cured in death.

KINKADE: It's the resurrection of the body—just as Christ promised me long ago, at Safeway, where I thought of adding little bits of diamond dust to every drop of soil, to give life a kick.

PICASSO: Was it Christ who taught you to mount old-fashioned trains around and around the Christmas tree?

SIRI: Yes, he was taught by Christ.

PICASSO: Next stop, Candy Cane Junction.

DORA MAAR: Hear that noise?

SIRI: The people of the living have captured a fugitive.

[*Enter JASON and THIEF BOY.*]

JASON: I've got him! I've got him! The little boy who stole the painting!
THIEF: Did not.

JASON: Where is everyone? Finally I do something for humanity, and there's no one here to praise me.

THIEF: I'll praise you, mister. Let me go I'll give you a hand job.

JASON: Ugh, you're only 9 or 10, come back in say, oh, I can't add up that high.

DORA MAAR: So it was a little boy! And yet he looks queerly familiar.

PICASSO: I could use him as the boy who brings in the horse in that painting.

THIEF: So you'll let me go?

JASON: I suppose they'll stick you in, what's it called, where kid criminals are born.

THIEF: In juvie? Hell no, I'd rather go to the French Academy.

[*Enter MARY.*]

MARY: Jason Johanson, you've done it again. How did you find him?

JASON: Grindr—but it's too complicated to explain, Mary dear. Where's my Dad?

THIEF: A child walks the moonlight, climbs the steps to the tower of his father.

KINKADE: The words of Jim Morrison, my master.

[*Enter INSPECTOR and RACHEL.*]

INSPECTOR: Ah, here we are at last, eye to eye with the little thief.

THIEF: I stole nothing.

INSPECTOR: A father and son have both sworn you took Picasso's painting of Dora Maar off the empty easel in the outer room.

RACHEL: Don't yell at him, Jordan. Remember your blood pressure.

THIEF: First of all, I took nothing.

PICASSO: He's got negativity—I like that.

THIEF: And first of all, what I took belongs to me.

RACHEL: But that was my painting!

THIEF: It was of Dora Maar, so it belongs to me.

INSPECTOR: Dora Maar, my former wife when we lived together in the Richmond? The artistic type?

DORA MAAR: It's Jordan Gadget! The man I married after I left you, Picasso!

THIEF: You are Jordan Gadget?

INSPECTOR: Sit down here on this bench, sonny boy. Come sit beside me. I was going to say, on my knee, but that brings back terrible memories of Anthony Hopkins as the mad ventriloquist in *Magic*.

THIEF (*sitting down*): Is this OK, Jordan Gadget?

DORA MAAR: There's something terribly wrong there.

[*Enter RODNEY.*]

INSPECTOR: Call me Inspector Gadget, son.

THIEF (*amused*): I don't think so.

PICASSO: Siri! What's going on?

SIRI: The activation of—

RODNEY: It's my fax machine, invented by me with patent # 115! It caused time to collapse in the kingdom of the living, just as I planned for it to happen. Soon as the system knew I was dead, it was programmed to activate the Faxenheimer time collapse!

DORA: Speak in English—I mean French. Speak in rose and blue for once, not your scientific mumbo jumbo!

RODNEY: He's talking to himself as a child—they're the same person.

KINKADE: For goodness sakes, are you just working that out now? I've known that for half an hour. —Christ told me.

GADGET: So you stole the painting because—

THIEF: Because it showed my wife to me, so I would keep it and in years to come I would know who to marry.

MARY: If only things were that simple!

THIEF: They are that simple—now.

[*Enter RYAN.*]

DORA MAAR: So later in life, that boy grows up, and becomes him, and marries me, rescuing me from my job at Flax Design on Market?

GADGET: Well! I don't know what to say.

RACHEL: Ask him where the painting is now.

RYAN: If only Rodney were here to watch this! I miss him!

MARY (*clutching RYAN's hand*): Me too.

RODNEY: To hell with the lot of you!

THIEF: The painting has disappeared, squeezed through a wrinkle in time—into a knothole of nothing—

JASON: What?!

THIEF: But, I'll know when my love comes along.

JASON: Why did you chloroform us, that was just rude. Many gay men suffer from substance allergies, though as it happens I'm not one of them.

THIEF: Okay, okay, it's back on the easel.

[*Enter HEIDI BROAN, with painting.*]

RACHEL: Oh my God, it's back!

RODNEY: Yes, but due to the time collapse, it's not yours any more.

SIRI: I will fax her and tell her.

INSPECTOR: But due to the time collapse, Ryan, you are now Jason's son instead of vice versa. All power relations switch.

JASON: Ryan and I own the gallery, and Mary and Rachel are our assistants, and they're running the office pool.

MARY: And JFK and Marilyn are still alive, and Michael Jackson.

HEIDI: Time collapse on Nob Hill? Who, what, when, where and—[*pause*] OK, I give up.

JASON: How?

RYAN: Why?

THIEF: And I can feel myself growing older minute by minute. Soon I will be the oldest man in the room.

INSPECTOR: And I will be the child.

THIEF: Jordan Gadget.

INSPECTOR: And you will grow, and you will already have loved and lost the beautiful Dora Maar.

DORA MAAR: And I will never know how much he loved me.

PICASSO: He just seemed like an American oaf.

THIEF: Stop the fax machine! I must find her!

RODNEY: Too late, little boy, or should I say, college student? Young cop?

THIEF: If you can hear me, Dora Maar, under the ground, move to the fax machine, where the air is thinnest.

DORA MAAR (*she does so*): Where the sky is like glass and I can almost see your feet.

THIEF: Hold out your hand like this—can you feel me?

DORA MAAR: I'll try.

[*Their hands touch, but they don't know it.*]

SIRI: "Tropical the island breeze/ All of nature wild and free/ This is where I long to be/ La isla bonita./ And when the samba played/ The sun would set so high/ Ring through my ears and sting my eyes/ Your Spanish lullaby."

END

"Box of Rain" took shape when the San Francisco Arts Commission Gallery, a city-funded agency boasting a sizeable exhibition space, presented an offering from the New York based ICI (Independent Curators International), a non-profit organization which allows curators unattached to institutional funding to create their own exhibitions, which the ICI then rents out to empty kunsthalles here and in many other countries. The show in question was slotted to reach San Francisco in the spring and summer of 2012, and it was called "Fax," organized by João Ribas.

Riba's idea was simple, that the world's greatest artists could fax the gallery one of their own creations, but because the facsimile (pace Baudrillard) was nowhere near as valuable as the original, the show could be installed very cheaply. People would be coming to see Wolfgang Tillmans and Tauba Auerbach and William Pope L and the like, but what would the difference be in the way they experienced rough fax versions of the work that never actually left the artists's studios? Each city to which "Fax" travelled would benefit from a new infusion of faxes sent by artist particular to that city. But the renting organization would have to buy a fax machine—even then approaching dinosaur status, like the typewriter of long ago—or rent one. At SFAC, director Meg Shiffler and manager Aimee Le Duc, fans of the San Francisco Poets Theater, asked me to write a play in which the fax machine would be front and center. I hit on the idea of a haunted fax machine, one that would run from earth to hell, and bring back communications from the dead.

The commission coincided with news of an actual crime in which a financial district gallery had been burgled by a tourist who came in and took a Picasso right out of the window. He was caught shortly afterwards, as surveillance cameras mounted on the streets of the city recorded his every move, block by block, as he trudged the Picasso back to his hotel room. So it was a lesson that rocked us a little—the idea that you were always going to be photographed, your every move, and always in the service of the State. I wrote the part of Inspector Gadget for one of our stars, the designer Rex Ray, who we loved having in our shows. For one thing, he had a huge studio in which he let us rehearse. But Rex had been sick for some time, and when our one rehearsal was done, he asked me to stay back a few minutes. When we were alone he apologized and said he wasn't strong enough to play the part, and he shouldn't even have participated in the rehearsal, but he had always had so much fun playing in our plays, he had hoped he could go on when we took the play onstage, a few days from then. But it was not to be. Rex couldn't even make it to sit in the audience, and he died in February 2015 of lymphoma. So I had to go on and play the part, which was a pretty melancholy one in the first place. We were all a little chastened as we acted "Box of Rain."

MARY MULHAIR,
director of the Rumaker Gallery .... Karla Milosevich
RACHEL RUMAKER, her boss... Laurie Reid
RYAN TREE COLLINS ....Ryan Funk
JASON JOHANSON, apparently his boyfriend, actually his son ....Matt Gordon
JORDAN GADGET,police inspector investigating a theft .... Kevin Killian
SIRI, computerized voice of a smart phone..Cliff Hengst
HEIDI BROAN, reporter for the *Nob Hill Gazette* ....Charlene Tan
PABLO PICASSO, the modernist painter .... Benjamin Vilmain
RODNEY, the inventor of the fax ....Craig Goodman
THOMAS KINKADE, the painter of light..Wayne Smith
DORA MAAR, French painter and photographer .... Tanya Hollis
LITTLE THIEF, a child of nine or ten maybe...Jordan Essoe

Directed by ....Kevin Killian
Designed by.. Matthew Gordon
Contemporary art ("Computronium" and "Coooh!") by ....Neil LeDoux
Rehearsal studio provided by .... Rex Ray

In Chicago, in December 2016, I rehearsed a new cast who revived the play for
the Second Annual Chicago Poets Theater Festival at Links Hall. Here our cast
included:

MARY MULHAIR,
director of the Rumaker Gallery .... Carmen Merport
RACHEL RUMAKER, her boss... Rebecca Walz
RYAN TREE COLLINS .... Ryan Pfeiffer
JASON JOHANSON,
apparently his boyfriend, actually his son.............................Jean-Thomas Tremblay
JORDAN GADGET, police inspector investigating a theft ....Arnold Kemp
SIRI, computerized voice of a smart phone....................................... J'Sun Howard
HEIDI BROAN, reporter for the *Nob Hill Gazette*..................................Jen Karmin
PABLO PICASSO, the modernist painter ....Daniel Borzutsky
RODNEY, the inventor of the fax ....Steve Reinke
THOMAS KINKADE, the painter of light...................................... .... John Neff
DORA MAAR, French painter and photographer ....Eliza Starbuck
LITTLE THIEF, a child of nine or ten maybe.......................................Stevie Hanley

New Light on Riboflavin

characters

JIMMY JAY
security guard at the Berkeley Museum

MAY TRIX
curator at the Berkeley Museum

MARSHALL McLUHAN
Canadian media theorist

BOB BISHOP
reporter for the Berkeley Barb

KEVIN KILLIAN
department secretary

LADY JAY
the janitor's wife

ANAIS NIN

DAN FLAVIN
sculptor of light

GORDON LIGHTFOOT
Canadian folksinger

[*Lights fade up: a car has crashed into the Berkeley Museum and though no one is behind the wheel, the headlights are still shining.*]

JIMMY JAY: Ms. Trix! Did you hear the crash?

MAY: Yes—I came running to see if—(*pause*)—well, never mind.

JIMMY JAY (*as he spots the car*): Whoa, dead ride!

MAY: Jimmy Jay, what has happened here? It's Berkeley and it's 1972 and we're on the brink of real social revolution.

JIMMY JAY: Sorry, Dr. Trix, let me start at the beginning.

MAY: The eternal cycle of starting at the beginning.

JIMMY JAY: At approximately eighteen fifty-five,—

MAY: When? Tonight?

JIMMY JAY: Yes. Tonight a male suspect was seen crashing his car, a late model Chevy wagon, into the concrete wall of the two year old Berkeley Art Museum and Pacific Film Archive, interrupting the premiere of Maya Deren's *Medusa Haiku*. The car door cracked open, reported Miss Deren, and the driver staggered away, possessed, she believes, by the divine gods of Haiti.

MAY: Those gods are real. They have real powers!

JIMMY JAY: He hasn't yet returned. Though he left behind—oh, never mind.

MAY: What?

JIMMY JAY: I don't know what you want me to say. Dr. Trix!

MAY: Jimmy Jay, have you heard of riboflavin?

JIMMY JAY: Did somebody say I did?

MAY: Tell me, have you met our Matrix artist Dan Flavin?

JIMMY JAY: I am a janitor, Dr. Trix. I mean, literally, a janitor. And my wife—

MAY: Yes?

JIMMY JAY: —is a janitor's wife.

MAY: Then answer me this, have you heard that scientists here on the Berkeley campus have invented a replacement for—

JIMMY JAY: For me? Like, a robot or something?

MAY: No!

JIMMY JAY: A robot janitor?

MAY: No! A replacement for the old electric light bulb of Thomas Edison?

JIMMY JAY: I'm here from Georgia, the land of rich peaches and much capitalist bullshit. There I was born without electric light. My mother had only the village nurse to guide baby Jimmy Jay into a cruel dark hot landscape.

MAY: I'm talking of course, about the modern fluorescent light.

JIMMY JAY: You got me there.

MAY: Wait, that man must be a scientist, look at his coat. He can explain it better than I can.

JIMMY JAY: Dr. Trix, you explain fine.

MAY: Fluorescent lights are the long tubes recently invented by NASA to provide illumination for the space program. Oh dear, you're shivering, and it's a warm June night.

JIMMY JAY (*shivering*): Tubes give me the creeps. Give me a flashlight any old day, with a Double A battery.

[*Enter MARSHALL McLUHAN in a white lab coat something like a scientist's.*]

McLUHAN (*whistling*): Some smash, eh?

MAY: A terrible dust-up.

McLUHAN: Yes…. The collision is the collage.

MAY: You were at the Gordon Lightfoot meet and greet.

McLUHAN: I am a scientist, and my focus is on understanding media. But I'm something of a quick study, and I couldn't resist the fun of a Gordon Lightfoot meet and greet.

JIMMY JAY: May Trix, this is Marshall McLuhan from University of Canada.

MAY: Oh, you're Canadian, then you won't know anything about NASA. Or vitamins.

McLUHAN: Try me.

MAY: Is there a NASA Canada?

McLUHAN: We are all one big nation today with our TV addiction and our long, cool, fluorescent tubes dusted with moon dust.

JIMMY JAY: When the rockets filled with Neil Armstrong landed, a terrible music hit the campus of Berkeley.

McLUHAN: Not music—not Gordon Lightfoot music—but what we in Toronto call "inhabitative noise."

MAY: You seem very familiar, Marshall, with Gordon Lightfoot's oeuvre.

McLUHAN: He's been looking like a queen in a sailor's dream, and he don't often say what he really means.

MAY: He hasn't been to the Berkeley Museum as often as he used to.

JIMMY JAY: Oh now I know who you're talking about.

MAY: The gallery girls would tease me that I had a new boyfriend, folk singer Gordon Lightfoot.

McLUHAN: Have you asked yourself why Gordon has not been to see you in months?

MAY: If you could read my mind, Marshall McLuhan, what a tale my heart could tell.

JIMMY JAY: Aw, who needs him? May Trix here's got a new show with an American artist we're nuts about.

McLUHAN: Just like a paperback novel, the kind that the drug stores sell.

MAY: As one Berkeley professional to another, sir, will you help me?

McLUHAN: The vacillation is the visage.

MAY: Have you ever seen or touched a fluorescent light?

McLUHAN: I have, Miss Trix.

MAY: And?

McLUHAN: Like TV, they are the cooler emblem of a new cybernetic age. Our ancestors used heat, tamed dragons, roasted meats on spits, had sex. In the new age the temperature drops [*voice drops*] way down.

JIMMY JAY: Fluorescent lights are the devil's dick, Miss Trix! Bulbs filled to bursting with a miasma, a thick crummy miasma, that can wilt a cabbage at thirty paces. Break a tube, you die screaming.

McLUHAN: That miasma could wilt a full size sequoia if one chose to harness fluorescence for evil, but luckily the miasma don't know its own strength.

JIMMY JAY: Ms. Trix, Dr. McLuhan, what are you driving at?

MAY: I woke up this morning and said to myself, "May," (*for I am May Trix, founder of the Matrix program*)… "May, it's your day off but you better go down to the Museum and see what's going on."

JIMMY JAY: So you came in….

MAY: I came in and….

JIMMY JAY: Wait! Was the disoriented driver—are you trying to tell me—Maya con Dios, was the driver Dan Flavin? The man they call (*pause*) the sculptor of light?

MAY: Wait here please.

JIMMY JAY: Do I wait as witness or suspect?

McLUHAN: Wait nearby the car, sir.

JIMMY JAY: Inside the car is there miasma?

MAY: I would never ask you to endanger your health, Jimmy Jay.

McLUHAN: Just get over there.

JIMMY JAY: All right, I will stand near by the death car.

[*He walks over to the car and puts a hand on the trunk, as though linked to the car.*]

MAY: Heavens to Betsy—Dan Flavin and his quest for a new vitamin—has it led to this car crash?

McLUHAN: Wasn't there an American cartoon where they say, "Which way did he go, boss? Which way did he go?"

MAY (*to herself*): Ironic how I, a respected West Coast curator, am reduced to acting like a private eye in a film noir movie, like *Kiss Me Deadly*, who gets burned in a three way strip.

[*Enter BOB BISHOP from the Berkeley Barb.*]

BOB: Dr Trix. A few questions from the press?

MAY: Why not?

BOB: I'm Bob Bishop from the Berkeley Barb.

MAY: The radical underground press.

McLUHAN: I will say goodbye—for now. I'm here on a Fulbright interpreting the ways our two countries differ. And I have a full load, as you say here.

MAY: The coursework alone must be an ample burden, Dr. McLuhan.

McLUHAN: In Toronto we say, "The coursework is the corsage."

[*Exit McLUHAN.*]

MAY: Bob Bishop of the Berkeley Barb.

BOB: Dr. Trix, is your protégé, Dan Flavin of New York, smuggling the new fluorescent lights into the museum under cover of darkness?

MAY: Dan Flavin is not my protégé. He belongs to the world, like all great artists of his stripe. I am but the humble curator, flicking a switch onto 1972.

BOB: Does the University receive funds from NASA?

MAY: Certainly not! I'm with the Matrix program and we're doing a show with Dan Flavin. That's all I know. I mean I know my Michael Fried and Clement Greenberg. And now that it's 1972 my Linda Nochlin.

BOB: Does Marshall McLuhan work for NASA? The Canadian man.

MAY: Bob, you grew up in the shadow of the atom bomb, didn't you?

BOB: Yes, from an early age I, a baby boomer, ducked and covered under the school desk or if I was at home, under the sturdy tool bench my Dad had put up in his basement.

MAY: Did Dad, or Mom, for we must not discount the power of the woman, ever tell you about vitamins? Or give you one or more to swallow?

BOB: Flintstones vitamins.

MAY: Here we are in the last rays of the sun, can you feel the heat dying on your face?

[*BOB turns his face to the sun, rubs his forehead, his cheek.*]

BOB: Yes—the dying, June sun.

MAY: Sunlight is a potent source of vitamin D.

BOB: In grade school they used some of the letters for the names of vitamins, there was vitamin C for orange juice, B for beans, A for apple…. There were so many letters left out, I felt quite sorry for them, I did.

MAY: Under the desk you felt sorry for them.

BOB: Kissing my ass goodbye I felt ever so sorry for F, G, H, I, J et cetera.

MAY: Dan Flavin is a talented sculptor using his art world push to provide a place here at UC Berkeley to help others invent a new, site specific vitamin – which we are calling Riboflavin.

BOB: Riboflavin? Isn't that a thing already?

MAY: Is it? You know Dan was one of twin brothers, and the other one died.

BOB: I actually don't know much about Dan Flavin.

[*Enter ANAIS NIN.*]

ANAIS NIN: Why not ask a woman?

BOB: Anais Nin!

ANAIS NIN: Yes, and this is the Chevy that Dan Flavin stole to make love to me in.

MAY: That's a bare-faced lie!

ANAIS NIN: Is it, Dr. Trix? It was a love making site specific in its details. And what do you care, Dr. Trix? I, Anais, have loved many men, from Henry Miller to Gore Vidal, to Charles Mingus and Jackson Mac Low. Even my own father, if my legend is true. Yet no man has moved me such as the young Dan Flavin.

MAY: I see.

ANAIS NIN: Well, perhaps Gordon Lightfoot.

BOB: "If I could read your mind, girl, what a thought my mind could tell."

MAY: Nothing annoys Gordon as much as a fan who cannot remember the lyrics

ANAIS NIN: Or makes them up.

MAY: His singing voice is a tenor perfectly suited for our cool, minimalist era.

ANAIS NIN: Yes, like a Canadian sunset. His actual Delta of Venus is small, quite small when compared to those of Mac Low or Flavin.

MAY: You will never be a Matrix artist! You are far too presumptuous.

BOB: Miss Nin, you have lived in California for nearly thirty years, what changes have you observed in your decades of sexual experience?

ANAIS: The long hair on the men. Like yours, Bob.

MAY: Dan's twin brother was called Robert, but little Dan couldn't pronounce it, and called him Ribo. So sad.

BOB: You act almost as if there was a tragedy in the Flavin family.

MAY: Young Ribo died of polio.

ANAIS: The chicken.

MAY: No, the disease, polio. Not pollo.

ANAIS: In Spain, when twins are separated, we call it the sundering of the two.

BOB: Impressive!

ANAIS: Old Spanish saying: "Take what you want, saith God—but pay for it." God bought Dan Flavin a box of lights, the brand new miasma tubes in pastels and primary colors, and Flavin lit up the sky with them.

BOB: No wonder Dan Flavin feels such torment. Here he is, dean of American minimalism, yet his brother's in Colma gathering dust.

ANAIS: I can still hear Ribo scream out, "Dan, Dan! Can't you invent something? A vitamin or something?"

MAY: The terrible screams of a man drained of life.

ANAIS: "And name it after me," cried the brother.

BOB: Didn't you say something, earlier in this play, May, about how one always has to start at the beginning?

ANAIS: Very meta, May Trix!

MAY: Yes, I did. I remember now. "The eternal cycle of starting at the beginning."

[*Enter KEVIN KILLIAN, May Trix' executive assistant.*]

KEVIN KILLIAN: Dr. Trix, the press conference is beginning and nobody can find Dan Flavin.

BOB: Maybe he's still installing.

MAY: He had nothing to do with this car crash, nothing, or my name isn't Mabel Trix and this isn't Kevin Killian, my personal assistant.

ANAIS: Who designed this building? [*After a pause.*] I slept with him! It's coming back to me now. He was a brutalist, just like the heavy concrete that stopped this, how do you say, Flavin's, how do you say, "hot rod."

BOB: What strange green light hovers over this concrete creation?

KEVIN KILLIAN: Miss Nin?

ANAIS: Yes?

KEVIN KILLIAN: The building was designed in 1970 by a Mario Ciampi. A mere two years old, like my little boy at home.

ANAIS: Yes, Mario! I gave myself to him and he was like a boy at Christmas to whom Santa had delivered his first architecture set of glass, concrete and steel.

MAY: Let us disperse and leave this scene. Kevin, how do I look?

KEVIN KILLIAN: Lovely.

ANAIS: Frazzled.

BOB: Like you're hiding something.

MAY TRIX: Has Gordon Lightfoot been located? He swore to me he would sing some of his folk hits.

ANAIS: Like "Early Morning Rain."

BOB: "Carefree Highway."

MAY: "For Loving Me."

BOB: "If you could read my mind, girl,"

BOB and ANAIS: "What a tale my thoughts would tell."

KEVIN KILLIAN: "Just like a paperback novel,"

KEVIN KILLIAN, BOB, ANAIS: "The kind the drugstores sell."

MAY: "In a castle dark—"

KEVIN KILLIAN: Dr. Trix, reporters are waiting under the huge Hans Hofmann.

MAY (*to KEVIN KILLIAN*): I hate to leave you alone like this.

KEVIN KILLIAN: Go and do your duty as the first female curator at Berkeley.

MAY: Will Gordon Lightfoot be there?

BOB: Follow me. Maybe we'll find Dan Flavin.

ANAIS: I for one would welcome that opportunity.

[*Exit MAY TRIX, ANAIS NIN, and BOB.*]

KEVIN KILLIAN: It's growing dark. Soon the whole world will be glowing red with radiation. Or green, if Marshall McLuhan is correct [*Sings.*] When the world gets cold—I'll be your cover. Let's… just… hold… On to each other. When it all falls, when it all falls down, we'll be two souls in a ghost town.

[*Enter LADY JAY.*]

LADY JAY: Jimmy Jay! Where you got yourself off to? I declare, Jimmy Jay, you are the hardest man to pin down.

KEVIN KILLIAN: Why hello!

LADY JAY: Hi, y'all. I'm Lady Jay and my husband is your janitor—you know him, little bruiser of a guy, Jimmy Jay?

KEVIN KILLIAN: Of course I do! He's the heart and soul of the Berkeley Museum.

LADY JAY: But now he's AWOL! He had a break at six and I was supposed to meet him in the janitor's closet. I was right on time and where was he? Don't know! It's like he's being held hostage.

JIMMY JAY: Help! Help me, Lady Jay! I'm like stuck to this old death car.

[*But his cries go unheard.*]

KEVIN KILLIAN: Sorry, I haven't seen him! He likes the salad bar at the student center.

LADY JAY: I put up his lunch, every day, in a brown burlap sack, like they do where we come from. He don't need no salad whatever it is.

KEVIN KILLIAN: Bar. Salad bar. Invented in Berkeley in 1964, the salad bar is the modern-day equivalent of the smorgasbord of the Scandinavian Viking people.

JIMMY JAY: I don't like salad bar, that's government lies about me! Kevin Killian is bullshit, man.

LADY JAY: Everything's the modern-day version of something superior. What happened to love—the love of a good woman. Jimmy Jay! Come and git it!

KEVIN KILLIAN: Lady—is that your name? "Lady Jay"?

LADY JAY: Yes—like Lady Bird Johnson.

KEVIN KILLIAN: I've worked for Dr. Trix for two years now, ever since the opening of the museum and the very first Matrix artist was Ursula Schneider.

LADY JAY: How many you up to now?

KEVIN KILLIAN: Oh goodness, we've done so many. Dan Flavin is Matrix 6. Or seven.

LADY JAY: That is a lot, but when I see the green lights in the sky I get a little—apocalyptic, Mr. Killian. There's a man in the forest over there by the way.

KEVIN KILLIAN: Oh my God that's our Matrix artist, stumbling from the trees! Dan Flavin!

[*Enter DAN FLAVIN, stumbling from the trees.*]

FLAVIN: Where do I go from here?

JIMMY JAY: And don't forget, there's me over here!

LADY JAY (*approaching FLAVIN*): Poor boy, you have suffered a bump on your head? May I feel?

FLAVIN: If you must.

LADY JAY: My mom taught me phrenology, long ago, in the backwoods of Georgia. It is the art of picking up the vibes of a man from the bumps in his lap. I mean, on his head.

KEVIN KILLIAN: He looks so woebegone!

LADY JAY: And you, Dan Flavin, are complicated.

FLAVIN: One bump's brand new, woman of the South.

LADY JAY: Very complicated he is.

FLAVIN: I'm not complicated, lady, I'm just an ordinary guy whose twin died of polio, and so I seek a way to bring him back to planet earth, with a new forthcoming site-specific vitamin named after him..

[*Enter ANAIS.*]

ANAIS NIN: I have known and loved many artists, minimalists all of them, where it counted, in their lack of true value.

FLAVIN: It is here at Berkeley that multiple vitamins were developed, and now I want them to make me a Flavin vitamin. [*To LADY JAY and KEVIN KILLIAN.*] Find them and bring them to me.

LADY JAY: Hey, I'm still looking for my husband, Jimmy Jay.

KEVIN KILLIAN: He's probably at the Hotel Durrant. He likes to go there and eat from their salad bar.

JIMMY JAY: Lies! Untruths! Lies of Nixon dimension!

FLAVIN: My scientists?

LADY JAY: We'll find 'em, skinny.

[*Exit LADY JAY and KEVIN KILLIAN.*]

ANAIS: Is there not a "Riboflavin" already?

FLAVIN: People keep saying that, Anais Nin. But I don't think so.

ANAIS: Henry Miller said, "Anais, the inventor."

FLAVIN: My brother was called Ribo.

ANAIS (*with a sharp intake of breath*): Ribo Flavin? Polio?

FLAVIN: Did you know him?

ANAIS: He was my lover, like most American men born in the 30s.

FLAVIN: But Ribo had little or no experience with women, due to his illness.

JIMMY JAY: Maybe that's what he told you! Men are just lying dogs!

ANAIS: He was in the Navy, and the Navy was in me, like molecules in your light saber, Dan Flavin. We used to see him nightly on the docks and wonder who would be the first to explore the crevices, the edges, the curls of his body.

FLAVIN: Some say that I am the greatest American artist, but in my heart, I know I am but a stand-in for my more talented twin.

ANAIS: Elvis says the same, Elvis Presley.

FLAVIN: Twins lie conjoined inside each other, like chrysanthemum stalks bundled for market.

ANAIS: Twins and triplets were my meat, when I walked Navy Pier. Your brother was strong man, Matrix artist. His little legs and arms were nothing, weak, flapping like flypaper, but perhaps in contrast, his qu'est-ce-que c'est, his Poteau was vast, like the north pole, Dan Flavin. With many penguins around it to give it noble strength and intensity, like a hundred stalks of mums bundled together for market.

FLAVIN: Well, I'll be!

ANAIS: Flash that light in my eyes, make me feel even a thousandth part the dazzle I felt with your dead twin boy. If that is polio, every man in America needs it.

FLAVIN: OK, you're from France?

ANAIS: Born under the Seine.

FLAVIN: Do you know Niki de Saint-Phalle?

ANAIS: Tell me more about Ribo, the man who destroyed me.

FLAVIN: Top scientists from the Berkeley Biochemistry department, and the physics department, arrive at eight pm to combine their flasks of atomic miasma. From the four corners of the earth they come, with crystal tubes open at one end.

ANAIS: I see, for the ultimate cocktail.

FLAVIN: From the Nobel Prize of Sweden, I bring you Stephen Hawking, walking towards us before his diagnosis, bringing with him the beaker of DNA he invented.

[*Enter JIMMY JAY.*]

ANAIS NIN: That is Stephen Hawking?

FLAVIN: Wait—that's the Matrix janitor!

JIMMY JAY: Trapped in a web of Berkeley lies, I saw me a vision. I say, a vision to rival that of Oppenheimer and Edward Teller, the Berkeley men who brought forth the atom bomb. I tell you this, I, Jimmy Jay of Georgia!

ANAIS: He's a strong, handsome man but he's been through [*pause*] très ordeal.

FLAVIN: Tonight is the night! [*To JIMMY JAY.*] Where's that beaker of DNA?

JIMMY JAY: Here it is, like alphabet soup of the soul.

FLAVIN: Green rays of fluorescent light penetrate the concrete hulk of the museum.

JIMMY JAY: And I have seen—look, from the forest floor, the animals bringing gifts of acorns and squash—the healthy food from which riboflavin is derived.

ANAIS NIN: From cold Canada comes the media theorist Marshall McLuhan,

[*Enter McLUHAN.*]

Author of *The Medium is the Massage*!

JIMMY JAY: He brings with him large cup of maple syrup and Canadian Club.

FLAVIN: Pour it into my beaker, McLuhan, hurry do, and don't be stingy, baby.

McLUHAN: The tedium is the tiramisu.

FLAVIN: Step back, it's about to blow!

McLUHAN: Rub it on the rear view mirror.

FLAVIN: Like this?

McLUHAN: We will consult the modern day gods of speed and resurrection.

JIMMY JAY: I have spent forty days and forty nights in that car, and have been vouchsafed a revelation.

McLUHAN: The mirror is the mirage.

FLAVIN: What was once hot is now cool.

McLUHAN: The garish is the garage.

[*Enter LADY JAY.*]

LADY JAY (*to her husband*): There you are, little rascal! Where have you been? [*As he tries to explain.*] Never mind, I know, you were at the salad bar, see I know your little temptations.

JIMMY JAY (*slowly*): Yes. I was at—the salad bar, Lady Jay.

LADY JAY: You don't fool me with your disappearing act. Now hush up, this man is about to invent a new vitamin.

JIMMY JAY: I saw it in a vision, at the salad bar.

McLUHAN: The Manon is the mayonnaise.

JIMMY JAY: The Manon is the mayonnaise.

[*Enter MAY TRIX.*]

MAY: Dan Flavin, bad boy, you cracked up your car to give your curator a scare. Is that the riboflavin?

ANAIS NIN: It needed a woman's touch. A woman with experience—and a woman with innocence. A curator's naivete.

FLAVIN: Yes, it is ready.

MAY (*looking around*): But I am missing a man. The Apollo of our day, with the cool, mechanical voice of the 70s.

JIMMY JAY: I saw him at the salad bar. Look, here he comes now, in my vision.

[*Enter BOB BISHOP of the BERKELEY BARB.*]

BOB: Were you missing me, May Trix, or the Gordon Lightfoot of your imagination?

[*Enter GORDON LIGHTFOOT.*]

ANAIS: He is Gordon Lightfoot—the John the Baptist of Riboflavin.

McLUHAN: Sing, Canadian brother, sing.

MAY TRIX (*to BOB*): Don't ask me who I miss! Just as my dreams of a woman-led Matrix come true. Gordon! I'm here.

BOB: "The eternal cycle of starting at the beginning."

GORDON LIGHTFOOT: Hi everyone, I'm Gordon Lightfoot from Canada. "If you could read my mind, love, what a tale my thoughts would tell.

Just like a paperback novel, the kind the drugstores sell.

In a castle dark, or a fortress strong, with chains upon my feet, but for now, love, let's be real.

I never thought I would feel this way, but I've got to say that I just can't take it.

I don't know where we went wrong, but the feeling's gone, and I just can't get it back.

[*Enter KEVIN KILLIAN.*]

KEVIN KILLIAN: What about me? I had a vision of an active, committed poets' theater that would change the world. And yet it still seems to be 1972!

DAN FLAVIN (*taking center stage, spreading his arms wide, palms outstretched.*) Ladies and gentlemen, behold, I give you riboflavin!

END

Here in San Francisco live three of my favorite people, artists, writers and curators all, who have formed a quasi-independent entity called 'Will Brown." "Will Brown" has been responsible for many of the most exciting curatorial projects in the Bay Area over the past few years—quirky, heavily researched, jumping out of fact into speculation and theory at the drop of a dime. I've admired Jordan Stein, Lindsey White, and David Kasprzak for ages, and I was thrilled to hear that they had been awarded the coveted Matrix fellowship at the Berkeley Art Museum and Pacific Film Archive—BAM/PFA they call it for short. The Matrix program has been going on since 1978—small exhibitions of international work, sometimes the first local museum shows of artists who go on to have great careers, everyone from Basquiat to Eva Hesse. Will Brown's Matrix show was Matrix 259, and when they asked me to write a play for them to stage I jumped at the chance.

Wasn't until I started work on it that I realized the unusual numbers of constraints I'd be working under. The entire Museum would be shut down for retrofitting, so the show had to be able to be seen outside, and that included our play. Will Brown found a vintage car and arranged for a simulated crash into the front entrance, as though it were outraged the museum doors were locked and barred. The play was supposed to happen outdoors in the patio area emanating from this totaled old car. Because it was outside there would be no chairs or seating, except for the shallow steps of the old museum,, and practically speaking it meant that they didn't want a very long play, because people would tire if they had to stand through a play of, say, two hours in length. "If you could make it 32 minutes," said one—"or 29 minutes," said another, "or 35 minutes, that would be great," advised the third. So I cut out half my characters and began again. And then it became apparent that all three of the Will Brown artists expected parts written for themselves, and Jordan Stein really wanted to play Dan Flavin. But I find that sometimes the more "have tos" you're saddled with, the stronger your imagination grows in response. Through some mystic Marvel Comics legacy you grow able to work around and through the manacles of sanity. The text of *New Light on Riboflavin* was featured by Lyn Hejinian and Christopher Patrick Miller in issue #3 ("Absurdity") of their online journal *Floor* in August 2015.

JIMMY JAY, security guard at the Berkeley Museum..................David Kasprzak
MAY TRIX, curator at the Berkeley Museum...................................Lindsey White
MARSHALL McLUHAN, Canadian media theorist..........................David Brazil
BOB BISHOP, reporter for the Berkeley Barb.............................Paul Ebenkamp
KEVIN KILLIAN, department secretary...................................Theo Konrad Auer
LADY JAY, the janitor's wife...May Wilson
ANAIS NIN.. ....Suzanne Stein
DAN FLAVIN, sculptor of light............... ....Jordan Stein
GORDON LIGHTFOOT, Canadian folksinger....................................Kevin Killian

Kevin Killian is the author of more than 40 plays for San Francisco Poets Theater. His collaborative poets theater works include *Stone Marmalade* (1996, with Leslie Scalapino), *The American Objectivists* (2001, with Brian Kim Stefans), and, with Barbara Guest, *Often* (published in a limited edition by Kenning Editions in 2001). Killian and David Brazil are coeditors of *The Kenning Anthology of Poets Theater: 1945-1985* (2010).

Killian's poetry collections include *Argento Series* (2001), *Action Kylie* (2008) and *Tweaky Village* (2014). In 2017 appeared two new volumes, *Tony Greene Era* (Wonder Books) and *Les éléments* (Joco Seria). He is also the author of three volumes of *Selected Amazon Reviews* (2006-17), the novels *Shy* (1989), *Arctic Summer* (1997), and *Spreadeagle* (2012) the short-story collections *Little Men* (1996), which won the PEN Oakland award, *I Cry Like a Baby* (2001), the Lambda Literary Award–winner *Impossible Princess* (2009); and the memoir *Bedrooms Have Windows* (1989).

With Lewis Ellingham, Killian coedited Jack Spicer's posthumously published detective novels *The Train of Thought: (Chapter III of a Detective Novel)* (1994) and *The Tower of Babel* (1994) and cowrote the biography *Poet Be Like God: Jack Spicer and the San Francisco Renaissance* (1998). With Peter Gizzi, Killian coedited *My Vocabulary Did This to Me: The Collected Poetry of Jack Spicer* (2008), which won the American Book Award from the Before Columbus Foundation. With Dodie Bellamy, he edited the anthology *Writers Who Love Too Much: New Narrative 1977-1997* (2017).

Juana I, by Ana Arzoumanian, translated by Gabriel Amor

Waveform, by Amber DiPietra and Denise Leto

Style, by Dolores Dorantes, translated by Jen Hofer

PQRS, by Patrick Durgin

The Pine-Woods Notebook, by Craig Dworkin

Propagation, by Laura Elrick

Tarnac, a preparatory act, by Jean-Marie Gleize, translated by
Joshua Clover with Abigail Lang and Bonnie Roy

The Kenning Anthology of Poets Theater: 1945-1985, edited by
Kevin Killian and David Brazil

The Grand Complication, by Devin King

Insomnia and the Aunt, by Tan Lin

The Compleat Purge, by Trisha Low

Ambient Parking Lot, by Pamela Lu

Some Math, by Bill Luoma

Partisan of Things, by Francis Ponge, translated by
Joshua Corey and Jean-Luc Garneau

The Dirty Text, by Soleida Ríos, translated by
Barbara Jamison and Olivia Lott

Who Opens, by Jesse Seldess

Left Having, by Jesse Seldess

Grenade in Mouth: Some Poems of Miyó Vestrini, edited by Faride Mereb
and translated by Anne Boyer and Cassandra Gillig

Hannah Weiner's Open House, by Hannah Weiner,
edited by Patrick Durgin